Lucky Lamson

In Her Own Words

The Story of the
USS Lamson, DD-367

FRONT COVER IMAGE: A 2007 bow view of the wreck of the Lamson at Bikini Atoll,courtesy of diver/photographer Andrew Pitkin.

REAR COVER IMAGE: The USS Lamson in Ormoc Bay after being struck by a Japanese kamikaze. Painted by US Navy combat artist Dwight Shepler.

We were miserably tense. But dawn came and the planes left. We had it all our way at the landing. But we'd wondered how long it would be before the first suicide attack would come in. -Edgar M. Adams

Another member of the Repair Party landed on my back just as the plane hit the superstructure and exploded. We both got up shaky, and scared as hell, and I went back to the shop after taking a quick look at the carnage just forward of the blower shield. —Stanford Lichlyter

Flames flashed more than masthead high and enveloped the ship…the crew gathered on the forecastle, while all survivors aft of No. 2 stack, together with fireroom and engine room crew, quietly gathered on the fantail.- Samuel Eliot Morison

The casualty toll in the Ormoc Operation from 3 through 11 December 1944 amounted to approximately 565 killed and more than 300 wounded. Some of the wounded died later. - William L. Griggs

U.S.S. Lamson, DD-367 at Yorktown, Virginia, April 1939 (Naval History Center)

TABLE OF CONTENTS

INTRODUCTION

Almost 70 years ago, Martin Earls, a high school English teacher in Southbridge, Massachusetts, (and my father's first cousin), put aside his passion for literature and went off to war by joining the U.S. Navy, where his age (he was already over 30), education, and natural skills as a leader brought him immediately into the ranks of the officers. His war time duty, particularly the hazards that came his way on the *USS Lamson*, became part of family lore. I last saw Martin Earls at a family reunion I organized in 1999, shortly after the death of my father, Robert K. Earls, himself a World War II navy veteran (a sonarman who served with the harbor defenses of Majuro Atoll during 1944). By the time of the reunion, the years had taken a toll on Martin, too, who was compelled to depend on a wheel chair for mobility. Martin died in June of 2001.

Hoping to preserve his story and that of the *Lamson* and its crew, I laid plans to create a book. Rita Earls, Martin's widow, was immediately helpful and shared a collection of *Lamson* memorabilia and documents detailing Martin's services in the war. Through the connections afforded by the internet, I was also able to locate a few individuals with *Lamson* connection, most notably Stanford Lichlyter – who generously shared the "diary" he had created by melding the *Lamson*'s deck log, which he obtained from the National Archive, with his own notes and recollections.

Pondering this substantial body of material I considered a number of approaches that might lead to a book and put the project on my to-do list. Unfortunately, that's where it stayed. Excuses abound for a writer supporting a family with young, active children that deserve time and attention. But, most of all, I think I was held back by a sense that I alone couldn't really do justice to the story of the *Lamson* or Martin's portion thereof.

After the passage of a further nine years, my elder son, Eamon, who had grown into fine writer in his own right, with a deep and passionate connection to history, made my dereliction with regard to the *Lamson* the focus of his attention. The requests to revive the project grew too insistent to ignore. Thus, late in 2009, I humbly contacted Mr. Lichlyter again to ensure that I still had his permission to publish the material he had sent. Again, he was gracious and agreed. Anything to ensure that the *Lamson*'s story was preserved. He also informed me that while I had dithered, other able hands had taken up the task, leading to the publication of **Tin Can 367** by *Lamson* crew member, Richard Phelan. This book I immediately acquired, finding in its pages much that I had not known and much I had hoped to convey about the *Lamson*, including substantial portions of Lichlyter's diary as well as recollections by the late Edward M. Adams, which Stan had also provided to me in manuscript form. In addition, the story was delivered with the authority that only one who had been there could render. Still, without taking anything from Mr. Phelan's accomplishment we, my son and I, determined that a second *Lamson* book, including more of Lichlyter's writings as well as our small trove of Martin Earls recollections, would still be a worthy project.

So, we began again, this time with the father following and the son leading, with the latter performing prodigies of typing and editing. To refresh and strengthen the effort, we again contacted Rita Earls, who graciously agreed to meet with us and share her story of war-time peregrinations and worry, as well as facts relating to Martin's responsibilities and activities. She also introduced us to her nephew, J. Paul Lanza, a destroyer man of a later generation, who grew up, figuratively at least, on Martin's knee, sharing local travels, fishing trips, and fellowship over a period of many years. Like a veritable Rosetta Stone, Paul's intimate knowledge of the Navy and of Martin brought clarity, insight, and whole new chapters to the story of Martin and, in particular, the events during and after the Battle of Ormoc Bay that cost so many men their lives and nearly lost the U.S. Navy a fine destroyer.

So, with these resources and a fresh sense of energy, we have crafted a book that we hope will be appreciated equally by surviving members of the *Lamson* crew, their family and friends, and anyone who appreciates history and the vital role the U.S. Navy played in bringing a hard and bitter war to a victorious conclusion. The material from Stanford Lichlyter and Adams constitutes the bulk of the book, supplemented by a short section on earlier *Lamson*s and the ship's namesake by Eamon and the Appreciation, which touches on our known oral tradition about Martin Earls, supplemented by a handful of documents and an article which the *Worcester Telegram* newspaper published about Martin in the 1980s. We hope all who explore these pages will find a value in this labor and will thereby better remember and appreciate the crew of the *Lamson*.

-- Alan R. Earls

MARTIN EARLS: AN APPRECIATION

"Uncle Martin's experiences on the *Lamson* meant a lot to him," noted his niece, Anne McGann. Nephew Paul Lanza would probably go further – for Martin, the war and especially his association with the *Lamson* seemed to put everything ever after into perspective and gave him the measure of men.

As noted in the introduction, our documentation related to Martin Earls's World War II years, including his months on the *Lamson*, is sparse. What we do know is that Martin Earls joined the Navy (his two brothers, Gerald and Francis, joined the Army Air Corps and Army, respectively) and received his commission on Jan. 7, 1943.

At some point in his time with MacArthur's Navy, Martin is supposed to have volunteered to deliver dispatches to a US submarine cruising in the area by boarding a rubber raft, armed only with his 45 caliber pistol, and waiting for the sub to surface and find him after dark…

Martin joined the *Lamson* in June of 1944 as an ensign, and stayed with the ship until July of 1945.

At Ormoc, Martin was apparently on or near the superstructure where the kamikaze struck and made it into the water and then to the *Flusser* or ATF-31. He was also part of the crew that eventually reclaimed the damaged ship. During the long return voyage to the West Coast, Martin told of helping Captain Noel with navigation duties and was eventually rewarded for his services by getting assigned to teach at a naval training program at the University of North Carolina, Chapel Hill.

After the war, Martin returned to Massachusetts and ran a successful business, Wachusett Welding and Tank. He died in 2001

Martin Earls, left, shipboard during World War II, right, in the late 1990s...

Stanford Lichlyter

U.S.S. LAMSON (DD367) ODYSSEY
THE WAR YEARS '41 - '42

17 DECEMBER 1941. WEDNESDAY. I said my farewells to the family, and my buddy Kenneth Lloyd drove my '37 Pontiac coupe and me to Los Angeles. He dropped me off about 1300, and I began a military career. In the meantime Ken locked the keys in the car and had a problem.

There was a line of men at every desk, and I was told to fall in line at the end of one of them. After the initial paperwork there was a physical so there was another line of mostly unclothed guys. The formalities took almost all afternoon, but those of us who were accepted were lined up in some semblance of order and sworn into the United States Navy. I thought that my worries were over.

It was dark when we were marched out of the Federal Building and down the street to a restaurant, that accommodated the crowd, and provided the evening meal. About 2000 a couple of busses pulled up and we boarded for the trip to San Diego where the Naval Recruit Training Center was located. It was about 2300 when we were ushered into a barracks, dimly lit with blue lights, and assigned bunks for the night, and told that we could expect to up bright and early.

18 DECEMBER 1941. THURSDAY. A Chief Bos'n by the name of Salinger rolled us out at 0500 for a short speech, telling us that we were in Company #41-184, and a light breakfast that would have held a field hand over until noon.

After breakfast there were shots, haircuts and uniforms, not necessarily in that order. At the outfitters we received the basic sailors V Neck Gown and other items of clothing plus a Sea Bag and Hammock. The latter was accompanied by a mattress, pillow, 2 wool blankets, and lashings. The Sea Bag took all the clothes, and was then mated to the rolled up hammock. With a little urging one could swing the 85 pound package to one's shoulder and march off with all that was needed by any self respecting Sailor.

Chicken was served at Lunch, and then we were introduced to the Tailor Shop where some adjustments were made in the Dress Blues, and a white 'watch mark' was sewed to the right shoulder of Dress and Undress Jumpers, signifying that we were to deck hands as opposed to firemen. One thin white stripe on each cuff of the Dress Jumper indicated our lowly status as Apprentice Seaman. At the Barber Shop it did not take the man long to relieve the boys of those beautiful locks. A #1 blade did the trick, and we began to lose our individuality very quickly.

There were thousands of men at the Training Center, and an overflow compound was set up at Balboa Park in the old Balboa Exposition buildings. After spending only three days at the Main Training Center we were bussed up to the Park and got a look at our new home. The structures were huge exhibit halls that had been modified by hundreds of double deck iron bunks. Our hammock, mattress and pillow became useful immediately and we moved into buildings that had little heat, and no washroom or toilet facilities. These civilized comforts were provided outside in makeshift fashion. A small boiler provided hot water at least.

December turned cold, and it began to rain, making Balboa Park a rather miserable place to be. Sherman was right. "War was Hell!!"

24 DECEMBER 1941. WEDNESDAY. Electing to enlist before Christmas was bad judgment upon my part, for now I was sequestered with a bunch of miserable kids, and could not get home. The Navy tried to make the season less miserable with a big Christmas tree, and excellent food. A troop came down from Hollywood so we had professional entertainment to help keep our minds off our troubles which seemed to mount with each needle and shot.

Each Company had its share of Mess Cooking, taking care of the Mess Hall and Galley that fed the thousands of hungry boots that mobbed the place. We served food from behind the steam tables, set tables, cleaned up afterwards, and helped scrub the gear in the Galley. A couple of days of this and we were relieved by another company.

25 DECEMBER 1941. THURSDAY. We had not been issued rifles, for there were not enough to go around, and did not have to drill with them daily. On this day of peace and goodwill we had our first chance to become acquainted with the U.S. standard Springfield Mod. 03 left over from World War I. Later we would see the British Enfield which was heavier than the Springfield.

Close order drills with the gun were interesting, and we marched up and down the parade ground then through the wilderness and ravines of the Park. The weather was cold, and the sweater felt good under the Undress Jumper. The wool watchcap itched like crazy though.

There had been lectures on seamanship, and knots, but the main purpose of our stay was the quarantine and shot period that required three weeks. At the end of that time the formalities ended and we were shipped out.

1942

10 JANUARY 1942. SATURDAY. We had endured! The Company photograph had been taken for posterity, and now we were ordered to lash the seabag and hammock together and get ready to leave this lovely setting. I was so weak from Cat Fever and the shots that I needed help getting it all pulled up snug, but managed to get to the bus with everything intact.

We were taken to the train station in San Diego, loaded on the old Pullman cars and headed north. Los Angeles was the first stop for dinner at Union Station. Over the hill to Oakland took all night, and from there we were bussed across the Bridge to a waiting transport that would take us to Hawaii. The *President Garfield*, was a converted President Lines freighter, and we spent 7 miserable days enroute to Pearl Harbor.

18 JANUARY 1942. SUNDAY. At 0900 we were ready to go through the anti submarine net, and when we got to Hospital Point there was *U.S.S. Nevada* (BB36) aground where she had been ordered beached on the west side of the channel. Bunker crude oil was thick on the surface of the harbor as we went by Ford Island and the other damaged battle ships. The media had not conveyed the real extent of the damage, and the topside of the *Garfield* was very quiet as we surveyed the sunken ships, and the destruction on Ford Island.

Company #41-184 was sent to *U.S.S. Whitney* (AD-4), a Destroyer Tender, and it would be our home until we were assigned to destroyers as they came alongside for upkeep. We were just in time for Sunday dinner, and the pork chops were superb after the miserable rations on the *Garfield*. The mess deck was spotless and airy, and we later found out how it was kept that way, for we were assigned to X Division. This was the transient labor pool, and we scraped oil off boats in our whites, handled ammunition, painted magazines, and did about every other menial task that was required on the tender. We had not been issued dungarees in boot camp, but our Division Officer finally found some after our whites had been ruined.

There was no space in the berthing area for our hammocks so an awning was rigged topside aft, and we spread the hammocks on the teak. The blankets felt good at night, but the Catalina Patrol planes took off over our heads at daylight. There was one submarine scare too, but we had lost so much sleep that it was minor.

30 JANUARY 1942. FRIDAY. As destroyers came alongside members of the company were sent aboard in alphabetical order, or so it seemed. When they got to the H 's about 20 of us were sent to *U.S.S. Chicago* (CA-29) in the Pearl Harbor Navy Yard. It was late in the afternoon when we boarded, and after the evening meal we were introduced to five inch 25 cal. fixed ammunition loaded in box cars on the dock. Our job was to get it aboard *Chicago*. Each round weighed about 80 pounds if I recall, and we carried it up a ladder and on board instead of using skip boxes, for all the cranes were busy.

That night we bunked in a spacious compartment, and thought we had fallen on better times, but our relief was short lived, for an outbreak of measles, or something, caused us to be moved to the Mess Deck where we spread the old hammock on deck again. At least there were regulation hammock bins on either side of the Mess Hall, and we were able to stow the baggage, but did not have to swing the hammock. This peacetime cruiser had large portholes in the messhalls; the food great, and the mess cooking better than in San Diego.

1 FEBRUARY 1942. SUNDAY. *Chicago* was underway for Suva, Fiji Islands. We were told that we would be transferred to a destroyer that would meet us there.

6 FEBRUARY 1942. FRIDAY. *Chicago* crossed the equator at 1327 hours, 159 Deg. West Long, near Jarvis Island. The initiation of Pollywogs by the Shellbacks was not severe because there were so many of us and so few Shellbacks. They did not want to risk anything. We had steamed south from Oahu because we were alone, and did not want to run into any submarines. The crossing of the International Dateline came on Tuesday and the 11th was lost forever.

I enjoyed the trip, for I ran into Kenneth Harris from Wilmington, and he gave me a tour of the ship. The launch and recovery of the SOC patrol planes was spectacular. The 'Cruiser Navy' looked just as it had when I visited the ships anchored off Long Beach in 1938.

12 FEBRUARY 1942. THURSDAY. In January *U.S.S. Lamson* (DD 367) had been detached from the Task Force headed by *U.S.S. Enterprise* (CV-6). Admiral Halsey sent several cans, including *Lamson*, to escort the fast Matson line troop ships that were headed for Samoa.

Lamson was fitted out as a Squadron Flagship, and was ordered to pick up Rear Admiral Fairfax Leary who would become Commander, Southwest Pacific Command. The Admiral was in Wellington, New Zealand and had the skipper invited correspondent Joseph C. Harsch to go along as a passenger. The correspondent was dropped off in Wellington, and the ship brought the Admiral up to Suva, Fiji, and the ANZAC Squadron was formed.

HMAS Australia (CA), *HMNZS Leander* (CL), *HMNZS Achilles* (CL), *HMAS Waramunga* (DD), *HMAS Arunta* (DD), *U.S.S. Chicago* (CA-29), *U.S.S. Perkins* (DD377), and *U.S.S. Lamson* (DD367) made up the new task force.

U.S.S. Lamson (DD367) was moored in a nest in Suva, Fiji Islands when we pulled in, and it was not long before the 30 sailors, 21 of us from Co. 184, were standing on her Quarter Deck complicating the life of the OOD, and the Deck Watch. Our draft would fill out the War complement of the ship.

On 7 December there were 176 men and 11 Officers on board, 34 more men reported prior to 10 January 1942, and there were 21 boots plus 9 other sailors who reported on 12 February. There were now 240 men and 11 Officers on board, and the ship was crowded.

The Shipfitters had been making canvas bottomed bunks that were triced up in the Mess Halls, but there were no bunks for several of us so we were told to take our gear to the Forward Mess Hall, and await instructions. I ended up swinging my hammock to hammock hooks just as sailors had done for centuries. I had not swung my hammock before, and it took some experimenting to get it taut enough to be comfortable.

13 FEBRUARY 1942. FRIDAY. My first liberty in Suva enabled me to do some sight seeing, and I managed to spend a dollar. The beer was excellent, and the pink gin a surprise.

The entire port area was surrounded by barbed wire and policed by New Zealand and Australian soldiers wearing heavy hobnail boots. As I got back to the gangway, BM2C Martin was being carried aboard, for he had made the mistake of calling the guard detail, "A bunch of F----- Limeys." For this indiscretion they knocked him down and walked up and down his white uniform causing his clean uniform to tear, as well as his skin which allowed his blood to leak upon the whites. I learned a valuable lesson in 'foreign relations'.

14 FEBRUARY 1942. SATURDAY. *Lamson* got underway at 1305 with the Squadron for the first time, and the ANZAC Squadron, *Australia, Chicago, Achilles* & *Leander,* with *Lamson* & *Perkins* as the screen. The Squadron went to sea for exercises with Task Force 11. The U.S.S. *Lexington* (CV2), was accompanied by *U.S.S. Portland* (CA24), *U.S.S. Indianapolis* (CA35), *U.S.S. Minneapolis* (CA36), and a screen of destroyers. I had been on all of these ships while in High School, and could recognize them by their outlines which surprised my shipmates.

We were paid half a months pay by the Division Disbursing Officer. My first watch was after the evening meal (18-20) on the Port wing of the Bridge as a lookout. I promptly got sea sick so the Quartermasters got me a bucket, and I continued the watch, but it was miserable as well as embarrassing. The sea was like glass, but I felt like we were rolling 40 degrees. That hammock was great until I had to hit the deck, and then I had real balance problems. After three days I finally got a bunk over a mess table, and still did not get any sleep--maybe five hours a night.

17 FEBRUARY 1942. TUESDAY. Two months in the Navy and I was a hardened Old Salt. The Cruise Seamen said life was not so hot on one of these tincans, but what I had seen so far was not bad, and I had gotten used to the ship's motion. In the Deck Force I was handling lines on the Foc'sle, and stood lookout watches. We stood the old 4 on 8 off and 2 hr. dog after the evening meal. This morning it was a bit damp and the liquid sunshine poured down my neck. We had not received mail since Diego.

22 FEBRUARY 1942. SUNDAY. One of the men that came aboard with our group, Hank Briggs, was sent by high line to the *U.S.S. Platte* (AO-24) with appendicitis. He later died in a hospital in Samoa.

24 FEBRUARY 1942. TUESDAY. We ran into a small cyclonic storm and we didn't do much for a few days. The swells were fairly heavy, but we could still eat and move around in comfort. We had to hold our plates down on several occasions though. One fellow's coffee slid across the table into the lap of the guy across from him. We woke this morning to a calm sea and a clear sky. This meant Field Day, or sprucing up the ship. After a storm we could find enough salt on the superstructure to start a salt factory.

Note: Company #41-184 sailors had not been paid since coming on board for there was no Paymaster in Lamson. *He was on the* Flusser, *the Squadron Flagship, somewhere else in the Pacific, and even $21.00 would have given me something to spend. During this period we were operating between Dumbea Bay, Noumea, New Caledonia and Suva, Fiji Islands so there were not many places to spend our money.*

The Disbursing Officer on the U.S.S. Chicago *was talked into paying everyone $25 or $30.00 whenever he thought we needed it. LCDR Mercer was persuasive too.*

16

The Fleet Locater System had not been set up either, and mail wandered all over the Pacific. I went over a month without mail while others in my group got theirs.

Note: The ANZAC Squadron was still working in and out of the Coral Sea carrying mail to the various units of the Task Force headed by U.S.S. Lexington. I was on the Fo'c'sle, handling lines. Later I was assigned to the Midship section of the Deck Force under BM2C Howard.

7 MARCH 1942. SATURDAY. *Lamson* was ordered back to Suva, and took 5 Army Officers to Noumea. We arrived on the 16th and received orders to go to Brisbane, General MacArthur's Headquarters. We were excited over the prospect until a seaplane from *Chicago* dropped a message on us when we were 5 hours outbound, telling the Old Man to return to Noumea. There was much bitching over that change--all over.

In another month I would become a Seaman 2nd Class with a raise in pay to $36.00/month. I figured that to date I had over $40.00 on the books. We were all hoping there would be a Disbursing Officer in Brisbane.

18 MARCH 1942. WEDNESDAY. Back into Noumea to fuel--had a swim party and liberty for 30 men--about 5 hrs. Not much in Noumea.

19 MARCH 1942. THURSDAY. I got ashore for four hours; 1400 - 1800, and found all of the bars closed, but did find a glass of claret. I did manage to spend $3.00; about 130 francs. Noumea was a small colonial city, and not a good liberty port, but it got me off the ship for a bit. There was also a swimming party for the crew on the beach instead of over the side.

The French were not friendly, but Vichy supporters, and I understood that several U.S. soldiers were killed when we occupied the Island.

21 MARCH 1942. SATURDAY. Captain Mercer held Personnel Inspection, and a Chaplain from the seaplane tender *U.S.S. Tangier* (AV-8) came over to take care of the Catholics. The day was enhanced by a Stores Working Party on the *Merkur*, our Aussie supply ship; out of Singapore originally, and a quart of Aussie beer was served on the freighter after the work was finished, and it did hit the spot. The boilers had been torn down on Friday so we were not going anywhere for a few days.

22 MARCH 1942. SUNDAY. The Navy was on a 7 day week work schedule so there was no Holiday Routine. When underway, reveille was at dawn for anti-sub GQ. I would get off watch at 0400 and curl up on a life jacket until GQ which was secured after the sun was up about 1/2 hr.

In port, the Noumea area was hot because of the surrounding hills. There was a liberty party after 1400, a ball game with another ship's team, and movies on the Fantail. On Saturday night the movie was, "Hold Back the Dawn."

Howard let me work on "Charlie Noble" a smokepipe for the galley that runs up the forepart of No. 1 stack. It had to be scraped, wire brushed and primed before I could paint this lean pipe. Most of the time I was hanging by my heels and a safety belt banging and painting for all I was worth. It was one hot and miserable job.

The Midship Section had the fancy accommodation ladder, and two whaleboats to keep us busy too, but it was better than the Foc'sle.

My Insurance allotment had gone through and now I was insured for $5,000. This policy could be kept and converted to an annuity at only $3.25/mo.

Note: When the liberty party returned there was a report of another soldier shot. Many had been killed since we occupied New Caledonia several weeks ago.

23 MARCH 1942. MONDAY. BM2C Howard had us scrubbing canvass all morning. In the afternoon a pair of seaplanes from *Chicago* ran mock attacks against the anchorage so we went to General Quarters. My station was on Secondary Con with LT Jenkins; the Executive Officer. I was a loader on a 30 Cal. WW I machine gun. We had two 50 Cal. and two of the Browning pan magazine 30s. What a farce they were, but it was a lot of fun anyway.

It had been a full day, for the *Lamson;* played cricket against HMAS *Australia* and we aired bedding. Despite the rain "Sergeant York" was shown on the Fantail.

25 MARCH 1942. WEDNESDAY. About 1000 we left the anchorage and fueled alongside the British oiler *Falkefjell* at 1000. Rigged for getting underway. After lunch the Special Sea Detail was set, and Howard and his stalwarts hoisted in the boats as we got underway with *Perkins* (DD377) about 1300. The two cans went to General Quarters as they formed an ASW Patrol screen off the mouth of the channel at 1400, and waited for cruisers to come out. The day was stormy and chilly, with wind and rain from easterly direction, and as we set a southerly course I got sick again on the first watch of the dog. Too much time in port.

27 MARCH 1942. FRIDAY. Still rough, but I was feeling better; at least I did not have to turn into my bunk, and I could go down the ladder into the Mess Hall without feeling queasy.

Ship's Company was eating off plates; and still by Divisions wherever possible. A Mess Cook was assigned to each table, and his job was to bring the tureens of food down from the Galley on the Main Deck, and set them on the table. The Senior Petty Officer at the table was served first, and then he passed the chow to the rest of us. As each man finished the Mess Cook took his place setting to the Scullery. In the tropics the After Mess Hall was a steamy, hot, and noisy place to eat.

HMAS *Australia* and HMNZS *Leander* held Main Battery target practice against each other's wakes, by offset firing, in the morning.

I had the 18 - 20 Lookout Watch on the 50 cal. machine gun platform forward of the Bridge, and had gotten the reputation of being one of the sharper eyed Lookouts, but this did not appeal to me much, and I saw no future in polishing the main deck in preparation for painting.

The best part of the day was when I was notified that my chit for transfer to the Engineering Department had been approved. I would leave the Deck Force and go into the Black Gang, changing from Seaman Second to Fireman Third on April 1st. This meant a Fire Room, leaving the unending task of chipping, scraping and painting to some other poor soul.

28 MARCH 1942. SATURDAY. Another 04-08 on the platform in front of the Bridge. Talk about being under the gun; the OOD could really keep the two of us on our toes.

Inspection of personnel, lockers and berthing spaces was held this morning at 1000. Now that I had a bunk in the after Mess Hall I had to keep my place ready for inspection all the time. Since I did not have a locker I had to lay everything out of the seabag out on my bunk over one of the mess tables.

A convoy of 2 single stack cans, 1 tanker, 1 freighter, and 1 transport came over the horizon just before inspection. We acted as the Postman and picked up mail from *HMAS Australia* and other ships. There was an unexpected Holiday Routine in the afternoon, and the sea has calmed down and sun was out most of the day. Things were looking much better.

29 MARCH 1942. SUNDAY. Dawn General Quarters had not been relaxed, and as daylight broke we sighted land low off the starboard bow. The convoy turned into port, but we kept on course. *Achilles* and *Leander* had moved away during the night. Things were beginning to relax a little, for there was another Holiday Routine. I could not turn in because my bunk was over the table where people played cards.

30 MARCH 1942. MONDAY. The Quarterdeck crew turned to on the deck again. It was calm enough that we could scrape, wire brush and red lead some more. After a week at sea, we had to start all over because salt water took the paint right off. Howard had a couple of "Cruise Seamen" helping him keep us busy, and I was glad that I had the afternoon watch.

31 MARCH 1942. TUESDAY. There was a Main Generator lube oil failure on the 04 -08, and I saw the Bridge fly the 'Break Down Pennant' for the first time. After the generator was back on the line we fueled from *Chicago* which required line handling by the Deck Force, and we got to use the winch. There was more work on the rust and paintwork.

LCDR Mercer passed the word to, "Save your money." Those that had tangled with the gamblers did not have much left to save. Frank Ganem was one of the professionals, and really cleaned house. This 'scuttlebutt' could have meant a liberty port in the offing. *Perkins* came alongside for a mail transfer, and watching her bob gently on the swell was a beautiful sight. First, a heaving line went over with a piece of light manila bent to it, and before you blinked the mail bags were gone, and so was *Perkins*. The seamanship was excellent, as it had to be with Mercer and Jenkins, for things could get very exciting if the sea was rough and the two ships were pitching and yawing. It was really great to see the sonar dome come out of the water when the other can pitched its bow into the air.

1 APRIL 1942. WEDNESDAY. Today was the beginning of a new Quarter, and my request to go into the Engineering Department. I was approved. This got me off the miserable topside, and removed me from the supervision of BM2 Howard, and began my career as a 'snipe.' I would receive a rate change from Apprentice Seaman to Fireman Third Class, and remove my white 'watch mark' on the right shoulder, replacing it with a red one on the left side. I would become an artificer too, and on 17 April my pay went from $21.00 to $36.00 a month after four months in the Navy. I was no longer a "Boot."

The New Hebrides Islands had been in sight most of the morning. We would enter Havanna Harbor, Island of Efate, and drop anchor in the afternoon.

The Engineering Officer was Mr. Pond, but ENS Conley was the Comm. Officer with the collateral duty as his assistant, and he assigned me to Number Two Fire Room, and I began to stand watches under the supervision of Watertender First Class Roy Edwards. My first job as an apprentice Burner Man was to learn the front of the boiler and how to operate the burner valves that controlled the oil flow into the fire box. The fire room was enclosed, that is, pressurized totally, and there were two airlock doors to pass through before getting to the boiler room itself. WT1C Edwards controlled the blowers that provided the combustion air to the boilers and pressurized the space.

2 APRIL 1942. THURSDAY. 0800 and my first 'Quarters for Muster' with the Engineers. There were general drills and then I was able to hit my bunk in the after mess hall, until lunch, when I had to trice it up for the noon meal. After lunch I was back on the floor plates in front of #4 Boiler. I learned how to clean atomizer tips, and was assigned a cleaning station.

The southernmost portion of Loyalty Islands came into view, and from our vantage point low on the horizon they seemed flat. Standard speed was 15 knots, and we were rolling heavily with water over the main deck periodically.

The word came into the radio shack that we would not have to buy postage stamps. There would be "free" mail service back to the States. A small pay raise, but a welcome one, for stamps were not always that easy to find.

3 APRIL 1942. FRIDAY. Rough water, and waves over the main deck, washed out Quarters for Muster on the Fantail. Back on watch again and this time a lesson on the gauges and what they meant. Hourly readings had to be taken and logged. Another benefit of the fire room was being able to wash one's clothes in a bucket, hang them over a rail on the upper level, and fold them for the locker by the end of the watch.

The Loyalty Islands were still visible, and we passed down a low flat chain about 1800. Some parts appeared heavily eroded, and others were like the desert mesas covered with a stick-like growth with no apparent foliage on top.

4 APRIL 1942. SATURDAY. The scheduled inspection was canceled. We had cruised along the islands all night, and as we closed them there was more foliage apparent. I was told of their volcanic origin, and that the crater was below the surface of the water.

We pulled into Uvea Harbor about 275 miles from New Caledonia. It was a moon-like part of the larger island upon which grew copra palms. *U.S.S. Chicago* and *HMAS Australia* were in the harbor, and we mustered in whites topside as we moved alongside *Australia* to fuel. *Falkefjell* was in the process of fueling *Chicago*.

There were a few white buildings back away from the beach, but they were screened by palms and other trees so I could not really identify them. Along the edge of a gleaming white sand beach a few huts were visible, and it reminded me of a Dorothy Lamour movie set. Wave action had undercut the rocky edges of the shoreline, revealing the volcanic origin of the island.

Just as soon as we finished taking on black oil, we relieved *Perkins* on ASW patrol and she came in for a drink. We got back in about 1845 and dropped anchor in 13 fathoms of water with 30 fathoms of chain out at the water's edge.

One of the things that I liked about the Engineering Department was the fact that watches were dogged on a weekly basis instead of daily. On Saturday we shifted, and meals were taken care of by watch stander relief for half an hour or so. My body adjusted to the new watch hours quickly, and I slept better than I had when the routine changed daily.

5 APRIL 1942. SUNDAY. Underway at 0820, and back to sea. We were headed back to Noumea, and thought we would escort *Falkefjell*, but she took a different course once away from Uvea.

A welcome, cooling rain fell all afternoon, and washed the salt off the superstructure. A movie was shown in the forward mess hall. That was a crowded exercise, and guys were laying in the bunks, sitting on the table tops, and wherever they could get a purchase. The old 35mm movie projector was a relic, and the films were almost as old, breaking frequently. 'Phantom Submarine' in black and white, was the epic for the afternoon

I checked out a course book for Fireman Second and First, for I did not want to waste any time in making Fireman Second Class just as soon as I had the time required in rate. All I had to do was learn pumps, boilers, and the steam cycle. That was in addition to working hard and keeping my nose clean.

6 APRIL 1942. MONDAY. There was another routine Anti Submarine GQ at 0500, and I got a few winks on my life jacket after coming out of the Boiler Room. Noumea was on the horizon after daybreak, and we were in the outer channel by 0730 and breakfast. The morning was spent alongside *Merkur* where we drew provisions. The pleasant surprise was the fact that it was American chow, not Australian, and we would be able to eat it.

While alongside an Auxiliary watch was stood in the Boiler Room. The main steam blowers were too much for a single burner so an electric auxiliary blower provided combustion air, but little ventilation so the temperature on the floor plates would go up to about 130 degrees.

The boilers do not cool down very rapidly, and the two of us on watch really sweat. Relief was provided every half hour, and I got a breath of fresh air at the top of the hatch when relieved..

We were ready to get underway at 1630, and prepared for 25 knots. Two boilers could handle that easily. Scuttlebutt had us headed for the Tonga Islands, where larger fleet units anchored, south of Samoa.

My Boot Camp trim had grown out, and I got a haircut, and when I was finished I found that a bulletin had been posted telling the crew about our next duty assignment. *Lamson* was to go to the Coral Sea, and report to Task Force 17 as part of the screen of a carrier task force led by *U.S.S. Yorktown* (CV-5) which had been built in 1937. Enterprise was the CV-6.

General Quarters was sounded for the Anti Aircraft battery about 1800. The engineering spaces were almost always manned at a battle level so there was not much change unless one of the fire rooms had been secured. At GQ the plant was usually split with #1 taking the starboard turbine, and #2 taking the port side. 5 men could handle a fire room easily. At 2000 'Lady Eve' was shown to a full house in the Forward Mess Hall. The projection lamp did not fail, nor did the Photoelectric cell on the sound track so all we had to contend with was the changing of the reels at some critical point of the plot.

7 APRIL 1942. TUESDAY. There was a library on the ship. It was not very big, but there was a good variety of books, and I was able to read when not on watch; or working on the course manual. I managed to get through "Great Impersonations" before going back on watch after the noon meal.

The weather was kicking up again, but I did not have the problem in the fire room that I had topside, for we were right in the center of the ship, and the vessel seemed to work around our center of gravity. I could hang onto the blower reach rod that ran over my head in front of the boiler, and counter the movement of the ship with the balls of my feet, swinging to the rhythm of the sea, and enjoying the sound of the boilers.

Wednesday was very rough, and we were bucking the sea, taking waves over the bow, and even the after superstructure. The Lookout Watch below the Bridge was secured. Everyone not required topside stayed below, but regular meals were served in the Mess Hall so it was not too bad, and I enjoyed the storm, and did not get seasick. Heavy weather was not a problem.

I stayed in my bunk until the Mess Cooks ran me out. On watch there was little to do but keep the fire going, and it was relatively cool with the rain topside. The afternoon cleared, and aircraft from *Yorktown* came over for an exercise. That evening I had a chance to see 'Lady Eve.'

9 APRIL 1942. THURSDAY. Another underway replenishment, or UNREP, was scheduled for the morning. We fueled from *Chicago* at 0900. The Firemen handled the big 6 inch hoses, and the Seamen handled the lines. A guywire was run between the ships, and the hoses supported on pulleys that enabled us to pull them across where they were lashed in position at the fuel intake openings. A signal was given to the provider, and they would start pumping. God help us when they started too soon, or we did not get everything out of the hose before capping off. The main deck would be awash with black oil, and we would get saturated too. Thankfully, that did not happen very often.

Word came from *U.S.S. Platte* (AO24) that Henry Briggs, an Apprentice Seaman who came aboard with me, had died in Samoa on 28 February. He had been transferred at sea with appendicitis, but must not have gotten the proper care soon enough.

At 1500 I was called below to man #4 boiler. We were building to flank speed to close the carrier task force. This was great fun for all hands, especially the Black Gang, for maneuvering gave us a chance to exercise the whole plant, and we enjoyed the pulsing throb of the ship as it pounded through the water.

Captain Mercer was a great seaman, and must have enjoyed showing the "Big Boys" the dash of the destroyer Navy as he whipped *Lamson* around to come on station. I watched him park this bucket between *Leander* and another ship at the wharf in Suva, Fiji just like he was parking a car at the curb. The Line Handlers stepped off on the dock and dropped the loops over the bollards and we doubled up and secured. He stepped over the gangway in his tropical white shorts and gave the British a real lesson.

10 APRIL 1942. FRIDAY. A little sleep, despite the racket in the Mess Hall, and then to General Quarters at 1400. I was still assigned to Sec. Con. with the XO, but had advanced to loader on one of the water cooled 50 caliber machine guns. We could barely track the fighters off the carrier, but fired at the sleeves anyway. The 5" .38 did not do much better although they made a hell of a lot more noise. We were caught between guns #3 and #4 of the main battery, and when they trained to either side we took a lot of the muzzle blasts, and powder fragments too. There was a GQ team for each fire room so if I was on watch I would be relieved and head for the gun.

We caught another Guard Mail detail, and carried mail between the units of the Task Force including *Yorktown*, *Astoria*, *Portland* and *Australia*. I was glad that I was no longer on the fo'c'sle, especially when it was choppy, for the detail got saturated.

The Radio Shack Press News told us of the fall of the garrison on Bataan. We were still taking a beating, and trying to regroup after Pearl Harbor. There was no relief for the Army, and the Navy was trying to stay out of harm's way for the present.

11 APRIL 1942. SATURDAY. *Lamson* was still taking water over the topside regularly while keeping station on the carrier. Inspection was canceled because of the weather, and I got a little sleep. The Mess Hall went up and down like an elevator and I longed for the day I would have a bunk back aft in the Engineer's Compartment, and did not have to worry about being awakened by the Mess Cooks & crew.

At about 1000 we were detached from the Task Force to escort *HMAS Australia* back to Noumea, arriving off Bulari Passage about 0700 the next morning. The watch was dogged, and I was getting familiar with the routine and found it more defined and the machinery more enjoyable to work with than the stuff topside on deck.

14 APRIL 1942. TUESDAY. A general Field Day was ordered. 'Pappy' Edwards kept #2 Fire Room so squared away that all we had to do was titivate a little bit. Admiral Chrise, a British Officer, came aboard to inspect the ship. He was pleased with the looks of the *Lamson* and her crew.

1400. Swim call for two hours. I had the 16-20 Auxiliary Watch, securing just in time for the start of the movie, a double feature with "Thanks a Million," a cartoon, and then "Coconut Grove" again.

An Australian Chaplain came aboard to talk with anyone that wanted religious counseling, and to watch the movie which was almost rained out between features.

15 APRIL 1942. WEDNESDAY. Reveille was at 0630, and we went topside to an overcast sky with showers that helped clean and cool the topside.

A school of tuna-like fish were sporting in the harbor, chasing the smaller fish for breakfast. Number Two Fire Room took all of my time in the morning, and Edwards gave me a chance to learn about the bilges. I cleaned the pockets between the frames under the floor plates, and attacked a little rust with scraper and wire brush before applying the trusty red lead. At least it did not come off as fast down here as it had topside.

The break for lunch was a real treat, for the menu included turkey, cranberry sauce, and all the trimmings. It was just like a holiday. We were being prepared for another "All Hands" working party on board *HMAS Merkur*. This time we found fresh fruit as well as dry, and bulk stores. The party enabled me to capture a couple of Sunkist oranges and an apple. Cookies also came aboard for the little Ship's Service Store: 60 cases would be sold at 15 cents a pack. With my new pay for Fireman Third I could afford to splurge on them. The movie on the Fantail was appropriately titled, "Night in the Tropics." I watched the film, napped afterwards, and then was called out for my Auxiliary Watch at midnight.

16 APRIL 1942. THURSDAY. WT1C Edwards had me in the bilges again. He was a real taskmaster, for he did burden us with labor. I had another hour with him in the afternoon, but had a chance at some recreation that was out of the ordinary for Fireman.

A party from *HMAS Australia* sailed over in a cutter, and I was given the chance to join the sailing party. LT Jenkins, ENS Conley, and Lt. j.g. Hayes as well as S1C Coke, S2C Freese, myself and S2c Taylor made up the LAMSON party that dropped into the cutter with the Australians. We had sandwiches, cookies and fruit to keep us alive while sailing the cutter around the harbor. It was a beautiful afternoon and 1700 came too quickly. I have never forgotten the sailing instructions or the enjoyable afternoon. 'Shepherd of the Hills' was the movie, accompanied by a few showers.

17 APRIL 1942. FRIDAY. This was my fourth month in the Navy, and I celebrated it in the bilges again. The fresh fruit had given me the runs which complicated life, and I was queasy. There was a swim call in the afternoon, and another sailing party. That night the movie was "Dance Hall."

18 APRIL 1942. SATURDAY. Number 2 Fire Room was lit off at 0430 by the 04 - 08 Aux. Watch. I had the 16-20 for the rest of the week. Our 'in port' upkeep period was at an end, and at 1000 we left the anchorage for Efate, New Hebrides Islands with four Army passengers, including a Major

General, Major and two Lieutenants. We had the Flag space for the general. Course 158 degrees then 000 true to Vila.

About sunset an island appeared on the Port beam. It had a high symmetrical cone on the south end, and sloped into a long graded plain on the north side. The sun was setting behind it making a deep red sky which silhouetted the island beautifully against the horizon.

19 APRIL 1942. SUNDAY. Quarters for Muster again. The Division Officers were required to read 'Rocks and Shoals' to their men periodically. Navy Regulations and the Courtsmartial Manual were the Bibles of the Navy, and were read to acquaint sailors with the pitfalls and punishments that could lie ahead if we were not careful.

Just before lunch we encountered a small French freighter, and the Captain challenged it as we made a sweeping high speed circle around the ship with our main battery trained out just in case the '*Polynesia*' was armed and unfriendly. There were still a lot of loyal Vichy French units in the world, and we were taking no chances.

After lunch the Boatswain's Mate of the Watch passed the word that the uniform of the day was Undress Whites. We entered Vila Harbor about 1330 and dropped the hook with about 45 fathoms of chain out of the hawse pipe..

ENS Samuels had been given the wrong dope, and we just about put the fantail on the beach so we had to move and do it again. The fantail was so close we could see the outriggers on the beach, and they were just like those in the movies.

Liberty was piped about 1600 for 80 men of Section 3. Four hours were granted, enabling us to stretch our legs a bit. The light rain did not dampen the sailor's spirits either, or keep any aboard. A movie on the fantail showed 'Dulce,' and 'Girls under 21.'

VILA HARBOR, EFATE, NEW HEBRIDES ISLANDS.

The approach was generally from the south just as with Oahu. The island was mountainous with a very rich green covering. As usual, there were small hills surrounding the harbor which sheltered it, and provided excellent vantage points for viewing the surroundings. The channel took us to the right as we came in, and dead ahead lay the small town similar to most of the tropical villages and communities that we had visited. Our anchorage was in a clover shaped harbor with Vila at the top of the center leaf. The light yellow buildings were roofed with red tile, or rusty corrugated iron which made them stand out sharply from the luxuriant green backdrop of the hills. The scene from the harbor was quite beautiful, and it was not until we got ashore that the true composition of the buildings, and the primitive nature of the town, was revealed.

We had anchored in the center of the right clover leaf, and to our right was a small mission, or school building, with many natives in the area. They appeared to be mostly women and children, and much like those we had encountered in Fiji. There was a high bluff in back of the town, and facing the sea. On the opposite side of the bay were thousands of tall, thin coconut palms in a tended grove. These provided the copra that was the industrial base for the town.

On the left side of the main channel there was what appeared to be a natural park. Some of the palatial dwellings were on this point. One large place was clear of trees except for a clump in the center. The field was grassy and exceptionally green, for the annual rainfall is high in this region. I would go ashore for a closer look the next day.

20 APRIL 1942. MONDAY. Two liberty parties were scheduled for the day. I went ashore in the morning from 0900 to 1130, but there was nothing in town so the short time was about right. There was a large general store on the main drag, which was like an alley, and several smaller shops run by the natives. The currency was English, and the rate of exchange was 6 shillings to the dollar.

Back of town, on the hill, was a Catholic church, and several of us walked up to see what it looked like. There was a machine gun nest nearby, manned by Australian soldiers, and we chatted about the duty in the islands. We were treated to coconuts cut right off the tree, and they were ripe and very good.

After returning to the ship, and lunch, we lounged around topside for a bit and watched the natives in their outriggers (bum boats) trying to sell their fruit and carvings. The Supply Officer had made arrangements for fresh oranges and coconuts to be delivered to the ship, and I got called out for the stores handling working party.

21 APRIL 1942. TUESDAY. Boilers 2 and 4 were given a rest and the forward Boiler Room was lit off at 0430, and we were underway shortly after Quarters for Muster. The sea was rough outside the harbor, and I turned in until called for my watch.

Passed Lifu Island on the starboard side on our southerly course for Noumea. The day became very interesting for all hands. Suddenly the head would not accommodate the crowd, for the fresh fruit had given all hands the runs. The Shipfitters and Carpenter's Mates rigged stages just forward of the prop guards on the main deck, and the First Lieutenant relied on the rough sea to take care of general cleanliness.

When we got in about 1630 we went alongside a Royal Fleet Auxiliary, *Bishopdale*, for fuel. We fueled at every opportunity, for there was no telling what sudden surprises might overtake us, and full tanks gave us a lot of confidence.

The movie was set up on the Fantail again, this time "Northwest Mounted Police," but I was called away for a stores working party that went to *U.S.S. Tippecanoe* (AO-21), *Perkins*, and *Tangiers*. Another sea plane tender, *U.S.S. Wright* (AV-1), had joined us. Some of the larger flying boats were making the run between Oahu and Noumea with mail, passengers, and high priority cargo so there was a need for service at this end.

At 0330 Wednesday morning the Deck Force was called out for Special Sea Detail and we moved alongside *Perkins* and then *Merkur* for more provisions. We were going to leave Noumea after Quarters. On our way out of Bulari Passage we passed *Leander* waiting for our ASW patrol. Once we had set up the screen she came out, and we escorted her to Suva, Fiji.

24 APRIL 1942. FRIDAY. As we were about to enter port a convoy crossed our track port to starboard, with a four piper escort, and disappeared over the horizon. Probably headed for Australia.

HMNZS Leander led us into the harbor and tied up to the wharf. We went alongside and took on fuel and diesel oil. Then there followed an exchange of visits between the crews of the two ships. I went aboard and talked to one of the firemen who invited me to go below and visit their boiler rooms. It was even worse than the *Chicago's* and I was glad that I did not have to serve those boilers.

Liberty for Section 2, and I went ashore from 1600 to 2200. After to bottles of excellent Aussie beer, and a glass of wine, several of us found a taxi and made a tour of the city. I enjoyed the Aussie Ice Cream and candy bars too. We found a roller rink and skated for awhile then heard of dances at the local parish hall, and the New Zealand Club. Not being picky, we looked in on both, and found the floors crowded with sailors of all three navies.

Of course the girls were outnumbered, and one had to cut in to dance, but it was a very nice change after the few weeks at sea. I almost got into a fight over one girl whose partner accused me of patting her on the fanny. It was so crowded that all of the girls probably got a few pats here and there. The big bloke was outnumbered by U.S. sailors so he put me down.

25 APRIL 1942. SATURDAY. Visits between *Leander* & *Lamson* increased. I was invited to one of the engineering messes, and found that the British sailors slept, ate and generally lived in a compartment by Division. We were in time for the rum ration, and were able to share that fine English custom. My host showed me the whole ship this time, and we were able to get an ice cream from the canteen. I invited him to come over for dinner.

The evening meal was crowded with New Zealand sailors, for many of us were returning the favors of the afternoon, including the rum. They thought we ate well, and enjoyed the canned beef stew that the cooks put up. We had lots of guests during the three days we were there.

26 APRIL 1942. SUNDAY. Mass was celebrated, and I lounged around most of the morning, but managed to wash my whites before visiting *Leander* again. There was a piano in their Recreation Lounge, and I worked on the keys, but was stiff and could remember some of Gramercy Square and 12th St. Rag. One of their chaps played very well.

Before going on watch at 1600 I saw *U.S.S. Sims* (DD409) and *Ramsey* come into port.

27 APRIL 1942. MONDAY. I had the 4 to 8 Auxiliary Watch on #4 boiler; and at 0530 the Steaming Watch came down and lit off boilers 1,2, and 3, making us ready to reach 35 knots if needed. By 0710 we were underway as a screen for *Leander* heading for Samoa. About 1300 we sighted two large volcanic islands and sailed between them. I found out that *Leander* had just been fitted out with new 20mm anti aircraft guns, and was taking some to *Achilles*; the light cruiser that had tangled with the German pocket battleship *Graf Spee* off Montevideo.

28 APRIL 1942. TUESDAY. The clocks were set ahead an hour from 2330 to 0030 as we crossed the International Dateline; screwing up the watchbill. After daylight there were 'flank speed' maneuvers, an abandon ship drill, and air bedding in that order. The sea was almost dead calm as we passed Kappel Island at over 10,000 yards. All we could see was a part of the 2,000 ft. volcanic cone from such a distance.

There were two Tuesdays, and we raised Samoa about 0800 on the second Tuesday, celebrating the event with an anti aircraft drill at 1000. *Achilles* and two *Gridley* class cans joined us and 7 Grumman fighters came out from the island to attack the force.

A convoy of troop ships came out, and the two single pipers and the cruisers took off with it in the direction of Australia. The Army was staging in Australia in preparation for the drive north, and to protect Australia from the menace of the Japanese Army.

We took station on a Liberty ship, *John Paul Jones*, that I had helped build while at Cal Ship on Terminal Island, and escorted her into Pago. The large deep blue breakers at the mouth of the channel threw up a beautiful misty spray that caught the morning sunlight, making our landfall something out of a movie travelogue.

Once inside the deep harbor we found the DESRON 5 Flagship, *U.S.S. Flusser* (DD368) and transferred the ANZAC signal flags to her, indicating that we were through with *Leander* for awhile. We also found many units of the fleet including *U.S.S. Honolulu* (CL48), *U.S.S. Harris* (APA2), *U.S.S. Zeilen* (APA3), and *U.S.S. O'Brien* (DD415).

The Harbor Master instructed the Captain to moor the ship between two large buoys aft of *Zeilen* which was unloading cargo into Marine landing barges. It was dusk at 1830 so we could not see much of the beach. Winter was approaching below the equator.

29 APRIL 1942. WEDNESDAY. *U.S.S. Mustin* (DD413) was alongside and a couple of us went over to see what the boiler rooms and living spaces were like, for we had not had a chance to look at one of the newer cans. She was Sims Class built in 1939, and a little more than two years out of the yard. The boilers were encased, taking the air pressure directly, so the space was not as hot as ours with the whole space being open to the boilers. Living was about the same, for not much could be done with a berthing space.

The Master at Arms requested that I join them on a working party on the *Harris* that was loaded with Marines, and very crowded. After taking on provisions we moved out to the anchorage and dropped the hook only to get underway about 1600 to go alongside *Honolulu* for fuel, canteen and deck stores, and then it was back alongside *Mustin* at the buoys.

The *Mustin* had just come down from San Francisco and the guys told us that there were 7 battleships there. The Pearl Harbor Ship Yard had done a monumental job getting them out of the mud.

30 APRIL 1942. THURSDAY. There was a field day in the fire room, but liberty was on the Plan of the Day for 1400 - 1800 and that was something to look forward to, but the morning was spent on my Cleaning Station. It was only 110 deg. in the fire room and fairly comfortable.

I shared the starboard bulkhead, upper gratings, 1 set of bilges, 1 bilge pump, and the Emergency Feed Pump with another Fireman. Things were kept spotless, and the bilge was clean; no grease or oil. I had scrubbed the bulkhead earlier so all we had to do was titivate the space, and that went quickly. Topside, the First Lt. was trying to paint the ship in the rain.

When liberty call was sounded Gaines and I landed at Tutuila with the liberty party in our Undress Whites, and went directly to the Marine Canteen where there was beer and ice cream. A quart of beer and two cones made a wild dessert after lunch, but they tasted great so we took off to see what the town offered. There was a small business district, but behind it was a residential area that drew us on. The Samoan houses consisted of a thatched roof on palm tree trunks embedded in a platform of oyster shells and rock. The floor was covered with coco mats and tapa cloth. Woven blinds, almost like Venetian blinds, could be lowered from the roof line to give privacy, or protection from the elements.

We talked to the girls and found that the Samoans made love at night, not during the day, and we were out of luck for liberty expired before sundown. They were fun to talk to, and we enjoyed the banter.

The island was extremely verdant with a veritable jungle of vines, palms, ferns and large tropical trees, for the rain came down like I had never seen before. Tutuila had some shell and rock paving that stretched along the south side of the harbor for about a mile. Pago was at the west end of the long east to west harbor, and about 5 miles from the mouth of the channel that faced south to the open sea.

We decided to walk to Pago, and found the road along the water's edge to be a sea of mud after we left Tutuila. The high mountains on either side of the harbor made any other roadway impossible. Our whites were saturated with mud to the crotch when we got back to the landing.

1 MAY 1942. FRIDAY. *Lamson* would get underway again. There was the usual muster in the morning, some titivating in the fire room, and after lunch #3 boiler was put on the line in preparation for getting underway. As a part of the Harbor Master's ship shuffling we had *U.S.S. Sumner* (AGS15) at our side for most of the morning. She was a brand new Survey Ship that would help chart the unknown waters of the western Pacific.

At 1400 we slipped our moorings and were outbound again, passing *McCall* (DD400) on her way in. The bright morning sun picked up the spray on the long swells and breakers headed for the beach, making a foggy boundary between the clear ocean and the green, high landmass.

We had been assigned the job of helping *McCall* escort a barge of machinery to Apia, British Samoa. They came out about dusk and we were off again.

2 MAY 1942. SATURDAY. While I was on the 8-12 on #4 boiler we started into Apia Harbor, and I got a burner barrel crookedly into its socket on the valve seat. A backing bell was received, and as I cut the burner in the hot oil sprayed out of the bad seat, throwing a fine spray of 160 degree hot oil over the face of the boiler; and the watertender, Roy Edwards. I was in deep trouble, for Edward's dungarees were always immaculate, and I had changed all of that. He was mad as hell, and I stayed below to clean up the fire room while the watch went topside to the cool of the morning.

I did get permission to go ashore in the afternoon, after #4 was polished, and found the women friendly, and the Samoan home brewed beer refreshing. As at Tutuila, the girls wanted us to come back at night for there was no 'jig, jig' during the daylight hours. Tafolla, and Colaizzo must have taken them at their word, for they were not on board when we got underway that afternoon. Liberty had generated a conflict and we were treated to a short 'honor battle' on the fantail that settled the matter with no hard feelings.

The run back to Tutuila was quick at 25 knots, and we were back between *Zeilen* and *Harris* by 1700. *U.S.S. Boise* (CL47) was in port after her action with the Asiatic Squadron and the Dutch. She looked very rugged, and scabrous, in the black paint that she wore. We heard that the cruiser was on her way to the States for a major overhaul, and new anti aircraft weapons.

4 MAY 1942. MONDAY. Pay Day, and another $30.00 for All Hands, including the Captain. The *Flusser* had departed with the Disbursing Officer and our Pay Records, but it was not all bad, for the rain and overcast caused the cancellation of an underway Anti Aircraft exercise. The overwrought gunners' mates had to go to the Marine Canteen with the rest of us and drink beer. I walked back to Pago and bought a beautiful palm frond 'corking mat' as a souvenir. Many bought tapa cloth, but I did not care for it so passed it up.

5 MAY 1942. TUESDAY. The buildup in the Pacific was increasing, but the Japanese still controlled the direct routes to the Philippines from Hawaii so everything was routed through Samoa. As we got underway early in the morning with *Mustin, O'Brien,* and *Honolulu* an incoming convoy came on the scene as well as the Destroyer Tender *Rigel* (AD13) with a tin can escort. We would get a tender availability after almost 6 months at sea with little, or no maintenance other that by Ship's Force.

Minor crew changes began, and one Fireman injured his hand and went to the Hospital so I got his bunk in the Engineers Compartment. I was out of the crowded Mess Hall where the crew seemed to play cards all night on the table under my bunk, and could sleep until 0700 instead of 0530 when the Mess Cooks began to set up for breakfast. My next problem was to deal with the guy that owned the footlocker under the bunk, for if he needed clothes I had to roll out so my bunk could be lifted.

17 MAY 1942. SUNDAY. While sheltered in Tutuila Harbor I celebrated my 5th month in the Navy. I had survived, and all of us were busy cleaning and repairing the ship as rumors flew that we were about to get a new Skipper.

I was studying the Fireman Second Class manual, and was to turn the work sheets over to the Division Officer, and take a short progress exam once I had the required time in grade. The course material was interesting and close to the work so it was not difficult, although the material on the engine room was new. I had no experience with pumps, or condensers. The care and feeding of boilers, and boiler nomenclature was detailed, and I would become more intimate with the details later as I crawled around the tight, hot spaces.

The war in the Pacific was still full of Japanese successes. *Lexington* had been sunk, and *Yorktown* damaged, on 8 May in the Battle of the Coral Sea, and our forces were still trying to recoup from the initial losses at Pearl Harbor, and build for a counter attack. The Army Air Force raid on Tokyo helped morale, but did little damage. We were still staying out of the way, and *Lamson* needed anti-aircraft gunnery modernization badly.

After our stay in Samoa the crew was treated to another visit to Suva, Fiji;

leaving the ANZAC Squadron, and returning to Samoa the last week in May.

28 MAY 1942. THURSDAY. 0620. Underway again, and this time everyone was pleased to be headed back to Pearl even though it was as a screen for the *U.S.S. Tippecanoe* (AO9). This World War I oiler had a top speed of about 9 knots, and *Lamson* toiled back and forth out in front for about 9 days. Once the oiler had an engine room failure and the C.O. asked if she wanted a tow. The skipper of the oiler outranked LCDR Mercer, and did not take kindly to the offer. Later we found out that the oil was going to be made available for the Battle of Midway; just in case. George, F1C was given a summary court for gambling, and reduced to F2C. This was one of the big sports on the ship, but the Navy Regs came down hard on the activity.

MONOTONY
JANUARY - MAY 1943

1 JANUARY 1943. FRIDAY. We started the New Year on ASW patrol off the harbor of Espiritu Santo, temporary home of *U.S.S. Dixie* (AD-14), and Cruiser Task Force 67. This was also our recreation and beer party home after the Guadalcanal runs with the cruisers, or a convoy.

Lt. j.g. Behan had become the Engineering officer with the transfer of Mr. Conley, and he gave me my Certificate of Completion for the Electrician's Mate Third Class course. It was dated 27 December 1942, and signed by Commander Fitzgerald.

4 JANUARY 1943. MONDAY. TF 67 had been split for action against Munda on New Georgia. *Drayton, Lamson,* and *Nicholas* (DD-449), escorted *Louisville* (CA-28) on a diversion while remainder of Task Force bombarded Munda. The next day we were steaming off the port side of *HMNZS Achilles* when the force was attacked by dive bombers. *Achilles* was the main target and took a small bomb on number 3 turret. There was little damage and she did not leave formation.

10 JANUARY 1943. SUNDAY. Yesterday was Payday again, and since I had been saving my cash I sent $90.00 home. I would want some money easily available when we got back home again.

NOTE: We had an availability alongside an old repair ship, *U.S.S. Vestal* (AR-4), built in 1913, and damaged on 7 DEC. The *Lamson* Electrician's Mates had to stand watches on one of *Vestal's* Auxiliary Electrical Generators that was supplying power to *Lamson*. I had the mid, and when my watch came around I found that they darkened ship almost completely. Well, I got to the watch station OK because my eyes were used to the dark, and I could see the ladder railings gleaming in the dim light. In one of the auxiliary spaces I spotted a pump with a *U.S.S. Georgia* nameplate on it. My Dad was in *Georgia* for training in WW I.

When the watch was over, it was a different story because I had been in a well lighted space. I made the first ladder OK, but from there I was lost. I guess I bumped into all the machine tools in the shop, and walked over half the crew before I found a hand lantern and got out. I found later that every one of us standing that watch had the same story.

20 JANUARY 1943. WEDNESDAY. LCDR W.T. Jenkins had left the ship when we got back into Espiritu, Lt. Hayes was signing the logs, but

would be relieved by Lt. H.B. Sanders, USNR our new Executive Officer.

The Task Force had returned to Espiritu Santo, and *Lamson* was alongside *U.S.S. Dixie.* Everything seemed to go awry, or quit, at once so there were switches to clean, motors to repair, lights to install, batteries to clean and charge, and the Captain conducted the routine Personnel and Lower Deck Inspections as well.

Note: After the short tender availability TF-67 got underway for Vila, in the Russell Islands.
TF 67 was now four Light Cruisers and seven destroyers.
One day we were cruising along very slowly, and because of the calmness of the water, we could see several large shadows following alongside. They were large sharks, and the CO authorized a little target practice for the riflemen that were assigned anti-shark duties during swim call. They did stir up the water when hit by 30 cal. bullet.

Speaking of fish, schools of porpoise would sport along the surface of the water. Flying fish skipped away from the bows and really travel. They'd hit the water traveling one way, and in a split second be out again and moving swiftly in a completely different direction. Once in awhile we could see a shark's dorsal fin cutting the water just behind the flying fish.

Large schools of porpoise had suddenly appeared near by. They swam on the surface, arching their backs out of the water in such a way that the sun caught their gleaming backs, and they seemed afire.

It was not all monotony. More than once the lookout watch reported the surfacing porpoise, while far off, as torpedo wakes, for the fish would head for our bows and play in the bow wave. One evening about dusk a larger fish, presumably a whale, came to the surface close aboard, spouted and submerged again. Things like that were always interesting and part of the many beauties that were to be found if one could only take the time to see them, or even smell them.

The smell of land was very pungent and strong after a few days at sea, whereas the sea breeze was at its best after being below or just coming out of harbor. One had to look for beauty, or this life became too drab with regulation and routine.

A destroyer knifing and rolling along at high speed, or a fleet maneuver with all the signal flags flying, and planes overhead made an exciting moment if one could pause long enough to watch it. This was one advantage the topside sailors had. They saw more than we engineers did. The elements were a never ending source of interest too. Different shadings in the clouds, the sea, and the effect of a sunset or sunrise on a ship seemed to soften all the harshness about one.

On a particular evening the sunset was especially lovely. Deep reds and purples blending into blues, green and yellow beyond description. Shadows on the western slopes of the small islands, so green and clear in the sun seemed intangible and made the land an unreal blob on the horizon. The way the clouds piled up over an island like a protective cover could be spectacular. All of this produced on a canvas would make a person famous.

Dusk too had its charms. One evening as I sat on deck enjoying the coolness of the shadows the southern sky built up into a forbidding darkness of towering clouds. The rain wisps were like fine grey curtains hung from them, and there might be lightning playing back and forth from their deepest parts. I enjoyed watching this show of the elements and only wished that I might be watching as I used to when we, Ken, Stew, and I drove the old Chevvie into the Palos Verdes hills and the rain.

Flash and fork lightning made a varied program for its audience of one, but it was great pantomime and the thunder did not take its part because of the distance. As night came on each flash illuminated the ship like a powerful light. More than once it helped me find my way down a darkened deck--it also could help a submarine skipper.

Note: 21 JANUARY 1943. Nimitz and Halsey met on U.S.S. Curtis (AV-1) while we were at Espiritu Santo. The Japs bombed Segond Channel.

23 - 24 JANUARY 1943. Task Force 67 bombarded Vila, Kolombangara. Again, *Lamson* was in a support role with *Honolulu* and *St. Louis* as a diversion force.

1 FEBRUARY 1943. MONDAY. I took, and passed, the exam for Electrician Mate Third Class last month, and effective this date was advanced to EM3/C. Tom Hebard was advanced to Electrician's Mate First, and my buddy Frank Ganem made MM2/C. I had a months pay on the books, $55.00, and drew it all.

Our glass smooth sea had replaced itself with rolling swells. With this came clouds, rain, wind and cooler compartments. We rolled, and dipped gently to the waves slightest whims and when speeding along it was interesting work keeping in an upright position while walking down the heaving deck. There had been little spray which was a relief because that continuous salty/oily feeling got old after a day or so.

1-14 FEBRUARY 1943.   The Task Force, and *Lamson*, operated for two weeks between Santa Cruz, Guadalcanal, in the Coral Sea area. We were still working with TF 67 around Munda and Rabaul on hit and run bombardment missions. U.S.S. *Chicago* was lost to enemy aircraft. Those Washington Treaty cruisers had little protection, and when a torpedo slowed her down bombers were able to sink the ship a day later.   I thought of our two weeks in transit on the cruiser, my old high school buddy-Kenny Harris, and those deep fire rooms.

14 FEBRUARY 1943. SUNDAY. There was another 'Tender Availability' alongside *U.S.S. Dixie* at Espiritu Santo. The Japanese mounted several air raids while we were "cold iron" alongside, and it is a real kick when the ship is unable to defend itself; except for a few exposed 20 mm guns.

One time, I had the gyrocompass motor-generator on the tender and we got word to put everything back together and get out of the harbor. The Black Gang heaved around all night long, and we were able to get the gear back before the repair people got to it. I had the gyro up on meridian about daylight when the enemy alert was cancelled.

16 FEBRUARY 1943. TUESDAY. The *Lamson* sailors looked forward to the rain squalls that came almost every afternoon because it gave us some fresh water for a bath. We caught water in any container handy, and bathed out of a bucket; often on the main deck in the downpour.

Since the ship was still tied up alongside *U.S.S. Dixie*, those sailors hung over the rail and had a real laugh as we scrubbed. They had plenty of water, and our evaporators were torn down. *Dixie* could not make enough fresh water for the cans alongside, and so we fended for ourselves.

About the time I got soaped down one afternoon, the rain squall passed, and about that time there was an air attack alert with the General Alarm chasing us to battle stations before I could rinse off. A dry soapy skin is very uncomfortable. The Tender's policy on repair parts was negative too. The Repair Officer figured that we would be sunk at Guadalcanal, and the stuff expended on us would be wasted.

We were eating well though. For awhile we were on short rations, but that was over and we were having 4.0 meals. Steak and eggs, or two fried eggs and bacon, the usual beans and cinnamon rolls twice a week (Wed. & Sat.) for breakfast. Beef roast, pork chops, carrots, peas, spuds (dehydrated foods mostly) powdered lemonade, cocoa, coffee, etc., etc....for dinner; and cold cuts such as tongue, spam or bologna for the evening meal.

There was another payday, and the increase to EM3C gave me $95.00 on the books. The pay raise was welcome. Base Pay for Third Class with less than three years in service was $78.00 a month.

23 FEBRUARY 1943. TUESDAY. There had been another patrol run, and we were back in Espiritu Santo again. On Washington's Birthday we had turkey for chow. Work went on as usual--there was a Fleet Letter telling us to 'carry on.' We did! I was able to go ashore with a recreation party in the afternoon for a bit of a hike and a swim. The beach where we swam was in a cove and tide didn't get in there very much, consequently the water was as the Long Beach Plunge in fact it was almost hot.

The bottom was coarse sand with a smooth, rocky beach. It was shallow for about 75 ft. and then dropped off. There were patches of a spongy 'hand-like' sea plant down there too, and it was startling to be swimming on ones back and bump into the rubbery roughness.

Note: The Recreation Area was in the former copra grove, and the flies were fierce. It was also very hot and humid, but the beer tasted good.

There was something that we really looked forward to after the rigors of a patrol run to Guadalcanal. It was called "Going Alongside a Tender."

In preparation for this big event the Chiefs would get their men together and conjure up all the work that they could think they could get the Tender Repair Department to take on. He then prepared the draft repair orders and made sure that everything needed was requested. Repair orders and requisitions were typed and put it priority order. These were presented to the Department Heads.

The Department Heads went over the requisitions with the Skipper, and they were delivered to a highly skeptical Repair Officer on the big Tender. He throws about half of the work in the waste basket, and Ship's Force ended up doing all of the dirty work.

The Firerooms were secured which in turn secured the power and water in the Main Plant. A huge shore power cable is hauled across the other cans to the tender, as well as a flexible metal steam line so the galley can still function. There were several cans alongside we could expect to be # 3, or 4 out from the Tender because of the low seniority of our Skipper. That meant hauling fuel and power lines across about 150 ft. of deck space and narrow gangways to get to our ship. Much heaving and hauling and a lot of sweat too. We fueled ship, put across steam and power connections and were all set, but there was fresh feed water only in the ships tanks since the Big Ship could not suckle all of us at once. That meant little water for personal use, and rationing.

The next problem was the "Working Party." All descriptions, sizes and shapes were these. Stores, provisions, big pieces of stuff, and just general miscellaneous what evers. The Masters at Arms, and whoever was put in charge, ran wild and piped, hollered and generally made a nuisance of themselves getting all of the "non-rated" men to 'turn to' on the stores, or, "Lay Aft on the Fantail" to handle provisions. It looked like we are loading for a year long cruise when all the stuff was scattered on deck topside. It lasted no time though when this hard eating crew dug in--maybe two weeks-- and we started all over.

After the Stores Working Party there was the general ship's work to do. The Deck Apes promptly roped off all of the Main Deck so one could not move fore, or aft. They beat, chipped, scraped, wirebrushed, and polished the steel in preparation for a coat of red lead which was liberally applied to everything!

The ship was a madhouse of cables, air hoses, steam lines and wet paint. If there was no paint, the deck had been swabbed some place or other, and some "swabhandle" was screaming, "Wet deck," at you as you tried to go about your own tedious tasks. Normally the 'Deck Ape' carried a big club, or wet swab as a persuader.

In the Afternoon, the gedunk (ice cream) stand opened on the Tender, and the crew disappeared to be found standing in line half the length of the tender, waiting for a pint or two, a sundae, or two drinks--coke or cherry--which I mixed. I'll bet that I had eaten gallons of the mixture. We were all Gedunk Sailors now. About this time everybody had enough of the "tender duty," and wanted to go back to sea, or home, or any place else for that matter.

Movies were available at the Movie Exchange on the Tender, or the beach. We got them --some new, some old -- by trading those we have for an equal number of different ones. Electrician Mates ran the movies so we had a degree of power over selection. At Movie Call the men dragged their benches, boxes, and chairs out of the shops and other spaces up to the Fantail in preparation for the Movie. The Officers and Chiefs had their mess chairs brought aft by the respective Stewards and Mess Hall Attendants and they flanked the sailors in the center.

There was usually a record recital of jazz and swing before the show to keep the bench warmers from getting restless. If it did not rain the show was a pleasure, but rain spoiled it very little 'cause the guys stayed and watched, rain or not, for a tarp was thrown over the projector, and the movie continued for as long as the Captain let it go on. If he stayed, everybody stayed.

The word finally got around that we were shoving off in the near future, and then the scuttlebutt ran awash with the "Straight Dope" as to where we are going the next time out.

Finally, the boilers were lit off again, the rainmakers re-commissioned and the power plant put back on the line, and we are ready to do our duty once more for Home and Uncle. Back go the thousands of feet of fuel hoses, power and steam lines. The decks are cleared of line and we are ready to cast off just as soon as the outboard can clears. Too often we are it, and get to be the first out on ASW Patrol. Especially if the C.O belts the Port Captain.

One military event alongside was stirring. First call always reminded me of the race track. The "Call to Colors" followed shortly, and the band on the tender got to practice with a short concert. The Lamson crew was called to attention by one blast on the mouth whistle, and we came to attention quickly. A look down the ranks, and one notices that the men are swaying gently in unison. Can't be still at all after rolling on the ocean for awhile.

26 FEBRUARY 1943. FRIDAY. The short wave radio set in the shop helped pass away many spare moments for all of us. There were orchestrations are Australian, and news from about four sources. Berlin, Tokyo, USA, and London or Australia. The broadcasts from the first two were in excellent English with the German broadcast the more interesting than the Japanese.

The Germans broadcast a more American style program, while the Japs talked more like the British, and said nothing for the whole period of air time. One Jap program of news was devoted solely to a review of their capture of Singapore a year ago.

1 MARCH 1943. MONDAY. Neal McShane and Dave Powers made Second Class, and the boxes of cigars helped break the monotony too. When I made Third I upgraded from White Owl to a better brand of cigars; as they did too.

11 MARCH 1943. THURSDAY. One of the Division's duties was the watch in After Steering, a very noisy, stuffy, and rough Compartment in the very stern. This was a very dull, but responsible, watch over the electrical/hydraulic steering machinery. There was nothing to do but sit and wait until something failed, or an emergency drill was run from the Bridge. When under way the topside hatch was open during the day, but dogged down at night and then it became hot and reeked of hydraulic oil. The Seamen's Compartment was just forward, and they suffered from the noise and smell too.

Before I started these watches I'd never steered a course as helmsman. One afternoon we were in company with some other ships and the O.D. held a casualty drill on the Bridge. Result: A very erratic course and a wiser watch stander. The guys on the bridge said they got a kick out of it because first I tried to ram the ships on one side and then the next minute, I'd have us headed directly away from them.

A siren wailed when the Bridge shifted control to Steering Aft. It was enough to shake the Watch Stander out of his torpor, and cause him to head for the small wheel in a hurry. I think that I could answer two phones and take control in one movement once I became trained. A compass indicator was all there was to guide the operator, and the small brass steering wheel was about the size of a car's. The Bridge watch would give the course to steer over the phones and one would try to maintain course by watching the gyro compass indicator.

The other day there was a Ship's Recreation Party. The main attraction was two pints of beer. We have not seen any white women since Honolulu. It got a bit tiresome after 7 months, but we were able to laugh it off and say "Boy, wait 'till we get back."

Our only dancing was on the fantail, and McKeever and Lightfoot were the pros. Some raisenjack was made, and there was an occasional drop of Gyro Alcohol, but we looked forward to the beer parties. We were still supporting the Guadalcanal 'mop-up' work with Task Force 67; trying to keep the Japanese Navy from reinforcing, or removing their troops.

16 MARCH 1943. TUESDAY. Another draft came aboard in Espiritu, on a stop enroute to Noumea, and E Division received Vern Tatum and Richard Thomas; both EM3/C out of Class A Electrician's Mates School. Allen Shipman CM2C also came aboard and went into the Shipfitters Division. He had a trumpet with him, and would be a welcome addition to the little combo.

19 MARCH 1943. FRIDAY. Time zone Minus 11. The ship was back in the Noumea area, and E Division received two more men from the Naval Operating Base, Noumea. One was Willis Paull, and the other was Fred Sass. Both were EM3/C right out of Class A School.

Now there were changes in work assignments in the Electrical Gang. I moved from "Boats and Batteries" to the Interior Communications Circuits, and Chief Kerszis and Clinton Little were breaking me in on the Sperry Gyrocompass, and all of the Interior Communications systems within the ship. That included the selsyn transmission systems, navigating machinery, and Sound Powered Telephones and the interconnecting cables and boxes. There was a lot to it; scattered all over the ship from stem to stern and bilge to masthead. There were few instruction books, but lots of blueprints, and I began to learn the whole ship, and get to know people in all of the spaces, and how they supported the mission.

23 MARCH 1943. TUESDAY. We were a wing DD in the ASW screen for a convoy of freighters that were helping resupply the troops on Guadalcanal. About 0100 I was thrown out of my bunk when the ship brushed a coral reef with the Stbd. propeller, throwing the stern into the air like a ball. Another foot to starboard and the reef would have opened up the whole starboard side like a can opener, and at the speed we were moving we would have gone under very quickly. "Lucky Lamson" had not been ripped open, and we continued on station with the convoy, and patrolled off the beach while they unloaded at Lunga Point.

28 MARCH 1943. SUNDAY. Lt. H.B. Sanders was signing the Deck Logs as XO and Navigator.

31 MARCH 1943. TUESDAY. Again, we were back with our friends in Floating Dry Dock RD-2. While the screws were being changed so we would have a balanced pair, the Engineering Department got to go over the side and polish the hull again. As in October of '42 we spent about 3 days trying to use the services of the dry dock. From there we went alongside U.S.S. Whitney. The Whitney crewmen were not convinced that Noumea was better than Pearl Harbor.

7 APRIL 1943. TUESDAY. Mail had caught up with the ship again after chasing us for anywhere from a month and a half to two months. Lamson was still alongside Whitney in Noumea while Task Force 67 was in action off Tulagi. This was to be the last attempt by Adm. Yamamoto to attack the Solomons and relieve the Japanese troops trapped there.

We missed six runs up the slot (New Georgia Sound) by Adm. Ainsworth's cruiser task force as our forces thwarted Japanese support of Vila on Kolombangara. Air actions against the force off Tulagi sank the Aaron Ward (DD-483).

8 APRIL 1943. WEDNESDAY. Underway again with a tanker in support

of Task Force 10 in the Coral Sea. Once we caught up with the main body of three wagons, a cruiser and 8 destroyers we were assigned a position in the screen.

I finally got an upright locker in the Engineer's Compartment. It had taken over a year. I began to get my uniforms in shape, and properly marked with my new crows. It made little difference because we lived in dungarees, but I wanted to be ready for anything.

The Navy was calling for enlisted applications for Commissions, and college training that would lead to ensign. I applied, and when I took the physical I found that my eyes had gone to hell working in the I.C. Room in the bad light. Now I needed glasses.

16 - 26 APRIL 1943. Back in New Caledonia. Another draft of men came aboard from COMSERV Squadron South Pacific, and the Wardroom received an Ensign, D.R. Hixenbaugh.

Admiral Yamamoto was shot down and killed on 18 April, and there had been heavy action by MacArthur in New Guinea against a dedicated and determined Japanese Army.

As the new Fletcher class of 2,100 ton destroyers came to the Pacific we were taken out of the fast strike forces, and given some strange assignments. One was to determine the feasibility of having DD types tow a variety of Landing Barges at various speeds. Each night we would anchor off Amede Island Light, Bulari Passage, New Caledonia. A patrol boat ran aground there one evening in the poorly marked channel; the reef got it. In the daylight we would tow barges.

My mentor in the I.C. Room had been Clinton Little, EM2C. He was transferred to New Construction, and I had the IC Gang that consisted of myself, Tatum and a striker. I lived in the I.C. Room standing 4 on and 4 off watches, repairing Sound Powered Phones, and other instruments. Since it was also my Battle Station I did not get a lot of fresh air.

When in port the routine could become almost pleasant. Last night after chow the crew not on watch laid aft and the Radiomen rigged a mike and a speaker to a record player. We would have music and madness when the comics got hold of that mike. After watches the engineers and snipes would lay aft on the fantail, and soak up the cool of the night before going to bed. There were hot discussions carried on back there concerning the War, women and our future. The Interior Communications Compartment was one of the best on the ship. The bulkheads were painted aluminum, the switchboards semi-shiny black and there were many gleaming copper switches and a colorful array of painted switch handles.

With a few flashing vacuum tubes (thyatron) and the gyrocompass to boot, it was an impressive layout at first sight, and more than confusing. I enjoyed it because it was more than just routine work. There was plenty of chance for study, and that was something that I really had to do, for I got little help from above now that Little was no longer on board to guide me through the intricacies of the Interior Communication System.

27 APRIL 1943. TUESDAY. The monotony was reversed when we were ordered to get underway for Pearl Harbor with a merchant convoy. We experienced some very uncomfortable weather on the first part of the trip. *HMNZS Leander* and *Cony* (DD508) joined us on the 29th.

29 APRIL 1943. THURSDAY. Time Zone Minus 11.

30 APRIL 1943. FRIDAY. Time Zone Plus 11. Our little group crossed International Dateline, and on MAY second we crossed the equator again, but there were no Pollywogs that I can remember, although Davey Jones gave out Shellback Certificates.

6 MAY 1943. WEDNESDAY. The day started with the usual morning alert, and before breakfast the *U.S.S. Kingfisher* was sighted pulling a target. The early morning was taken up with gunnery exercises against a variety of targets before we secured from General Quarters about 0800.

Oahu was sighted about 1000, and we began to patrol the entrance to Pearl while the *Leander*, and *Fuller* entered the harbor. By 1244 *Lamson* was moored alongside Pier 17, Pearl Harbor Naval Ship Yard. *Leander* was in the Navy Yard to for long needed repairs. Another of the old Electrical Division hands, Clint Little, EM2C, left for New Construction.

We spent over a week in Pearl Harbor Navy Ship Yard. There was lots of Liberty in Honolulu, and there were lots of photo opportunities, chances to have pictures taken of shipmates. Also, I was able to get my uniforms updated.

8 MAY 1943. SATURDAY. I was sent to the Hospital for an eye refraction, and had to buy the glasses in town. After putting them on I almost broke my leg stepping off a curb because I couldn't judge distances.

9 MAY 1943. SUNDAY. Several more Chiefs and First Class left the ship for New Construction. Chief Pharmacist Mate Sweterman made Warrant, and was transferred too. My buddy McShane did not come back on time, and on Monday showed up 15 hours over leave.

A new beer garden called The Breakers had been opened since we were here last time--down by the Moana Hotel---where you could drink all the beer you could hold as long as you held only one bottle at a time. A bunch of us got a table then started an endless march to the beer counter. There was a big contest to see who could get 10 bottles of Miller's High Life down the quickest. I don't know who won. When the place closed we had to roll out and head for the ship.

13 MAY 1943. THURSDAY. We were given more Rest and Recreation at the Royal Hawaiian, and Scotty Harris and I found a taxi driver that would take our $20 bucks for a bottle of aged cane whiskey. I ended up spending the night trying to sleep in the bathtub, for some drunk New Zealander off the *Leander* had been invited to the room, and had taken the bunk that I had been allotted. I had too much cane whiskey in me to complain. The three nice beds per room, that I remembered from my last visit, had been replaced by 6 double bunks in an effort to accommodate more servicemen.

The Royal Hawaiian was still superb though--milk, fruit and greens. Every time I ate on the beach, I'd order a big meal, with a big salad then I'd sit there and eat very slowly. The pleasure was sitting in some cool corner in a nice dining room and knowing that you did not have to hurry and relieve some guy so he could come down and eat before the chow line closed. Then too, there was the cute waitress serving the table; which did not hurt at all.

Harris and I got back from the Royal Hawaiian later than we expected, after beating a bunch of Soldiers time, and found that we were about to get underway. What a hangover! It was a funny thing; the way the milk and water tasted at first. Very strange. On board ship the Supply Officer was able to provide milk, sweet and buttermilk, as well as lots of ice cream.

14 MAY 1943. FRIDAY. Time Zone +9 1/2. At 0105 the Firemen were called out and began to fuel ship, and by 0325 the tanks were topped off with 104,623 gallons of black oil. Replenishment of ice cream began at 1000, and 15 gallons was all we could take. MUSTER ON STATIONS at 1015, and the next thing we knew we were "underway" again for Noumea, New Caledonia. We had missed the actions around Rabaul, but now we had better guns, and an improved CIC.

18 MAY 1943. TUESDAY. *Lamson* crossed the Equator again at 1345 Local. 161 Degrees West Long. Jack Dalton was stricken with appendicitis, and was given a highline transfer to *U.S.S. Pokomoke* (AV-9). Fueled off *U.S.S. Fuller* (APA-7). Very close fueling operation--not more than 10 ft. between ships most of the time, and we were steaming at 15 knots over a very smooth sea.

20 MAY 1943. THURSDAY. Now we were back on routine watches and there was not much to do other than stand a watch, read a little- maybe do a repair job on a set of phones, or sleep. I got two nights in my bunk, and then one all night stand in the I.C. Room with a watch each day. This was not bad, for when I was on watch I was able to repair Sound Powered Phones, or work the small cubicle over. I was able to take my shoes off, and relax in my stocking feet because the "Red Deck" had not been taken up.

I had permission to keep the 'red deck' because we were below the waterline, and fire hazard was a minimum. Also we "lived" down here--Hylton and I --at GQ. The steel deck was covered with the only piece of linoleum left on the ship. The rest had long since been removed as a fire prevention measure incident to the burning of the cruisers at Guadalcanal.

The linoleum was almost a necessity down here because of all the electrical systems that were exposed at the face of the switchboards. More than once it had kept me from being grounded and getting a good jolt as the ship bounced around. I had been bitten so many times that I could test a circuit with a light bulb in my mouth. If it lighted everything was OK.

21 MAY 1943. THURSDAY. We crossed the International Dateline(180th) at 12 $^{O.}$ S. Latitude, and then on Saturday sighted the Fiji Islands again in the distance, and passed just off Suva, but did not stop at our old ANZAC home port.

26 MAY 1943. WEDNESDAY. After the recreation and yard period we were back at Noumea, New Caledonia, and were sent alongside an oiler to fuel, and had to call away the Fire and Rescue Party to help put out a small fire on the tanker. The blaze was brought under control very quickly, averting a disaster.

28 MAY 1943. FRIDAY. Our lax routine was about to change again, and we were underway for Townsville, Australia with another convoy. The Army troops were being moved forward to the northern training areas of Australia. Sighted one of the DESRON 5 sister ships, *U.S.S. Mahan.* We were to join a new amphibious organization, preparing for MacArthur's move up the New Guinea coast.

31 MAY 1943. MONDAY. Anchored out in the roadstead off Townsville. There were heavy ground swells on the trip across the Coral Sea from Noumea, but after passing through the Great Barrier Reef the sea was very calm.

We cruised all one night and day up the East Coast of Australia-- which appeared very rugged--similar to the California Coastline. The weather was very cool, and there were clouds over us at all times and frequent squalls, for it was winter south of the Equator. The Outer Harbor beacons along the coast were sighted at dusk, and it was very strange to be using running, and speed lights again after dark.

After daybreak the Harbormaster told the Captain to move *Lamson* from the outer anchorage into the harbor where we were to fuel. We were just about to get back into action again.

46

TRAINING FOR MACARTHUR'S NAVY JUNE - JULY 1943

1 JUNE 1943. TUESDAY. After moving alongside the tanker, the Engineers fueled ship, and we moved back to the anchorage. Liberty call was sounded, and the men were in Dress Blues again. About 1500 a landing barge came alongside and the Liberty Party got wet and salty on the way to the beach, but nobody really cared.

Townsville spread around the base of a large outcropping of rock called "Castle Ridge." A flat marshy landscape was broken by small hills, and a small mountain range was back a short distance; breaking the coastal plain. An overcast sky made the surroundings very dull, and the few scrub trees could not provide much of a break, for it was winter in Australia.

The city was typical of the semi-tropical towns along the Australian coast. They looked alike, and had the same smell; pungently tropical. We managed to find something to eat, and a little beer. The evening provided a show, and there was a dance hall that enabled us to hold a white woman after a long dry spell. The women were nice to look at after such a long time, and some were very good dancers, but not exceptionally friendly. One could not expect otherwise considering the fact that this was an Army staging and recreation area for the New Guinea Campaign. There were huge numbers of servicemen in the area preparing for the drive into New Guinea and on north. MacArthur was committed to driving up the island chain and into the Philippines.

There were no open bars, and bootleg gin was about 4 pounds with a rate of exchange of $3.20 US to one Aussie Pound. Most of us stayed ashore until 2330, catching the last boat back to the ship.

2 JUNE 1943. WEDNESDAY. Sections 2 and 4 rated liberty today, and tomorrow would be Pay Day again. I had $35.00 on the books which I would draw in the event we rated another liberty. *U.S.S. Smith* (DD 378) departed, and we followed on the next day, without getting ashore again, to join Task Force 74 up the coast. There was an encounter with an old ANZAC member, an Aussie DD (I-30) either *Arunta*, or *Waramunga*, who sent a boat over with guard mail.

About 1850 the hook went down off Palm Island. A small village on the beach of the island broke the monotony of the green rugged hillsides that protected the harbor.

4 JUNE 1943. FRIDAY. It was strange operating as a Division again, but *Lamson, Mahan, Perkins,* and *Smith* were old hands at high and low speed

maneuvers, and a thrilling sight to see as they worked; with an occasional wave breaking over the forward guns. The grace with which these cans moved, and the intricate patterns of destruction that were being planned, combined to make these operations the best part of sea duty. About dusk, after the day at sea, the Division returned and anchored as before at Palm Island. Liberty was a movie on the Fantail.

After the movie a bunch of us went down to the cool I.C. Room to shoot the breeze. J.C. Rackley had just made EM3/C, and he was laboriously sewing crows on his jumpers. Before the movie I had held a field day in the space, for there was to be another Personnel and Lower Decks Inspection, and scuttlebutt had it that Side Boys would be required.

The cool weather felt good, and it was good to put a skivvie shirt on and not sweat heavily. Sleeping under a blanket was a novelty too, especially in the I.C. ROOM where I normally sweltered. Now I turned the fan off, and kept out of the line of the blower. My cot was folded away, and I was able to sleep in the compartment, avoiding the noise from the Mess Hall overhead.

I still had a lower bunk over a footlocker, and there was little space between me and the bunk above. The guy complained that I kicked him so I slept in the I.C. Room when it was comfortable. If we were underway I could hear the water from the bow wave rushing by, slapping and shaking the side of the ship. The wake rumbled and gurgled, and had a lulling effect upon me.

I got a real pleasure out of ships just the way I always did, and I liked the feel of this floating iron splinter, especially when the turbines were revving up and the steam was hissing through the throttles. About the only thing uncomfortable was rough seas which made it wet topside and muddy below. I thought there would be no dirt at sea, but the big blowers picked up dust in the air and distributed it liberally below decks.

5 JUNE 1943. SATURDAY. The Below Deck Inspections were held as scheduled, but Personnel Inspection was called because of rain. The fuel tanks were topped off, and we were sent back down to Townsville to escort U.S.S. Fuller (APA-7), getting underway about 1730. I spent the night in the I.C. ROOM, giving the guy in the compartment no trouble.

The sea inside the barrier was smooth, but the rain and spray topside made it a little cool for the exposed watch standers.

6 JUNE 1943. SUNDAY. U.S.S. Carin (AK-74) reported a torpedo miss early in the morning. There was a very strong wind and rough sea even inside the Reef. Overtook AK-74 about 1000--she is OK. Nothing doing topside because of the weather. Stayed below in Engine House, or the I.C. Room most of the day. Still on a southerly course. Lamson stayed with APA-7 until she arrived at her destination then we were ordered back to sea

on the 7th with two Liberty Ships headed back to Townsville.

10 JUNE 1943. THURSDAY. Departed Townsville about 0630, headed South for Sydney at 25 knots. Ran all day at 25, reducing to 22 knots at 1530. Underway thru 11 June.

12 JUNE 1943. SATURDAY. Sighted land early in the morning. We laid off the entrance of Sydney Harbor for an hour or so until several ships ahead of us entered the harbor, and then when it was our turn; we were led in by Pilot Ship. The coastline was shrouded in mist, but through it you could see the huge towering grey rock cliffs. It seemed to be all rock in this part of Australia. There were suburbs of Sydney on either side of the channel after the first entrance. The architecture was English and most of houses seemed to be made of brick with high red gabled roofs.

We tied up at a wharf called Woolamaloo Dock, ahead of *U.S.S. Dobbin*, (AD-3). This was an inlet outside the large Harbor Bridge. As we came in there were Aussie Servicewomen signalling from a small ridge that rose from the inlet. Needless to say, the Signal Gang on the Bridge were having a ball. By 1030 the plant was shut down and we were on shore power again. There were some new items for the Radio and Radar shack that had to be installed, but I was not involved.

I had the Duty, and the 2nd and 4th Sections went ashore promptly. Late in the afternoon a wild looking redhead drove up to the gangway with the Captain in a taxi. She came aboard and told the Quarterdeck watch that she had our Captain, and that we should come and get him. He was carried to his cabin and put to bed rather early in the evening.

At 1640 the poor guys with Shore Patrol Duty left the ship.

13 JUNE 1943. SUNDAY. Sections 1 & 3 rate Liberty and I got ashore about 1000. McShane, Sessions, Walsh and Wisneskie went over with me and we had a walk through the Sydney version of Hyde Park before getting to the main part of the City. We stopped to talk to some girls on the street and one mentioned that I looked drunk, but I said, "I could sober up in 10 minutes," and promptly passed out. I had too much to drink on empty stomach. To keep from going back to the ship my shipmates put me in a hotel room and I woke about 0100 without any idea where I was so I cleaned up and went back to the ship.

14 JUNE THRU 17 JUNE 1943. What a hangover. On Tuesday I got ashore again, and found an Ice Rink which was a delight. It was fun to skate again then go dancing in the evening.

Sydney was a Sailors paradise. All you could drink up till 1800 when the bars closed down. After that you paid for a couple of bottles of bootleg stuff and were set for the night. The gals were plentiful and broadminded as any I'd ever seen. Things that we hardly say in mixed company fell on ears that didn't even turn pink. They seemed to team up and unless there were two of us, it was strictly 'My Girlfriend and me.'

The natives got quite a bang out of my skates and those red socks. I was glad that I had taken them back with me. They went well with my blues. The old girl running the place got mad because I was skating too fast. The fellow I was with was a good skater too, and he started off like wildfire until somebody got in his way and he took a nose dive. What a flop. He cut a neat gash in his eyebrow and when we left everyone wanted to know who hit him.

Dancing at the Trocadero was a lot of fun too. I never saw so many stag girls at a dance before, but with the Servicemen that was all right. I did not see many that appealed to me even after such a long time at sea. The one that was most interesting enjoyed necking, but could not be persuaded to go any further. I ended up Thursday night in one of the suburbs (Delmain) with Liberty up at 0200 and the streetcars and busses secured. Well, on the average the girls seemed a little plain. At least they were not as flashy as those fems around Southern Cal.

A lot was due to the war. No nail polish remover so they didn't wear polish. As far as I could see they didn't use lipstick as heavily as they did in the Northern Cities. No hose so instead of the cotton stuff, most of them went bare legged. I did not see how they took the cold. Me and my Peacoat shook like the devil. It was not a dry cold either, but you could go to a dance and cut the place up and not work up much of a sweat. I never saw a place heated while I was there. June was the dead of Winter in Sydney. I'd get a room in town and when I'd crawl in about 0100 and take a look at the icicles hanging off the bedpost, give up and go back to my cozy sack on board *Lamson*.

After dark Sydney was dead compared to L.A. but before the war it was probably pretty much alive. After midnight there was nothing, but the bars in Kings Cross where the red light district and honky tonks were located. I went into one all night joint that was supposed to be 4.0. but it turned out to be a hole in the ground with a table and a trumpet.

I found a good tailor and bought a beautiful suit of Tailormade Blues. After several fittings I could hardly wait until they would arrive in the mail.

Several sailors including Wetzig, Lollar, Plasse and Schroeder had so much fun that they didn't come back until just before the ship sailed, despite Cinderella Liberty on the last night in port.

18 JUNE 1943. FRIDAY. Underway again at 0800 and headed back north. *Dobbin* was still sitting on her coffee grounds. We heard that the crew were marrying the Sydney girls and really making themselves at home. All of us hated to leave, for this was a marvelous Liberty Port, but duty called and we escorted a large Tank Landing Barge headed for a place north of Brisbane.

We sailed close to the shoreline so the Navigator could see the lighthouses and searchlights on the beach at night. It sure was a rugged coastline with mountains backing it up.

21 JUNE 1943. MONDAY. Pulled in close to Brisbane with the barge. A river opens into a bay, but the city is up the river several miles, not on the coast. We left the landing barge with a pilot boat about 1130. There was a small town at the end of a long white beach that was very picturesque. Low hills rose inland -- several smooth and some jagged cones were separated from the rest.

Captain Fitzgeral was ordered to take the ship back to Townsville again, this time at 30kts, but had to slow to 28.6 because of overheating in the starboard shaft and engine. The topside was very wet and uncomfortable due to the flying salt spray.

22 JUNE 1943. TUESDAY. The skipper was still running the ship at high speed with a great rooster tail for a wake, for we had to meet the rest of the outfit to continue the training program. We were back inside the reef again and the spray was down. I sure liked it when the Skipper was able to ring up a flank bell. The wake came over the fantail, and you walked up hill going forward. Down in the Fire Room the blowers howled like the Devil himself. Nobody could talk, just wave hands, or read lips. We had developed a form of sign language that enabled us to talk between stations. The big turbines in the engine house had a sweet whine as the Throttlemen opened the valves, and those turbines built up RPM. This was one of the few times when being on a Destroyer was really right.

We were back in Townsville Harbor in the early afternoon. Loaded 5" projectiles and got underway for Palm Islands up the coast.

23 JUNE 1943. WEDNESDAY. Anchored in harbor of Pine Islands with two Aussie Cruisers *Australia* and *Hobart* with *HMAS Warramunga* and *Arunta* our former ANZAC tin cans. McKeever has the Black Gang calling me "Chum" because of my Sister. I had her picture in the I.C. Room, and in my locker.

26 JUNE 1943. SATURDAY. Moved anchorage from Palm Islands north to the Flinders Group. Engine Rm. Tachometer gave me a fit. No spare parts so all I could do was clean and adjust, and hope the Throttlemen can use it. They lived and died by the number of turns that showed up on the Engine Order Revolutions Indicator.

28 JUNE 1943 MONDAY. Beer Party for Section 2 --Flinders Beach. On 29 JUNE 1943 LT(j.g.) Behan gave me an oral exam for Electrician's Mate Second Class. There was no formal written test on board, but I'd been recommended by Chief Kerszis, and I'd turned in the Course Exam which was really an open book test. The real test was the way I was able to take care of the I.C. circuits.

30 JUNE 1943. WEDNESDAY. The training had ended and we were finally underway for New Guinea. While the ship was on patrol off S.E. tip of New Guinea we could hear radio traffic, and conversations between forces in action. One pilot spotted something and radioed that he was going in to investigate, and the Japs chimed in that he'd better not come alone.

1-5 JULY 1943. At last I had advanced to Electrician's Mate Second Class. I always thought that if I could make Second Class that would be it, for it was the best rate in the Navy. Now I was thinking about First, but that was a year away. My buddy Frank Ganem, a *Utah* survivor, made MM1/c. I would be getting a little more money now that I wore that Second Class Crow, but I had more headaches on the I.C. circuit too.

Somebody was always spoiling my day by saying, "Hey Lic, so-and-so is crapped out again." I had started from scratch, and hoped that the Instruction Books would be enough to get me started in the right direction. Chief Kerszis stayed in the Chief's Quarters and played Acey Ducey; while the First Class, Tom Hebard was not that familiar with the I.C. Room, so I was on my own.

We were still patrolling in the northeast portion of the Coral Sea off New Guinea.

4 JULY 1943. SUNDAY. Many brilliant pyrotechnic displays had been flashed before these eyes in the last year and some months. For beauty I did not think anything could surpass a row of brilliant star shells drifting slowly seaward on their chutes, especially if there was a thin cloud layer for them to pass through. Tracer streams could be our rockets. They seemed to float in the air with no past or future.

5 JULY 1943. MONDAY. *Lamson* anchored off Stanley Island, Flinders Group. Later we were ordered alongside a larger ship and were told that we could draw small stores, so over the side I went. The line from me to the Issue Window wasn't so long when I stepped into it, and I thought that it wouldn't be long before I'd purchased my clothes and returned to the ship. I was mistaken, for after the Chiefs, and the Officers, took their turns at the head of the line, it was some time before I got to move. By that time *Lamson* had moved from alongside and anchored several hundred yards away. Also, the Storekeeper decided that it was Lunch Time so he shut the window and departed. The line folded to await the return of the bum, and nobody was going to leave after the hassle we had been through.

When we thought of chow a bunch of us decided to barge aft to the mess hall only to find out that Ship's Company was still eating by Divisional Mess instead of the Cafeteria style that we were used to, but the Master at Arms said they would feed us if we would stick around, and there was anything left in the Galley.

We had to wait for the second seating, and by that time all the chicken was gone and spam had been substituted. It was still good though and we got back to the Small Stores Window and I managed to buy the crows and other items that I needed. A sailor was issued a set of clothes, or sea bag, in Boot Camp, and maintained it out of his pocket thereafter. A clothing allowance was authorized when the war broke out, and that helped.

10 JULY 1943. SATURDAY. After 5 days in port getting the ship tuned up, and resting a bit, we were underway again for the previous Patrol Area.

14 JULY 1943. WEDNESDAY. Increased speed and headed for Tulagi again. Before we arrived, orders were received to change course and head for Espiritu Santo.

16 JULY 1943. FRIDAY. As we came in, so did *U.S.S. Honolulu* (CL-48) & *U.S.S. St. Louis* (CL-49). Both had their bows damaged by torpedo attack during Battle of Kolombangara on the night of 12-13 JULY 1943. *HMNZS Leander* had also been torpedoed.

17 JULY 1943. SATURDAY. Underway again with TF-74. Four new 2100 DD joined screen and we changed course for Noumea, New Caledonia.

20 JULY 1943. TUESDAY. Just as soon as we got into the harbor we went alongside a Tanker for Fuel. A Japanese two man Submarine had been loaded on deck and was on the way back to the States for Display.

21 JULY 1943. WEDNESDAY. Back at sea again to rendezvous with *S.S. George Washington* and *U.S.S. Drayton* (DD-366). The *J. Franklin Bell* (APA-16) joined the small formation. Word came down from the Bridge that we were going to Brisbane, Australia.

25 JULY 1943. SUNDAY. After an interesting cruise up the river, through flat marshy country, we tied alongside a riverside dock in Brisbane, Australia. Asbury came aboard at 0650, and 6 more men reported at 1500.

Mail came aboard too. Besides the letters; my suit of Dress Blues arrived from the tailor in Sydney. They really looked sharp. The material was about a 10 ounce blue-black wool. It was almost like gabardine, but not quite. It was a very nice job of tailoring too, and I would wear them ashore here for the first time. If I should gain ten pounds like I did when I was back home last year I'd bust out of them.

Harris, McKeever and Sulpizio lucked out with Shore Patrol, and left the ship at 1715.

26 JULY 1943. MONDAY. BRISBANE, AUSTRALIA.

Overnight liberty for the first time in quite a while. Mac and I toured the main part of town, and took in a show called, "Star Spangled Rhythm." There was time for dinner and then a dance later in the evening. The girls were a nice change from the sailors on the fantail, for they did not sport beards, but they smelled funny.

The place was heavily crowded with Servicemen since it was a rest & recreation area as well as General MacArthur's headquarters. It was not like Sydney, for there were too many GIs, and the women were heavily outnumbered. The pubs were open for a few hours until the daily allocation of beer was exhausted.

Brisbane looked prosperous and from a distance and was very attractive. The landscape scenes along the river are flat with trees and grass. There were low mountains in the background, and from the mouth of the river to the city was about 15 miles. Guess it must have been too marshy to build on the coast proper. We spent just enough time in Brisbane to give the whole crew liberty, before going back to New Guinea.

27 JULY 1943 TUESDAY. Underway for Port Moresby, New Guinea with *H.T. Allen* (APA-15). On the 28 & 29 July 1943 the ship was back at sea again. Our wild man, Boyle, EM2/C was in trouble again, and made Third at Captain's Mast.

31 JULY 1943. SATURDAY. At anchor, Port Moresby, New Guinea. Liberty --2 Hrs. per section. All hands got ashore. I was given a tour of the airport in a Jeep somehow. Probably hitched a ride, and it was really a bumpy one if I remember correctly. This was no tropical paradise, for it was hot, humid, and very primitive.

GENERAL MACARTHUR'S NAVY IN NEW GUINEA AUGUST -DECEMBER 1943

1 AUGUST 1943. SUNDAY. After a brief visit to Port Moresby we headed south again to the small city of Cairns, a coastal community in Queensland, Australia. It is about the same latitude south as Suva, Fiji so we were not sleeping under blankets. Dave Powers advanced to EM1/C. He would go to new construction soon.

3 AUGUST 1943. TUESDAY. E Division had been quite stable since we left the States. Kerszis was still the Chief, Hebard had made First Class, and so had Dave Powers, who had been my main teacher in the I.C. Gang with the departure of Clinton Little. Everybody was kept busy on their individual assignments, for every time we hit port there was preventive maintenance, or repairs to perform. McShane and I worked on phones and spare parts all day.

The deck apes were chipping away at the rusty metal, and spreading paint around. About half the main weather deck was roped off. The Black Gang and Engine Room Force turned to for awhile and the Gunners Mates had tools and parts spread all over their respective deck areas too.

I finally got around to getting another hair cut. Al Cacioppo the tonsorial expert (?) really gave me a clip job and it seems to be in all the wrong places. It was cool anyway, and I was not worried about appearances.

5-15 AUGUST 1943. We sailed down from Cairns to Mackay, which was the center of a large rural area. It is a typical farm town anywhere and had a population of about 10,000. The harbor was artificially made with two semicircular stone breakwaters so the bay was almost circular with an outer opening. The coastline was lined with sand dunes and brush just about like that above Huntington Beach, CA. There were no breakers because we were behind the Great Barrier Reef just off the coast. We passed several small islands that appeared to be a part of the reef. A few miles back of the coast rose the foothills of the Great Dividing Range that separated the coastal plain from the dry out back of Queensland. Several rivers and creeks ran close by the town and all around these were fields of sugar cane. The large sugar mills close by gave evidence of the root of the local economy.

There were two wharfs in the harbor, which was about 4 miles from town, equipped with warehouses from which the sugar was stored and shipped. Everything was built on high pilings because the tides seem to run at least 6 ft.

The *Dobbin* (AD-3) had to move up here from Sydney, and knew those married sailors were really singing the blues; as well as the rest of the crew. Liberty here would not be quite as lively as it was in Sydney. *Perkins* (DD377), and *Smith* (DD378) were tied alongside *Dobbin* when we steamed into port, and we were outboard so had to pull everything across the other two cans. When we got settled, Liberty Call was sounded about 1330, and there was bus transportation from the dock to town. I did not delay.

Mackay itself had the usual two blocks either way from the main intersection. There were several good stores, including J.C. Penny's and Woolworths, which were a surprise. The restaurants were not bad, and for Sailors the main bill of fare was steak, eggs, chips and tomatoes. The restaurants served a fish dinner called 'Barramundi' which was excellent. No bones and it melted in my mouth. Several theaters were available and the pubs opened when they had beer, and closed when they ran out about 30 minutes later. Bootleg booze was very expensive.

The Red Cross had a big recreation hall with magazines, books and a lounge. Pool and ping pong tables made up the standard recreational equipment. Several other places in town provide halls for dancing, and there were milk bars that were well stocked with dairy products and ice cream. One very modern milk bar was built into Mackay's most modern theater, and it was very nice.

I spent most of my liberty lounging around, and relaxing. We all ate as if there had been nothing on the ship, with the emphasis on ice cream, and milk. In the evening we would go to the dance and kid the girls.

One young girl, a very lovely strawberry blonde, had lost half her left arm in a farm accident, but she was a marvelous dancer. One girl, when asked to dance said, "I'm knocked up Yank, Jazz my sister." Translated she was tired and suggested I dance with her companion. Too bad I didn't have a car. It would have taken something like that to compete with the soldiers, for there was no place to take a girl after the dance.

The Army used Mackay, and Brisbane, as a rest camp for soldiers who have been fighting in New Guinea, so they were well entrenched. We made out pretty well though although MacKay was really too small for the Army and the Navy together. The Army lived here and they had the hotels reserved and could raise hell inside while we were doing our small bit of hell raising in the streets.

I had one hell of a horseback ride here on a rented horse. I was tearing down the road with several companions behind me trying to catch up. There was a small intersection with a store on one corner ahead, and just about the time the horse and I approached, a bus came out of the street behind the store. The horse shied and skidded into the back of a truck parked in front of the store.

I went over the nag's head, and ended up sliding up the tin bed of the recently emptied charcoal, or coal, truck. I was lucky, for just my chin and arms were scratched up, for I was in dungarees with my sleeves rolled up. The men drinking beer on the porch of the store got a great laugh out of the wild band of sailors, and my mishap. It was lucky that I kept hold of the reins, for I was able to crawl out of the truck, glare at the horse, get back aboard and gallop off into the sunset. Back at the ranch I showered and put my "tailor mades" back on and went to the dance. When I got back to the ship I had to soak my new tailor made blues with water because my arms had bled into the fabric like scabs. When I got back to the ship I struggled to get that bloody jumper off.

10 AUGUST 1943. TUESDAY. Boyle EM3/C was ordered to Mine Warfare School. That takes a problem off the Captain's mind. I'd not seen a sailor busted so many times.

I caught Shore Patrol duty--my first time. Two of us were assigned a beat in a quiet neighborhood. At Dinner time we hauled out to an Army Dining Hall that we were supposed to protect from marauding sailors until a certain time. That part was no problem; except for the smell of the chow and the cute waitresses we had to watch. We stood around for about an hour and a half before we could get chow ourselves. After that we had to walk a beat of about 3 blocks up and back in a semi-residential area. Along about 2200 it seemed to get darker than ever and the street died. Once in awhile we'd get to the Station for a cup of java which would warm us up a bit and off we went again on our lonesome patrol. We saw one lost, drunk sailor in the seven hours that we were out, and he was no trouble at all. It was quiet, but that was not all bad because in a lively spot the Shore Patrol really earned its money fighting drunken sailors.

15 AUGUST 1943. SUNDAY. Our Tender Availability ended and the three cans headed back to New Guinea to join General MacArthur's Navy as Destroyer Squadron 5, 5th Fleet. This time the destination was Milne Bay, and we arrived 19 August.

24 AUGUST 1943. TUESDAY. We were getting a lot of eggs for breakfast and they were a welcome change from the old routine. We could still tell whether it was Wednesday, or Saturday though. Hard-boiled eggs, baked beans, with red lead, and either corn bread, or cinnamon rolls. The latter was best because the corn bread was all flour and soggy too.

The mail was fouled up again due to ship movements, but it was beginning to catch up with us, and there were newspapers all over the ship. The boys in the Engine Room finally got the coffee maker bowls that had been sent for some time ago. Now we could throw that gallon can over the side. That tin can coffee wasn't too bad, at least it didn't taste like water with a pinch of coffee in it.

The Messenger of the Watch made the coffee, and the Chief of the Watch usually had a devil of a time breaking in a good 'coffee maker.' One guy made it so thick and black that you could not tell whether it was 'Jo' or fuel oil. The other night he put the can on the hot plate and when the stuff was brewed the watch sent him to check the Shaft Alleys. When he got back his coffee had been consumed apparently. The trash bucket got it. Later when the water was hot again they sent him to check the Ice Machines up by the I.C. Room. They poured the grounds in to their taste. Some system to save the system.

Besides coffee the Black Gang enjoyed making sandwiches, or anything else edible for Night Rations on the Mid Watch. In the Engine House there was a big locker with a double hot plate for the Silex outfit and many compartments for the stuff that goes with it so nothing fell on the deck when it was   rough. A small skillet was overworked since all the eggs were available for the Night Rations. When we hit the beach we would try to buy spreads and red lead which came in handy with a couple of eggs and a loaf of fresh bread. The cooks in the Galley were having a hard time with their bread. They were either throwing it into puddings, or else they don't have enough for chow. Some of these bread eaters on here really set up a howl.

28 AUGUST 1943. *Lamson* was better equipped, as far as entertainment goes, than in 1942. When we were in Pearl Harbor last time Ship's Service bought an automatic record machine and plenty of records. The shop still had a radio and a now a phonograph. Movies were still the key element in the program and were a regular feature in port; or at sea. I wore out "Trumpet Blues" with Harry James.

The Movie Operator got a dollar per movie up to $30.00/month. It was not much of a job, other than getting the film from various ships and then setting the equipment up and showing the movie.

There was fishing too, and while in Mackay a shark was caught off the fantail. Hoisted on the aft davit, his tail was still in the water.

1 SEPTEMBER 1943. WEDNESDAY. McKeever was promoted to Water Tender 1/C, and selected for the V-12 College program for enlisted men.   I had applied, but could not pass the eye exam. Freese made EM2/C. He beat me on Third, but I jumped ahead on EM2/c.

4 SEPTEMBER 1943. SATURDAY. The Division participated in MacArthurs's attack on Lae, New Guinea, escorting the Army Amphibious force up from Buna. The landing party hit the beaches in the mid afternoon. As the Landing Force approached Lae an LST signaled that they needed help with their Gyro Compass. They sent a boat over to *Lamson*, and Chief Kerszis sent me over to work on it, and I made the landing with them.

It sure felt strange being on board a ship that was deliberately run up on the beach, but I got a good appreciation of LST operations; watching them unload the tank deck in a very short time, and was glad to be on a destroyer. I found that the young Electrician was not familiar with the compass, and had touched the sensitive Stable Element, taking it off the meridian. I was lucky to be able to process the gyro, getting it back on bearing in just a short time, and it settled down with no error. My reputation as a Tin Can sailor was made on that barge.

On the way back to Buna, the flotilla came under air attack off Morobe, New Guinea. Several of the landing craft were hit, but no ships were lost. Hylton and I were down in the I.C. Room listening to the bombs, and the chatter on the telephone circuits while our guns were trying to get to the Japanese bombers.

I went through another tight streak, for there was no place to spend the money, unless one gambled, and I was leaving my money on the books. Now that I was Second Class my base pay was $84.00 a month and I had about $200.00 on the books. I had $31.00 out in allotments for insurance and savings.

6 SEPTEMBER 1943. MONDAY. Note: Chadd, and McKeever were transferred by whaleboat to a ship headed back to the States. They had qualified for the V-12 program and Mc Keever went back to UCLA, then later he was sent over to USC.

7 SEPTEMBER 1943. TUESDAY. The Japanese were putting up stiff resistance to MacArthur's move up the coast, and the fleet units supporting the Army were under continuous pressure. There were night attacks by enemy float planes off Cape Ward Hunt, New Guinea, and the next night they tried again off Morobe.

21 SEPTEMBER 1943. TUESDAY. The Division was escorting the Army up the coast again, and Japanese bombers made a high altitude daylight attack when we were off Lae. I was in I.C. Room at GQ. Everything on the Mess Deck above seemed to fall on deck. I thought that every rack of flatware and trays in the scullery came down on deck over our heads. Captain Fitzgerald would watch the bombers, and when they released the bombs he would begin his turn. He was uncanny.

22 SEPTEMBER 1943. WEDNESDAY. There was another amphibious landing scheduled for Finschafen, as MacArthur continued his drive up the coast. It was a daylight run along the shore with the LCI and LCVP. The sea was like glass so the small boats had no problem, and we chugged along as a screening protective force that would provide the gunfire support to the landing.

En route we were approached by one of the LCVPs, and were asked to take the body of one of their soldiers killed in one of the Landing Craft we were escorting. They were getting their weapons ready for the landing and the man was accidentally shot. Our pharmacists took care of the casualty, and the body was stored in the reefer until we got back to Buna.

23 SEPTEMBER 1943. THURSDAY. Muster on stations. Ten more lucky sailors came aboard for transportation back to the States. *Lamson* was headed for a port down the New Guinea coast where they would meet another ship headed east. It could have been Purvis Bay, for we met a civilian oiler there for fuel.

One time we had a visit from the members of one of the local New Guinea tribes, and the men were invited aboard. Their bare feet were not up to the heat of the main deck though and they returned to their canoes.

We asked them to bring their families out, and several women, nude above the waist, came along with children and small pigs.

24 SEPTEMBER 1943. FRIDAY. In port again. Lt. Behan and Lt. Samuels split the day's duty. As a result of all of the action; there was extra work on telephones for us down in the I.C. Room, for the men on the guns, and other topside stations would run around like maniacs during an attack, tearing the phones up rather routinely. At the end of an air attack we would have a pile of phones on deck that was hard to see over. Instead of bringing one set down to be fixed when it first started giving trouble they waited until an emergency and then found the phone out of order.

It usually went like this:

1/ Phone needed badly. Phone out of order for days, but not discovered until GQ now.

2/ Rush phone to IC ROOM and add it to the pile stacked up on deck--phone needed plenty fast.

3/ My striker and I would no sooner start on the phone when bell rings and voice asks when phone will be ready? Naturally, I have to stop work to answer telephone query. I cuss a little and go back to work on phone.

4/ When phone is fixed I call 'em up and tell them to come and get their precious sound powered phones. After all the worry about the rush order, the people usually waited for a couple of hours to come after the dang things.

The day ended with a gruesome movie comedy called, "Whispering Ghosts."

I had been hitting the books pretty hard, trying to bet a better handle on the Interior Communications game, and improve my theoretical knowledge. I was trying to get Alternating Electrical Current theory down pat, but there was a lot of trig and algebra application that I had forgotten. The folks had sent me my old High School slide rule, and that helped cut the time in problem solving.

Most of our work had evolved into fixing the sound powered phones, or waiting for something to go haywire, and there was little work to do other than preventive maintenance when we had a chance. When off watch I spent my time topside soaking up the sunshine, or visiting the other spaces, including the Radio Shack, CIC, or the Bridge to see how all the selsyn repeaters were functioning.

If we were secured I would walk all over the ship, checking jack boxes, telephone storage and anything that pertained to my Interior Communication circuits. I'd hit the Engine Room for coffee, take in the fantail to see what arguments were going on there. Maybe go up to the Bridge where there was always a breeze and the signalman's telescope for a little 'long glass liberty.' The Quartermasters and the Signalmen taught me not to split my hand when playing Blackjack. For solitude there was always the bow.

30 SEPTEMBER 1943. THURSDAY. The ship's allowance was 209 men, and there were 226 on board at the end of the Quarter. I think that there were 13 Officers in the Ward Room, for a total of 239 souls on board. Fred Sass would make Electrician's Mate Second Class on 1 October 1943.

3-4 OCTOBER 1943. MONDAY - TUESDAY. A Japanese submarine torpedoed *U.S.S. Henley* (DD391) while with *U.S.S. Reid,* & *U.S.S. Smith* on night patrol above Morobe looking for submarines. The sub found *Henley* first, firing a three fish spread, and I'd bet the sonar operators were pretty shook up. With the uncharted waters there were lots of things the submarine captain could take advantage of, and often we felt like we were sitting ducks, especially in an open anchorage such as Buna.

Drayton, Lamson, and *Flusser* were ordered to depart the Buna anchorage quickly to join *U.S.S. Reid* (DD369) and *U.S.S. Smith* (DD378) off Cape Ward Hunt to help with anti- submarine search and to help pick up survivors.

We had been replenishing our depleted stores, and an all hands working party was called away after dark to load dry stores. I managed to get into a barge with about 2 ft. of water in it. Man, were those boxes water logged. It was mostly canned stuff and we stripped down to skivvies and waded in. We had mud, sugar and saltwater all over us by the time the landing barge was empty. Lots of physical exercise, and it was a miserable night.

Note: There was one period at sea when we missed the supply ship and really ran out of food, except for some noodles. Ship's Company was fishing in earnest. Palfalvey, one of the Machinist Mates, caught a huge Black Bass, or Jew Fish, and it served the whole ship's company one piece of fresh fish each. It was a very welcome change from noodles, and rat droppings.

24 OCTOBER 1943. SUNDAY. *Lamson* had been sent back to Milne Bay with another couple of cans from the Division, and we were tied up alongside *U.S.S. Rigel* (AR-11).

Sailors were usually an easy going group of men. When a group of cans tie up together you could go from one to the other and get an idea about this part of the Navy. After work I took a tour of the ships alongside, and ran across a ho-down with a fiddler and a couple of guitars on one ship. In the distance there was the sound of a sax and trumpet, and above the noise of a record player came the sound of an accordion. The other crews were taking in the slack, and relaxing after a hot days work; just as we were doing.

3 NOVEMBER 1943. WEDNESDAY. I celebrated my 21st birthday. Our passengers had been transferred to an LST, and McShane made EM1/C on the first of November, and would probably be transferred to New Construction soon. He and I had made a good team in the I.C. Room. It would be another 7 months before I would be eligible for First Class, and I knew I'd better start studying again.

6 NOVEMBER 1943. SATURDAY. The ship was once more back in port briefly. Commander P.H. Fitzgerald had been transferred, which we hated to see, and our new C.O. was Commander Rubins. He had served as an ensign on he second *U.S.S. Lamson* (DD-328), a World War I four stacker before it was decommissioned 1 May 1930.

The new Skipper conducted our first below deck inspection in some time. The I.C. Room looked very good, and the inspection mark was,"Excellent." The ship was as clean as I'd seen it since the paint was chipped off a year ago. The compartments had been repainted recently with a fire proof white. The clean bulkheads were a welcome change after the drab, dark bare metal bulkhead we had lived with for the past year.

19 NOVEMBER 1943. FRIDAY. Field Day. The C.O. made a thorough tour to take a look at his ship. Captain Rubin seemed OK and was not having much trouble handling *Lamson.* He found out that it had a lot of power, but relative to the old four piper? it was hard to say.

I scrubbed paintwork until I was blue in the face, while my striker gave the Switchboards the works. Man, did those boards shine. After getting the overheads and bulkheads we swabbed the deck with soap, water and a touch of disinfectant. The binnacle of the Gyro was oiled and polished until it gleamed.

Dave Powers EM1/C was transferred, heading back to the states for DE school, and New Construction. I had a new man to break in Vern Tatum, an EM3/c out of school, and he seemed pretty sharp. He and Thomas had come into the Division 26 in March so they were familiar with the ship. A future striker, S2C J.T. Ferris came aboard from 7th Flt. Allowance the next day.

27 NOVEMBER 1943. SATURDAY. We were ordered back to sea again, and were running up the coast to join the Division at Holnicote Bay, Buna, Papua. We had been given time again for maintenance and recreation so *Lamson* had gone back to Milne Bay, and spent Thanksgiving off the line. It sure didn't seem like Thanksgiving Day though, and the special meal wasn't as good this time as last year, but it was still a welcome change from the routine fare. (Last year we were cruising slowly on patrol off Guadalcanal and the sweat from the Scullery was dropping off the overhead like rain.) This year there was beer on the beach to make up for the difference in the quality of the fare. Our movie was pretty well rained out so I turned in early for a good nights shut eye.

Note: I think this was the beer party where a flying wedge flew down the dock and cleaned it of all hands waiting for boats back to the ships. The wedge flew off the end of the dock into the drink. The rain had poured all afternoon, and every one was soaked anyway.

I was working behind a very tight switch panel and getting thirstier and madder by the minute. Could not crawl out every time I wanted so had to stay in there all day, except for chow at noon. Along in the afternoon, Chief Kerszis who I was working with, went to the CPO Quarters and brought back a couple of glasses of very cool synthetic lemonade, and was it good after all the parching I'd been through.

28 NOVEMBER 1943. SUNDAY. The Division departed for Buna at daybreak. U.S.S. *Shaw* (DD-373), U.S.S. *Flusser* (DD-368), U.S.S. *Lamson* and U.S.S. *Mahan* conducted hunter-killer ASW search. On Monday the ASW work was followed by night bombardment of Sio, New Guinea. General MacArthur had his soldiers leapfrogging up the beach, and after dropping the required number of rounds where the spotter asked for them we returned to the anchorage at Buna again.

U.S.S. PERKINS (DD-377), our old ANZAC companion, was sunk by a collision with an Australian troopship at 09° 39' S. and 150° 04'E. First the *Henley*, and now *Perkins*. Somebody must have been asleep on the bridge. We were keeping our fingers crossed, for the two losses cut the Squadron by 25%.

29 NOVEMBER 1943. MONDAY. The destroyer division sailed from Buna again, and this time we headed for Madang to bombard the village at 0110 30 November, softening it up for the Army moving up from Sio. MacArthur was trying to defeat a Japanese Army that melted away into the jungle whenever he tried to mount an attack.

Shaw reported an air contact and some minor tracer fire was seen in the distance at 0500 as we withdrew. We were authorized to make a high speed run back to Buna, for an air contact report indicated there was a cruiser up north of us. The Engine Room Watch had to run fire hoses to the turbine bearings to keep them cool. *Mahan* lost steering control and porpoised across our wake at 31 knots, regaining control on our starboard side, but what a beautiful sight from our fantail.

15 DECEMBER 1943. WEDNESDAY. Task Force 76 conducted combined landing and bombardment operations at Arawe, New Britain in the early morning hours of 15 Dec. l943. We patrolled the area between Arawe Island and Pilelo Island covering troop landings. The Division provided gunfire support to the troops on the beach, and Air Defense cover as well. Upon release from the line we returned to Buna.

25 DECEMBER 1943. SATURDAY. Underway from Buna at 0237 headed for Cape Gloucester, New Britain with an amphibious invasion force. Task Forces 74 and 76 conducted a combined landing and bombardment operations in the early morning hours of 26 December 1943.

After the landing *Lamson* was ordered to provide gunfire support to the troops, and had to patrol close to the beach, inside the restricted reef area. It was at this time when the Naval Forces came under attack by Japanese dive bombers. We took a near miss off the starboard quarter that shook up the whole starboard side, causing a leak in the Starboard Shaft Alley, and the water hammer also knocked the Steering system out momentarily. Rackley was at his GQ station in Steering Aft, and took local control just in time to keep us off the reef. The skipper was twisting the ship as fast as he could in the restricted waters, and managed to save our hides.

U.S.S. Brownson (DD-518), brand new in 1943, was not so lucky, for she took a bomb amidships and went down very quickly, and we picked up what survivors we could. *U.S.S. Shaw* and *U.S.S. Mugford* were damaged by bomb straddles. Lucky Lamson squeaked through again. Air cover could not stop them all.

At General Quarters FC2/C Hylton and I manned the I.C. Room, and were dogged in at Condition XRAY. There was a scuttle in the hatch leading from our compartment to the mess hall, but it was secured as were the blowers. We had fans to circulate the stale air, but all we could do was lay there and sweat. After about 6 hours we would have to have relief. The men in the magazines below us had to work under the same conditions.

After all that excitement, during the initial attack, I had to come up from the I.C. Room for a breath of fresh air, hoping that things had quieted down. I was standing on the starboard side of # 1 stack, enjoying the view when another dive bomber came in high off the starboard side . All I could see was a pair of red meat balls, a flash of wings as he pulled out, then the waterspout before I dove under #1 stack and out of the way of flying fragments.

27 DECEMBER 1943. MONDAY. Commander Rubins was ordered to leave the formation and escort the damaged *U.S.S. Mugford* to Cape Sudest.

It was not far, and we arrived at 1359, completing our last action of 1943. Another old hand left the ship when we got back to port. Fred Lee WT1/c left for destroyer new construction. He would later be promoted to Warrant Machinist.

31 DECEMBER 1943. FRIDAY. Two years of the war down. How many to go? There was no wild celebration of the end of 1943, and we did not want to think about 1944.

TO THE STATES AND BACK AGAIN
JANUARY 1944 - DECEMBER 1944

1 JANUARY 1944. SATURDAY. The year began well in the IC Gang, for Rackley and Tatum were advanced to EM2/C, and Thomas received word that he was going to be transferred to New Construction. Chief Kerszis also received orders to New Construction, and would leave on 17 January. Gordon Lee Earl was promoted from F1C to EM3C today, and we departed from Buna at 1448 headed for a Gunfire Support station.

2 JANUARY 1944. SUNDAY. Task Force 76 conducted an amphibious landing at Saidor, New Guinea with 7,000 U.S. Army troops. *U.S.S. Lamson* was operating in Group 8 of Task Unit 76.1.42. The Task Unit arrived on station at approximately 0530. After supporting the landing the Task Group returned to Buna, with no opposition. While maneuvering in the dark, *U.S.S. Smith* (DD-378) and *Hutchins* managed to collide.

10 JANUARY.1944. MONDAY. *Lamson* escorted another group of LST to Finschaven, dropped them, refueled from *U.S.S. Trinity* at Buna, and headed south to join the rest of the division.

11 JANUARY 1944. TUESDAY. In company with *U.S.S. Nashville* (CL-43), DESRON 5 headed for Sydney, Australia for well deserved rest and relaxation. En route our little task force ran into a very bad cyclonic that bordered on a typhoon. *Nashville* had water in the mess decks from what we heard. We rode the tops of the waves and had lots of wind and spray but no damage.

15 JANUARY 1944. SATURDAY. When we got to Sydney we were paid again. I had $475.00 on the books and drew $150.00 I thought that would be plenty for the week or so that we would be in port. The ship was tied up again at the Wooloomaloo Dock again just down from Manley Park. This time the first liberty party ran into trouble in the dimly lit park, and a couple of the men came back badly beaten. There were hard feelings, for the Rats of Tobruk were back and mad at the Yank sailors because they had money, and their girls. We started going ashore in doubles, or more.

One night I was out in the suburbs, and I thought that I had missed the last tram so I started hoofing it. After about a half hour of plodding along I ran into a couple of sailors sitting on a corner waiting for a bus. Well, I joined them and luckily a car came along and picked us up, taking us darn near to the ship. Some luck, and only 4 bob too. He had petrol, not charcoal.

I guess that on average I turned in at 0230 or 0300 and rolled out about

0800 for another go at it. We rated 2 out of 3 Liberty which wasn't bad at all. The Duty Section caught the working parties, and I even tried to sleep behind the hot Main Board, but the Engineering Department Master at Arms knew all of the hiding places.

We'd come back from Liberty and head for the galley or mess hall, grab something to eat or drink and then hit the hay for a couple of hours. I don't think I had breakfast more than twice while we were there because I slept right on through it. I'd crawl out in time for a glass of milk and then clean up to go ashore again.

As usual when we would get to a place where we could get the chow; the Supply Officer fed us well. There was always a milk can convenient, and ice cream containers were aboard most all of the time. I walked more in a week than I'd walked in six months. One night we, two couples, went for a stroll and ended up getting lost. Besides having to walk it started to drizzle as I was getting the girl home, and that put the final touches on the date.

Taxi service stopped at 12:30 a.m. and the trams were a real problem. I was taking the girlfriend home another time on the streetcar, and we had no sooner boarded when the car was besieged by commuters. I was wedged in among more girls than I had seen in many months, and could not take advantage of it. The girl and I were even separated.

Besides walking there was one afternoon of skating and a few evenings of dancing. The same old girl was guarding the skating rink, and she kept growling at me for using her rink as a race track, but it was still fun. The ice was so darned hard that my blades didn't even touch it, and I'd slide all over the place. I wore those red socks that I had worn in June, and that's how she spotted me. I rolled my pants down once, and she couldn't tell one sailor from another. There was another distinction though; hockey skates. There wasn't another pair like them on the ice.

When McShane and I went over we went out to Bondi Beach to see what the bathing beauties looked like. We ran into a 'civvie' that managed a hotel bar on the weekends. He took us to his home where we met his wife, Jean, and 15 month old son. Jean cooked dinner, broiled lamb chops, for us and that was the best meal I'd eaten since I left home. They had a very comfortable Apt. and invited us to spend the night, for we had been to their private club, and it was rather late. I remember Thomas, EM 3/c crying that he'd broken his leg. We were walking back to the house from the club and he had one foot in the gutter, and was too drunk to know it. We slept that night on the floor in the front room with just a sheet over us, and the fleas ate us alive.

There were excursions around the Sydney area that were enjoyable, and the ferry trip across the bay took us to the zoo, and the amusement park about where the Sydney Opera House is now located..

I had another eye check while there and spent one day wandering around in a fog. The Base Hospital was a good distance out on the train line and the bunch of us that went out there had a good time riding the electric trains that made the run. The down town Sydney stations were all underground, and the rest of them were topside. We saw a lot of the countryside and it was very much like home in the summertime. Sydney spreads out just like Los Angeles, but the houses appear more English, being of brick and tile.

I was supposed to meet McShane in a small bar, and when I went in and looked around I saw that I would be the only Yank in the place, the rest were Aussie soldiers, so I sat at the bar, and waited with a beer in hand. The very drunk soldier next to me put a large combat knife at my throat, and I found out he wanted to sell it so he could buy more beer, but before the Bar Maid got over to us he scared the hell out of me. I bought him a beer, and he began telling me how he had strangled an Arab in the desert. Before I could get away he had both hands around my throat in a real life demonstration. The bar maid rescued me again and I departed as quickly as I could. McShane never showed up. I found out later that he was being transferred too.

17 JANUARY 1944. MONDAY. Chief Kerszis, McShane, and Thomas left the ship, headed back for new construction. It was strange without the Chief, but Hebard would take his place. We were short handed again.

22 JANUARY 1944. SATURDAY. The Duty kept me on board, and except for a few nuisance trouble calls it was a day that enabled me to catch up on my laundry, and my sleep. Fred Sass was sent to Hospital # 10, Navy 135 for treatment.

25 JANUARY 1944. TUESDAY. Our fun was over, and we were back at sea headed for New Guinea again. That had been the best 10 days I'd seen in some time. If it had not been for feeling sorry for myself; the last night ashore with the Swiss Miss would have been more enjoyable. I managed to drink too much muscatel wine while waiting for her to get off work, and spilled a cup of coffee in her lap at dinner then took off on a crying jag because we had to go back to New Guinea. I managed to sober up enough to get her home. At least we had been able to find a Taxi that took her home, and brought me back to the ship for just a few Shillings. We stayed in touch though, and she eventually joined the Australian Women's Air Force. By the 27th we were back in the old routine with a run to Finschafen, and back to Milne Bay.

31 JANUARY 1944. MONDAY. At sea. Note: We went back to Milne Bay then on up to Finschafen, but that near miss at Cape Gloucester finally caught up with us, and the run down to Sydney and back was enough to make the shaft and steam line develop severe vibration problems, and we were sent back to Milne Bay for a tender availability with *U.S.S. Fulton*

(AS-11), and finally alongside *U.S.S. Dobbin* in an effort to correct the steam line leaks, but there was nothing that could be done with the shaft alignment. Most of February was spent in Milne Bay until temporary repairs could be made, allowing us to return to the ship yard for a complete overhaul.

While I was working in the open on Secondary Control one afternoon; I came down with some wild fever, keeled over, and spent 3 days in Sick Bay. Most of the "walk in" patients were mainly the results of the wild parties in Sydney, and some strange V.D. The Doc had them taking sits baths in a big metal basin, and that was the high spot in my miserable day, watching them submerge their butt, and cry about the water being too hot. The Aussie soldiers had brought back some wild clap from Africa, for they must have been sleeping with the Arabs, or the sheep.

1 FEBRUARY 1944. MONDAY. Hebard made Chief, and would be moving out of the compartment and into the Chief's Quarters on the 1st of February, and I would get his top bunk in the compartment.

10 FEBRUARY 1944. THURSDAY. Lt j.g. Burkhart gave me my course certificate for First Class & Chief. He and Commander Rubins signed it. I would be eligible to advance on 1 July 1944.

14 FEBRUARY 1944. MONDAY. McKeever wrote that he was having trouble beating the women off, for the ROTC units were about the only men on campus. Since he was First Class he was made Company Commander, and had even more prestige. He really broke my heart. I was down to 135 pounds now, and envied him the Stateside food, and his problems with the girls. CFC Hutton made W-1, GUNNER, effective the 15th.

21 FEBRUARY 1944. MONDAY. ENSIGN Richard Phelan came aboard and was assigned to the Engineering Department as LT(j.g.) Burkhart's assistant.

24 FEBRUARY 1944. THURSDAY. Everybody was holding inventory in preparation for the yard. I had not realized that the I.C. system had so many spare parts on the inventory. I had to crawl into some void storerooms that I had not known about. I found some antique boarding sabres that could have come off of Old Ironsides, and had been put aboard when the ship was commissioned as a part of the Landing Party provisions.

One time I was down among the boxes when I got the word that it was raining topside. The fact that I had my bedding hanging over the lifeline, taking in the air, caused me no little concern.

Because of our status the routine was more relaxed than had been the custom. We usually turned to in the morning, and if nothing else interfered, there would be a ball game in the afternoon. There was hot competition and inter divisional games were pretty good. The Engineers played the Officers and Chiefs once and the latter had a hot hurler. Poor Engineers. Once in awhile the game would be rained out, but that was not all bad, for there was always a little beer. Everybody was getting toughened up and having a pretty good time too.

27 FEBRUARY 1944. SUNDAY. After laying at anchor, we finally got alongside *U.S.S. Dobbin* (AD-3) for temporary repairs before heading back to the States and the Mare Island Naval Ship Yard. A good part of our ammunition was left with the *U.S.S. Dobbin.* No use taking it back. We missed the actions and landings on Los Negros in the Admiralty Group.

1 MARCH 1944. TUESDAY. We left Milne Bay on Monday, 28 February, in company with *U.S.S. Conyngham,* heading home. Our return route was back through the Solomons, and we saw Savo Island and Tulagi again, but this time under less fearful circumstances. On Wednesday we were back on course for Pearl Harbor. Payday was on the 6th instead of the first, and I had $410.00 on the books, and left it there. I would be paid before we went ashore in the States so I knew it was safe.

12 MARCH 1944. SATURDAY. The crossing from Milne Bay to Pearl was uneventful, and the ship was moored at Pier K-1 so we could "off load" some more of the ammunition before leaving for Mare Island Navy Ship Yard (MINSY).

18 MARCH 1944. FRIDAY. The Signalmen had constructed a long 'Homeward Bound Pennant' that extended from the yard to the fantail. They broke it out just before we steamed under the Golden Gate Bridge. It was 1 August 1942 the last time we went under the bridge, and we were outbound. We had been gone almost 20 months, and it was a real thrill, standing there on deck watching the bridge overhead, and seeing San Francisco in the morning fog. Each member of the crew who had been gone a year got a foot of the pennant.

Lamson went directly to the MINSY ammo depot and we removed all explosives. I grabbed a shell by the butt, and the nose cap, and the cap came off in my hand so I dropped the shell on the deck. I picked it up and went on over the side with it, but that could have been it. After unloading we shifted berths to the repair dock. I was dressed for Liberty, and had drawn over $400.00 which I had in my wallet. I went to the head, and dropped the wallet in a pile of newspapers on the deck, another shipmate found it, and returned it much to my relief, for that was my leave and transportation money. Those were the days.

I was in the first leave party, with authorization for 30 Days Leave. I got home the next day. My Mom thought I was skin and bones, and I was more than a little jumpy, for when the clock on the mantel struck the hour I headed for my GQ station. My Dad disabled the chime, and I was OK.

Mom wanted a good picture of me in uniform so I went to Austin's in Long Beach and had one taken.

My manners at the table had gone completely to hell too, and I made the mistake of asking my Dad to pass me the F---- butter. I could not handle the small table ware either, and managed to turn a salad over in my lap while we were eating at a restaurant in Long Beach. There was a lovely girl sitting across the table from me too, for tables were shared wherever possible to take care of the crowds.

I tried liberties in Long Beach and Los Angeles, but spent most of the time at home with the family, gaining weight to the point where I could not get into the suit of tailor made blues that I had gotten in Sydney. I enjoyed driving the '37 Pontiac again, and my Dad and I played with the 22 caliber rifle, firing shots from the driveway into the garage where a padded target had been set up.

Before I knew it my leave had expired, and I was back aboard trying to figure out what the Navy Yard had done to my I.C. Circuits. The master gyro was gone, and being overhauled by Shop 51. The familiar telephone system had been yanked out, and the old 40 wire boxes had been replaced by 60, and 80, wire boxes that were filled with a new maze of color coded wire that looked like spaghetti. I hardly knew where to start on the system, but the Shop 51 people helped me, and I hoped that the wiring diagrams and blue prints would be correct.

This was a major overhaul, and refit for the whole ship. In addition to a complete overhaul of the main engines the Engineering Department was given an updated Interior Communications system, including new Sound Powered Telephone switching that tied the new gunnery and CIC systems together, and allowed more flexibility in station interconnections. In the I.C. Room there was a new gyro follow-up panel and selsyn drives to handle the increased load on the compass. I also found myself confronted with a new General Announcing and entertainment system. The big addition was to be the Mark 4 Fire Control Radar and a pair of twin 40mm guns that went in where #3 Five Inch had been. More 20mm were installed, and CIC had been completely modernized so the ship could act as a Fighter Direction unit. More Officers, and men, came aboard incident to the beefed up CIC and Gunnery.

27 MARCH 1944. SUNDAY. The Muster Report, and Record of Changes showed that new men were coming aboard to replace the experienced hands that were being transferred to the new ships coming down the ways at a fast pace.

On this date a 15 man draft came aboard from Camp Shoemaker. E Div. got two strikers from Electrician's Mate School; Adamson F1/c, and Amsler F2/C. Small compensation for the loss of McShane and Thomas.

When I got back off leave I kept the duty section supplied with 190 proof alcohol by running chits for cleaning alcohol through the supply office. It was nice to personally select a five gallon can by hydrometer. Du Bay turned the jeep over coming down the hill from a Married John's party, after taking the Duty Section back. Several men got married including Allus Moore MM2C, and they were quartered in Quonset huts in the housing area of the Navy Yard.

9 MAY 1944. MONDAY. I had to get new glasses and went to the base hospital to see about another eye refraction. I was getting tired of looking out on a fuzzy world. When I made my appointment I ran into my first WAVE.

13 MAY 1944. FRIDAY. *Lamson* moved away from the dock for sea trials, and I spent a bad day running around the ship trying to get the new Sound Powered Telephone System operational. The Navy Yard workers rode with us, and helped the crew get acquainted with the new gear.

19 MAY 1944. THURSDAY. Cdr. Rubins was relieved by LCDR John V. Noel, another Navy Academy graduate. Now we would go back to WestPac with a new green crew, and a new Commanding Officer that we knew nothing about.

21 MAY 1944. SATURDAY. I had been on the run all day long, and after 14 hours trying to keep up with Ship's Force and Navy Yard work on the I.C. System I was really beat. Even so, things were shaping up fairly well though, and the old bucket did not look the same. Everything was beginning to run smoother and with the Second Leave Party returned the ship's organization was beginning to return. It was still a bit of a madhouse, with everybody trying to get 10 cubic ft. of stores into a 5 cu.ft. compartment. I was unable to turn around in my old I.C. Room without banging into something different. The locker was gone, and the good workbench too, so I was packed in there with a lot of equipment I would have to study quickly. If there were Instruction Manuals and blue prints the job would be easier.

Note: We are about to leave the Yard after just over 9 weeks. Almost all the senior Petty Officers went to New Construction. We had a green crew, but E Division was not in trouble, for we still had about half of the old crew.

22 MAY 1944. SUNDAY. One morning after LCDR Noel had taken over I was standing on the O1 level looking out over the yard when I saw a tall officer carrying his bag down the dock. It was Ensign Neal Johnson reporting for duty. I was surprised and delighted to see him, and yelled a greeting at him as he came over the brow. LCDR Noel, who was standing just above me on the next deck, asked me if I knew the officer, and when I said, 'Yes,' gave me the word that our previous acquaintance would have to be submerged in formality while the Ensign was on board. I tried to be

very circumspect in our relationship.

23 MAY 1944. MONDAY. The overhaul was completed, and we were scheduled for Sea Trials on Tuesday, getting underway at 240725 for Post Repair Trials which included calibration of the degaussing gear, and all of the RADAR. I had plenty of work trying to interpret the new Sound Powered Telephone system, and the repeater system that had been added to the gyrocompass to handle the additional gear in CIC. When we pulled back into port the ship was berthed at Pier 33 in San Francisco so it was easier to get into the big city, and out to Roosman's. I did not have to worry about Greyhound back to Vallejo.

I had gotten home several times, after the main leave period, taking the train out of Oakland down the valley most of the time. The last weekend ended with the folks taking me to the LA Airport where I caught a first class flight with United Air Lines on one of their posh DC-3s. The lights of San Francisco Bay communities were lovely, and it was nice that we did not have to curtain the windows as was done in 1942. The States were much more relaxed now that the war was going in our favor. I arrived at the San Francisco Terminal about 2100, and had time to go by the Roosman's before catching a bus back to Vallejo.

Sea trials at Mare Island Shipyard, May 24, 1944

Lamson at Mare Island Shipyard, May 24, 1944 (National Archive & Record Administration)

A bow on view of the USS Lamson (DD-367) off the Mare Island Navy Yard, California, 24 May 1944. (Naval Historical Center)

Above, stern view of the U.S.S. Lamson (DD-367) underway off Mare Island, May 24, 1944 (Naval Historical Center). Below, 29 May 1944. Note men handling a skiff by the lifelines just aft of Lamson's K-Gun depth charge projectors; provisions piled on deck; 40mm and 5"/38 guns; after control station; torpedo crane (lower left), and tank wagon on the pier.White outlines mark recent alterations to the ship. (Photograph from the Bureau of Ships Collection in the U.S. National Archives.)

25 MAY 1944 WEDNESDAY. The Electrician's had plenty of work, for we went out to the Degaussing Range at Treasure Island, and I was able to check the calibration on the main gyro compass. Part of the tests, especially those on the Radio Direction Finder were cancelled in the afternoon because of problems in the Engine Room, and we went alongside *U.S.S. Claxton*, one of the new cans, at Pier 54.

26 MAY 1944. THURSDAY. Back to sea after the yard birds worked on the engines. All of the ordnance was checked out, and depth charges rolled, giving me a headache in the I.C. Room. The hull held though, and the Black Gang was able to give the old man 351 RPM on a full power run. Pictures were taken of the ship, and they showed us with a new paint job. White and black anti-submarine camouflage gave the ship a completely different look, and the First Lieutenant had to buy more paint. By late afternoon we were back at Pier 21 in the Yard, and taking on stores in preparation for getting underway.

29 MAY 1944. MONDAY. Liberty expired on board at 0800. It was just before the noon meal when we pulled away from Pier 21, and headed for Pearl Harbor. *Lamson* was being rushed out of the yard to make space for battle damaged ships. We left with a fancy anti submarine paint job of black and grey stripes. There would be no training on the West Coast. There was a lot of work to be finished, and it was to be done by Ship's Force, and the Navy Yard at Pearl. Several men missed movement, and would catch the ship in Pearl.

30 MAY 1944. TUESDAY. *Lamson* was finally under way, and headed for Pearl. There were more mechanical and electrical problems than we had anticipated, and it was going to be very rough with a green crew, and new officers too. Rumor had it that several of the green officers were hot to get into combat on a destroyer, especially the Navy Academy graduates.

My new Log Table was designed for a giant. I could not sit, but had to stand to make my entries, or write letters. I needed a high stool, and had yet to find one that would suit my needs.

F1/C Adamson started standing watches with me in the I.C. Room, and he became deathly seasick. It was worse for him in this tight space up toward the bow, and he could not work. The sea was relatively calm, but he was in for some very bad days. I could sympathize with him. I still had Tatum too. After Kerszis was transferred in January, Hebard made Chief, and Freese, Rackley, Sass, Tatum, and I made up an experienced group of EM2/C. There were three, or four, strikers so we were about four men short, but not hurting badly.

2 JUNE 1944. FRIDAY. Captain Noel started conducting drills and inspections just as soon as we were underway. There was a bag inspection

to determine the gear we were to draw in order to complete a full Seabag after being in the yard, and to indoctrinate all of the new sailors. All I needed was socks, and a new mattress cover and pillow case. Extra dungarees always came in handy though.

4 JUNE. 1944. SUNDAY. As Diamond Head appeared we were met by a target towing aircraft, and fired more gunnery drills before going into Pearl Harbor where we were sent to Buoy X4S mooring at about 0945. In the afternoon the Port Director ordered us to shift berths to B-1 at the Pearl Harbor Navy Ship Yard.

The Main Battery was out of alignment, and the Engineers were still having problems with the gland seal vacuum system on the main engines.

5 - 15 JUNE 1944 was our assigned a limited availability period. This turned out to be a farce.

Note: When we left Mare Island some of the work of the gunnery and Fire Control systems was incomplete and Pearl Harbor was supposed to finish it. We were supposed to have two weeks of yard availability, and training before going out to WestPac again. Officers and crew were sent to various Damage Control and Gunnery Schools that were available on the Island.

Now, a day started about 0600, and ended between 2200 & 2400, and I had to make out IC work assignments as well as see to my own workload. We were still able to see the movies and get a good night's sleep so things aren't all bad, and we were still not in the War Zone yet.

10 JUNE 1944. FRIDAY. I had the Duty and had been working on the Whale Boat that was tied up to the Stbd. prop guard. There were lots of body parts in the water, for there had been an ammunition ship explosion in West Lock, and the debris was still floating around on the gentle tide. When I finished working on the starter circuit, Freese, DuBay and Giannatasio decided to test the boat. On their way back Freese fell overboard by the hull of the Oklahoma and was not recovered despite the fact that Du Bay was an excellent swimmer. In addition to the loss of Freese, another EM3 named Gordon got busted to F1C and was transferred to the *Griswald* (DE-7) built in 1943.

What problems we began to have. One day we went out to shoot. The Director trained to starboard and the battery slewed to Port. We would not even get to the gunnery range and would have to turn around and come back to the dock. On another sortie for training, after a night at the Royal Hawaiian, we got as far as Hospital Point, when the Gyro follow up panel failed, killing all of the gyrocompass repeaters on the Bridge as well as the rest of the ship.

We were about to turn around and go back to the dock when I answered the call. Despite a horrible cane whiskey hangover; I was able to repair it with a bucket at my side. A resistor had burned open, and I spotted it easily, soldered a new one in, and we kept our schedule. This cost me Gyro School, for the Navigator, Lt. P.J. Townley, called me topside and congratulated me on the work and said he didn't think that the ship could spare me to go to school. He had watched me work behind that tight panel; while using the bucket next to the board. What could I say?

16 JUNE 1944. FRIDAY. 0600 underway for the fleet training area for torpedo and gunnery exercises. There was another engineering casualty, one of the spring bearings burned out. This took us back into the yard, and a two day availability was authorized over the weekend.

19 JUNE 1944. MONDAY. Back to the training area again for another day of calibration, and tests on the engines. When we got back into Pearl we were sent alongside the long wharf at the Submarine Base. For the rest of the month we spent each day in the training area on torpedo and gunnery exercises.

On the 29th the Main Battery was still erratic, and after an hour or so we secured and went back into port, first to buoy X-4, and then back to B-18 in the Ship Yard.

30 JUNE 1944. FRIDAY. We were back in the Shipyard at Berth 18, alongside *U.S.S. Rowell*, I was giving Adamson a chance to learn how to hold field day. Below Decks Inspection came off today, but the I.C. Room was still dirty, and cluttered up with work. Not up to my standards so the striker was hot on paint work just in case.

I was checking an instrument in the Steering Compartment and ran right into the new C.O.'s Inspection Party. About that time I was told there was no one standing by the Electrical Store Room. I did double time to the shop for the keys and had a devil of a time getting a tier of bunks raised in order to get at the hatch. I made it just in time too, because the Inspection Party was right on my heels. The place passed O.K. The philosophy of "Protect your Chief" was in full play.

The Bureau of Navigation provided *Lamson* with a new 16 mm movie projector. The newer movies were coming out in the 16 mm format. Down South last trip the Army had new movies and we got 'silent movies' for our 35mm projector. The new outfit was small and compact, and Rackley, the movie operator, did not need a 10 hand working party to set up. The deck apes would rig the screen and put a tarp over the gun barrel to keep the rain off, and we're all set. Not so many reel changes either. The 35mm rig needed a film change about time something good came along and there would be a long pause to change reels. Now there were about three changes instead of ten.

After lunch, Lt. j.g. Burkhart called me to his cabin and gave me an examination for Electrian's Mate First Class. Much was oral, but I had to write and draw details of the whole shipboard Electrical System. There were not too many questions, but when I started writing it took eight pages to get it down. As of July, all rates were to be retroactive after the War. That meant I'd go back to Second Class.

Two more Electrician's Mates came aboard today. Fred Borrell EM2/C from another ship, and Sam Tinsley EM3/C from school. We were getting back up to strength, but the loss of Freese was really felt because he was the expert on the motors and blower systems as well as the Main Board.

While we were retraining the war in the Pacific had heated up as MacArthur and Nimitz tried to outdo each other in the March north to Japan. General Doug promised to return to the Philippine Islands, and New Guinea was his base of operations. The Navy Carrier Task Forces were starting to attack the Japanese homeland, and we were heading for WESTPAC again..

1 - 21 JULY 1944. The work on the Main Battery required a major rewiring job by the Navy Yard, and our availability was extended so repairs could be made. I was able to use the time to get the IC system in order, and there was enough liberty to deplete my finances.

Note: While Lamson *was in the yard, MacArthur moved up the New Guinea coast to Vogelkop at the top of the island. Admiral Spruance had defeated the Japanese Navy at the Battle of the Philippine Sea, and the Marianas Islands were in the possesion of the United States. The tide had turned, and the Pacific Command was driving toward Japan.*

1 JULY 1944. FRIDAY. This was the date upon which I was authorized to sew the First Class Electrician's Mate crows on the sleeve of my jumpers. I started with the whites because that was what I was wearing, and I would take care of the blues when we got back to sea, and things settled down a little bit.

I was able to help Chaisson with the new radio transmitter installation, for the ship was being modernized with new motor generator equipment for the main transmitters, and a new VHF transmitter/receiver came aboard.

3 JULY 1944. SUNDAY. Holiday routine, and a very nice Sunday afternoon it was. There was a cool breeze blowing through the portholes in the shop, and I was just easing along with the Duty. Most of the crew was crapped out some place on board, or ashore drinking beer with the rest of the fleet. Eleanor Roosevelt had closed all of the bordellos in late 1943 so that was about the only thing one could do. The shipyard was quiet, for there were not many ships undergoing repairs, and in general it was peaceful.

I was broke. The last time I checked my financial condition I had about 10 cents in cash, an Aussie one pound note, and a $10.00 debt to the Ship's Welfare Fund. Pay day would not come around for another week, and I had to be frugal until I started drawing that $114.00 a month for E-6(EM1/C). I had gone through the $400.00 that I had on the books when we hit the yard, and everything that I could draw while we were in the States. I could not go ashore on anything but a sightseeing exercise so I stayed around the Naval Station and went to the gym, or swam at the recreation area pool. I had gained my weight back, and the scale said I was up to 148 pounds. I could not get into my Australian tailor mades.

The Navy Yard work had scuffed up the IC room rather badly so I spent a lot of time getting it back into shape, and paint plus polish had restored my "home" to some semblance of order. My sister's picture, and one of Connie's, decorated the bulkhead. Tatum's wife had her spot too, and we were ready for the long haul below decks where we spent our time during General Quarters.

14 JULY 1944. THURSDAY. I started the day out by doing an acrobatic act on top of the mast. I was trying to install an anemometer for the Navigator. It was tricky trying to hang onto the mast with both hands, and work on the little windmill. I was sorry that he had not gotten the device while we were in the Yard at Mare Island, for cranes were easy to come by at that time.

The afternoon was spent drawing 'Small Stores' for the next day's Bag Inspection. I was out of socks, and towels, but hated to have to spend money on articles that I knew we would not wear when a sailor needed extra dungarees. After drawing the gear I decided to go to the bowling alley. I had not bowled in years, and managed to keep the ball in the alley, but did not make much of a score. There was one other 'recreational' activity that I had to get out of the way before we headed to the war zone again. My locker was musty after all of the yard work, and I scrubbed it inside and out with a potent Lysol solution, and stowed everything away in order so I could find anything in the dark. I remembered going to the theater in Long Beach before the war, and being able to tell where the sailors were by the smell of their clothes.

15 JULY 1944. FRIDAY. Captain Noel wanted to see what our gear looked like, and we laid every item from the sea bag out on our bunks. Formal Bag Inspection was conducted by Duty Section, and it was a very interesting exercise, for most of the crew were still civilian bums, and their gear was in sad shape. I looked forward to getting my new strikers, and school boys, cleaned up and squared away.

19 JULY 1944. TUESDAY. Pay Day had replenished the finances, and gotten me out of debt to the Welfare Fund so R.C. Smith, CM2/C and I went to Honolulu and had our pictures taken at one of the 'Post Card' photo booths that provided a reasonable likeness for very little money, and fast. This was my first photo as an Electrician's Mate First Class. What a silly smirk I wore. I was able to make a Liberty with Stucky, Richard Davis

a MM2/C, and my fellow E Div. mate EM2/C Fred Borrell.

22 JULY 1944. SATURDAY. Back to the training area now that the yard work was finished. Things worked, and we did a lot of shore bombardment of Kahoolawe Island, and in general fired a lot of rounds at a variety of targets for the next week.

23 JULY 1944. SATURDAY. *Lamson* was back in port after more training exercises. Time was passing quickly now because a 10 to 18 hour day was not uncommon. One night we "Turned To" until Movie Call, broke for the show, and then went back to work. Sandwiches were available for an all night session, but this time we lucked out, and solved the problem before midnight, getting more sleep than expected.

The new Sound Powered Telephone System that had been installed by Mare Island was really giving me a fit. It was completely different than the previous one, and I had to re-learn everything from the beginning. The blue prints were not always helpful, and the smaller gauge wire, and the elaborate switching arrangements in CIC, and other control points, complicated life immensely. Operator errors were horrible, for there were too many different switch combinations, and the potential for error was tremendous.

25 JULY 1944. TUESDAY. 0700 *Lamson* was underway again enroute to the train in area for gunnery practice There was more trouble in the system, and when we returned to port the ship went to the tender *Sierra* in X-7 where we moored alongside *U.S.S. Smith*. The problem was fixed during the night, and we were ready for another day on the range.

26 JULY 1944. WEDNESDAY. 0627 Underway again for the training area. The Captain was taking us out on a daily basis, and then we would come back in at night. This time we fired a torpedo, and after a successful day returned to Pearl and tied up portside to *U.S.S. Flusser* in a nest at X-3.

Pearl Harbor, and Honolulu, was treated to some heavy visitors, for President Roosevelt decided to visit the Pacific Theater, and the new cruiser *U.S.S. Baltimore* (CA-68) was carrying his flag. He wanted to talk with Adm. Nimitz, and Gen. MacArthur about Pacific War Strategy, and whether to attack, or bypass, the Philippines. The President gave in to MacArthur's desire to re-capture the Philippines, but authorized Nimitz to attack the Japanese homeland, and minimize the island warfare that had been so costly. The General returned to Hollandia after lunch on the 27th.

28 JULY 1944. FRIDAY. 0634 *Lamson* got underway for Type Exercises with *U.S.S. Smith*. Torpedo exercises were conducted, and after dark the Electrician's got into the act when the star shell illumination was not right. The big 36" Searchlight on top of the shop was used during night battle practice.

29 JULY 1944. SATURDAY. At 0727 we were back in port, and moored to S-10 at the Submarine Base. The President drove by on his inspection of the naval installations at Pearl Harbor. I volunteered to "Man the Rail," for I wanted to see how much the man had changed since I saw him in Wilmington on one of his campaign trips before the war. I was impressed by his gaunt appearance, brought about by his illness, and age, as well as the rigors of the war. I noted the quickness of his observations as his party passed us close aboard, and very slowly, in the open touring sedan. After the President had passed we were moved, and moored to Berth K-11. Our moment of glory was over. The next day we moved again, back to X-4 and made our liberties courtesy of the Boat Pool.

One of the Fleet Boat Pool Liberty Launches came alongside, and there was a battle royal going on in the boat. It must have been caused by a drunken comment about another ship, and blood was running freely. On *Lamson* the topside was crowded with spectators, and gold braid was running all over the Quarterdeck. Our Master at Arms finally got into the action, and jerked a bunch of drunken sailors out of the boat, and fortunately none were from "Mighty L." A couple of the men had to be taken to Sick Bay for emergency repairs before being returned to their ships. What a break in the routine!

31 JULY 1944. MONDAY. Still at X-4, and getting ready to deploy. The training period was over.

1 AUGUST 1944. TUESDAY. 1030 underway with *Drayton, Flusser,* and *Smith* enroute to WESTPAC as screen for the *U.S.S. Massachusetts* (BB-59). Our liberty had ended, and we were headed for the war again as our forces began to put the pressure on the main islands of Japan.

When *Massachusetts* came out of Pearl the group went to the gunnery range so the battle wagon could exercise her battery. The next day began with the force still on the range while the heavy fired again. By afternoon we had finished the gunnery work, and headed west for Eniwetok.

5 AUGUST 1944. FRIDAY. The Armed Forces were finally bowing to the demands of the politicians that the servicemen be allowed to vote in Federal Elections. They wanted the votes of the Reserves, and draftees, in the upcoming Presidential Election. Absentee ballot applications were made available to all hands, and posters appeared on the bulletin boards, telling the crew how to obtain their ballots. I knew Roosevelt, but Dewey appeared to be qualified, lacking only the war experience. Franklin looked bad physically, and I wondered if he would survive his term in office.

Down on the Generator Flat the Main Voltage Regulators were giving trouble again despite, or because of, the Shop 51 Overhaul at Mare Island. Chief Hebard showed me how to adjust them, and told me that it was my problem now that I was First Class Electrician's Mate. He unloaded the whole Division, and the gear on me, telling me that I would earn my pay while he relaxed. Life would get harder.

8 AUGUST 1944. MONDAY. At 0800 our position was 11° - 43' N, 163° - 15' E. By 1300 the ship was moored in Eniwetok Harbor, Marshall Islands, and we were back with the Fifth Fleet, reporting to ComDesRon FIVE, and ComTaskForce 57 for duty. I had never seen so many ships in one anchorage. We had crossed the International Date Line, and at 1510 the date was officially changed to 9 August.

There did not seem to be much left standing after all the shelling, but the Sea Bee outfit had cleaned the island up with bulldozers, and there was a beer shack, and a recreation area of sorts so we were able to get off the ship for a short beer party liberty. The billeting area was dotted with small windmill which drove washing machine. At least the shore based crew had clean clothes, and did not lose the hair on their knuckles from sweating over a wash board.

Neal and I got a chance to do some snorkeling along the shallow reefs. The little fish ignored us, as we poked around the rocks, admiring their colors and the tremendous variety of sea life that the reef protected. I swam out to a wrecked LCVP landing barge in the surf, and found a brass compass on the binnacle. The electrical magnetic compensation system was shot, but the compass was good, and I still have it.

13 AUGUST 1944. SATURDAY. We were still at anchor in Eniwetok Harbor, and LCDR Noel scheduled a Personnel Inspection which was normal in port routine for Saturday Morning. I missed out on the inspection because the Chief had me up the mast trying to correct a problem with the recognition lights on the tips of the Yardarm. Seemed that somebody had screwed the wiring up, and the wiring diagrams could not be found so it was a trial and error exercise for me, and my striker, who was afraid of heights.

This work reminded me of the nights in 1941 when I was working on the Gantry Cranes in the Todd Shipyard at Terminal Island. I could look down on the Quarterdeck watch, from 60 feet above the Main Deck, and wonder what would happen if I dropped one of my tools. The OOD, I think it was ENS Shonkweiler, would think I was trying to bomb him.

Everything was a miniature of what I had seen on deck. One realized just how small the ship really was, and the people on the main deck did not seem real when seen from above. We were anchored, and rolling gently inside the lagoon, which made the ends of the yard arm seem even more interesting, and as mentioned, my striker was most reluctant to climb the mast, let alone crawl out to the end of the yardarm where the signal lights were mounted. Besides, he was a school grad, and above such menial tasks.

After managing to find the problem we knocked off for holiday routine, and I managed to make the Majuro Hilton with "E" Division for a couple of cans of beer, and a few cheese sandwiches. It was a good picnic, and the swimming was great in the warm salty lagoon.

Chief Hebard assigned me to the Work Shop, and that was a change after over a year in the I.C. Room. That compartment was still my GQ Station, and I could not escape the heat of the Main Battery thyratron drive system. The work around the shop was completely different in that it concerned the Main Switchboard, and the 440 volt power distribution system that included all of the main blower and pump motors. I had worked on the lighting circuits when I first went into the Division, but the main power system took a little more study. I was given the chore of making out the Watch Bills, and assigning work, but in a way I more of a racket than I had when I had just the IC system to worry about. Now, I could emulate "Pappy" Edwards and keep my shoes shined, and my dungarees pressed.

14 AUGUST 1944. SUNDAY. ComDesDiv 10 in *U.S.S. Smith*, ComDesRon 5 in *Flusser*, with *Drayton*, and *Lamson* got underway for Majuro Atoll in the lower Marshall Islands, and spent the better part of three weeks patrolling the islands of Mille, Maloelap, Woetje, and Jaluit. These islands had been leapfrogged by the Marines, and it was our job was to see that the Japanese Army garrisons were not resupplied by submarine, or taken off the islands.

Majuro, in the chain of islands, had been taken without casualties earlier in the year, and became a major supply base as the forces moved forward. It was almost in the backwater now, but there was a submarine tended in the lagoon, *U.S.S. Bushnell* (AS-15) with COMSUBRON 14 embarked as SOPA. When we finished a patrol we were able to enjoy swimming almost everyday in port. There was not much to do on the island, but it was good to get on dry land, and drink a couple of beers that were authorized for our liberty parties.

The Destroyer Commanding Officers had orders not to fire on the beach, and as we patrolled offshore we could watch the men in the garrison in their daily routine. The duty was very good, and gave all hands a chance to get spaces and equipment in top shape.

One night while steaming from one island to another the compass repeater being used by the Helmsman quit. A fuse had blown on the new compass repeater panel in the I.C. Room, and I was on watch. The 21 MC Squawk box got my attention before I could check the fuses in the Follow-up Panel. The Captain was on the horn, wanting to know what was wrong, and when would the problem be corrected? I let him know that I could not tell him until I got off the speaker, and back to troubleshooting. He hung up, I replaced the fuse, and the Watch Standers on the bridge were startled to hear me talk to the skipper like that, but they heaved a sigh of relief because we were very close to a coral reef. (This could have been around 17 - 19 August, for we were going back and forth between Mille and Jaluit.)

20 AUGUST 1944. While patrolling north of Jaluit Atoll the Sonarman on watch reported a sound contact. The day was spent chasing what was later evaluated as a large fish. It gave the ASW team some good exercise. The month ended with a hunter-killer anti-submarine operation

21 AUGUST 1944. By 2000 we were back in the Majuro Anchorage, for routine relaxation, and upkeep. Tearing down blower motors for bearing replacement was interesting though for we worked on the main deck outside the Electric Shop in the fresh air. Cleaning bearings with benzene, or carbon tetrachloride, was dangerous to our health according to later environmental studies, but we were up to our elbows in the stuff with no thought of any danger to our skin, or anything else. With the war our main worry, who cared about a little CCL4. It was also a fire hazard to heat a gallon can of diesel oil with a blow torch so a bearing could be expanded and slipped of, or back onto, an armature shaft without damaging the bearing.

How the Radiomen in the forward berthing compartment moaned when we took their ventilation system down to replace the bearings in one of the motors.

24 AUGUST 1944. 0500. Special Sea Detail was early, and we were underway again for Mille Atoll to relieve *U.S.S. Drayton*. Time was flying by, for there was enough work, or school sessions, to keep all of us busy, and I was trying to keep the new school boy Strikers working so they kept me jumping too.

On the lighter side: The ship had some musical talent aboard, and a Ship's Band was formed. There was trombone, trumpet, guitar, two saxophones, and a set of drums. Al Shipman played the trumpet, and I can't remember who rounded out the group.

They had plenty of time to practice, and it was great having a live group that buoyed up morale. The first two years at sea we were satisfied with the canned music.

One dark night I was reading in the Work Shop when a voice from outside told me that there were a couple of light leaks in the Electric Shop. When I opened the door to find out who was beating on it I almost knocked the Skipper down, for the door opened outward. I was more than a little surprised, and especially when I found out that the blackout switches worked, but the door gasket did not fit too well. I had to talk to the Shipfitters in the morning about tightening up the door.

1 SEPTEMBER 1944. FRIDAY. *Lamson* was back at sea again, steaming

from Mille to Wotje Atoll. At 0825 we began a patrol off Wotje, and later in the day watch our bombers use the Jap compound for a target area. We were assigned the job as "observer."

My routine was standard with the Watch Bill to take care of, and light repairs and preventive maintenance as necessary. I found out that Frank Kozlowski, an older Reserve who had come aboard in May 1943, had been a professional electrician in St. Louis. The Classification people had designated him a Fireman, but did not specify the details of the Electrical background that he had so he had ended up in the Engine Room and was now a Machinist Mate Third Class. Frank kept to himself, and the only thing that called attention to him was the fact that he chewed "Copenhagen" snuff. He carried a Planter's Peanut can with him all the time so he could spit whenever it was required. The Engineering Officer was agreeable to his transfer into E Division with a change of rate to Electrician's Mate Third Class. He was a great addition to the gang, but I bad problems trying to tell the older, more experienced, man what I wanted done since I was just a ripe 21, going on 22, and Frank was about 45.

Several deck seamen wanted to strike for Electrician too, and we took Joe Ferris, and Ted Hoffman off the deck to fill out the watch bill, and spread some of the dirty work around. With all of this extra talent I had to really review the old NAVY "A-N." This was the sailors introduction to the Navy, and I had spent time with it when I had the flu while I was still at Compton Jr. College. Olid Metcalf, a Gunner's Mate Striker on the battleship *Tennessee* loaned me his copy, and I went through the whole thing while I was in bed, but had not looked at it since.

The ' *Lamson* Organization Manual' was the document that contained all of the ship's rules, orders, and regulations, and I had to get familiar with that too. In addition to all of the organizational requirements I had to get acquainted with all of the "Advancement in Rate" requirements so my men would be promoted when eligible, and qualified. Unfortunately, most of the military and organizational material was out of date, or had been overtaken by the war.

While we steamed from Mille to Wotje we were assigned to observe air action against the Wotje base, for the dive bombers were scheduled to attack about mid morning just as they had done when attacking Mille. This routine went on for several days, and on the 5th we were relieved by *Flusser*.

COMDESDIV Nine was riding *Flusser*, and got a real surprise when they moved in a little close to Wotje, normally we stayed out about 10,000 yards, and the Japanese gunners could not overcome the temptation. They hooked a truck to a canon, pulled it down to the beach, and when *Flusser* came back in close on her patrol the gunners fired a round that went through the director trunk above the galley. Nobody was hurt, but it took the "Flagship" out of action, and alongside the *Bushnell* for some new wiring.

Our plush duty at the Majuro Atoll was about over, and we would have to leave the tender care of the *Bushnell* and go back to the anchorage at Eniwetok again, but the relaxed routine had helped us train a little more, and permitted us to do things that we would be unable to do once we got closer to the battle lines. For example; the other morning I had put the 'slopchutes' to shame by proving, to myself anyway, that this Navy 'side meat' could be prepared and still be edible. The "Cook's Manual" required them to cook it up in a big pan, and let it sit in the grease until it congealed on the steam table, becoming inedible. I used the old drain technique, and prepared a crisp bunch of bacon except once when I was distracted, and the Fire and Rescue Party noticed too much smoke coming out of the Engine Room Exhaust! The bacon wasn't burned too badly though, for it disappeared in a hurry.

The Black Gang was very inventive when it came to providing night rations for the watch Standee. The non- rated Firemen were always on the stores working parties' and would become weak from over exertion about the same time they approached the Engine Room hatch in the Main Deck between the two torpedo mounts. The individual's fatigue often caused him to slip, dropping whatever he might have been carrying as he attempted to regain his balance. An alert salvage party came up out of the hatch like gophers, to maintain the orderliness of the Main Deck, and preventing any personnel casualties that might be caused by tripping over the cans of ham, or other goodies that might have been accidentally dropped by the poor fatigued Fireman.

The Engineers did manage to cook, and eat well, on watch. That was one side benefit to the watches in the hot and noisy spaces. One week a bushel of spuds was found at the bottom of the Engine Room ladder, and by happenstance some lard was available too so the two items were put together as 'French Fries.' They were not bad either. Sometimes it was soup, and at other times various meats became available. All of these goodies were prepared on an "8" Hot Plate that was unfortunately located under the main exhaust blower on the Throttle Platform. Anything being cooked was noticed immediately in the vicinity of the Exhaust Outlet on the Main Deck.

6 SEPTEMBER 1944. WEDNESDAY. *Lamson* was still anchored in Berth 15, Majuro Atoll. A transfer for an EM2/C came in, and it was just right for my old I.C. Room Striker Vern Tatum. We had made a great team, and I hated to see him go, but he would be back home with his wife when the baby was born, even though he would be going to school, and then New Construction. I had taught the Texan not to brag about how much he could drink, among other things.

8 SEPTEMBER 1944. FRIDAY. At 1555 we were underway with *Mahan*, *Drayton*, and *Smith* headed back to Eniwetok. *Flusser* was still being rewired, and would catch up with us later. It took us two days to sail to Eniwetok, and we dropped the hook at 0935 on Sunday the tenth.

Note: 12 SEPTEMBER 1944. TUESDAY. The Battle for Pelelieu began this date, and the island was secured by the 18th. This was one of Adm. Nimitz's targets in his island hopping strategy. We were not involved in this action that gave the Army Air Corps a much needed air base. It served as a support base for the carriers too, and put air power much closer to the Japanese bases that were next on the agenda.

Sitting in the shop after the evening meal gave me a chance to see who was coming and going, for I was right in the middle of every thing. The movie on the fantail was going to be "A Guy Named Joe" and the Old Man, and his followers, had just headed aft so it was about to start. I drifted on back, and enjoyed the film.

While we were anchored I got a real surprise, My old buddy Olid Metcalf came aboard, and we spent most of the day in a real Bull Session. He had gotten transferred to shore duty, and the novelty wore off when his, money ran out. A cargo ship came into port, and sent out a request for a Chief Gunners Mate, and Olid talked the School Administration into rating him Chief, and letting him take the ship, Now, he was headed back to Long Beach, and would bring the family up to date on where I was, and what was happening aboard *U.S.S. Lamson*.

I took on the task of inventorying the "E" Division material, and found that over the years, as the newer gear was installed, that old obsolete spare Parts were not taken off the ship, and they cluttered up the small storerooms that we had, and added weight to the ship. All of the excess went into the "Deep Six" locker.

17 SEPTEMBER 1944. SUNDAY. The Bureau of Navigation was looking forward to reduced shipbuilding program. New instructions came out on advancement. Fewer ships meant fewer crews, and most of the rates were being closed, and that meant no promotions in most of the deck ratings. I did not know how it would affect me in the long run.

Our regular Navy Academy skipper was trying to make *Lamson* into a "cruiser." Everything was a little tighter, but the topside looked pretty sharp. The Engine House, and Fire Rooms were hot as ever, but all the lines, and the machinery had been painted a light silver gray, and the spaces looked good. On the Bridge the Signalmen, and the Quartermasters had used all of the bright work polish in the storeroom, and here *in* the Shop the paint work had been scrubbed so it looked clean too. All of this was in preparation for the frequent "Regulation Inspections" including one underway "Dress Blue Bravo" Personnel Inspection that was washed out as we took water over the main deck while underway. Salt water does not do a spit shine a bit of good, and small emblems began to appear around the ship that depicted male sex organs pendant on a field of crap.

There was recreation though when we were in port, and sometimes targets of opportunity presented themselves when we were underway. Once we spotted a school of small fish swimming off the side, and suddenly they were attacked, and took off, with the larger fish in hot pursuit. The hunters rounded up the small fish, herding them against the side of the ship, and then they had their chow, In the meantime the guys on the main deck were trying to rig tackle, and they were able to catch a few of the larger fish.

The Hot Plate got some action that afternoon, and the Engine Room Exhaust told the story, There were many fishermen on board now, and fishing lines went over the side at every opportunity, the whale boat was used by the Captain, and his coterie of fishermen that included Doc Carris, ENS Johnson, and several others that enjoyed deep sea fishing. They came back with several beauties that the Officer's Cooks prepared for the Ward Room.

23 SEPTEMBER 1944. FRIDAY. Ulithi Atoll was occupied without any real opposition, for it had been evacuated with the exception of some radio operators. Now the Navy had one of the best anchorages in the world. We pulled into the harbor, and by mid afternoon were moored starboard side to *U.S.S. Cascade* (AD-16) for a welcome tender availability.

One of my jobs was to train the men in the E Division to advance, and take on greater responsibility. Sass, EM2/C was an A School graduate, and I wanted to give him some experience on the Main Distribution system, and started breaking him in on the testing phase of the 440 Volt distribution system from the Main Board in the Engine Room. We were using a Ground Test "megger" to ring out some of the motor circuits, and I had given Sass a demonstration of the technique, and it was his turn to run one of the tests. He managed to plug the test prods in to the live holes instead of the dead ones beneath the circuit breaker, and I took the full 440 volts while turning the crank on the megger. He had his back to me, and did not notice that I had been thrown back against the generator, until his test leads went taut, and the circuit broken.

I recovered, and went to the Throttle Platform, drank all of the cold coffee in the pot, mumbled something to the Chief of the Watch, Gerry Giannatasio, and staggered up the ladder to the main deck. Doc Carris, and a group were standing by the lifeline at the top of the hatch. I tried to tell them that I had been electrocuted, but must not have been very effective, for there was no comment. I went below and] turned into my bunk. I should have gone to Sick Bay, but I was stunned, and my left arm would not go up very far for almost a month.

27 SEPTEMBER 1944. TUESDAY. Our next assignment was to take a

transport, *S.S. Cape Pillar* to Tarawa Atoll with supplies for the Marines. It was not a long trip, but slow, for we did not get into the anchorage until after noon on the 30th.

1 OCTOBER 1944. SUNDAY. *Lamson* was anchored in Berth ll, Betio anchorage, Tarawa Atoll in the Gilbert Islands. It was hard to believe that this acquisition had cost the Marines so dearly. At 0753 the ship was underway again for Eniwetok.

Anchor pools were a form of legalized gambling that all hands enjoyed.. The Quartermasters, and other enterprising individuals would sell chances on the exact time the hook came up, or went down. At $1.00.a chance, with 60 chances, the entrepreneur would make a few bucks, as did the lucky winner. The exact times were those logged in the Quartermaster's Notebook, and broadcast over the General Announcing System, 1 MC.

3 OCTOBER 1944. TUESDAY. It was early in the morning when we pulled into the harbor and fueled before moving to our assigned anchorage. When we got to Eniwetok again we were back with the main body of the fleet, and there we found the tenders and the repair ships that were vital to our existence. That night a full moon lit up the smooth surface of the water, and there was enough of a breeze to make the ship almost comfortable.

The movie was topside again, and a good night's sleep made the next day easier to take. The radio was giving us the latest war news, but Ship's Company was not always keen on the war news, preferring music, and I was one of this group.

There had been a swim call, and I had managed to get a little more exercise than usual so I was feeling just tired enough to look forward to a nap, hoping that my fan at the head of the bunk would not crap out again, as it done recently. Hebard had made Chief when I was advanced to First Class, and I inherited his top bunk on the centerline in the Engineer's Compartment. This was a far cry from the hammock in the forward Mess Hall on 12 February 1942. I could even sit up in my bunk without banging my head on the overhead. RHIP!

5 OCTOBER 1944. THURSDAY. Eniwetok. Another set of orders came aboard transferring Fred Sass back to the States for more schooling, and new construction. My training program went down the tubes. My sore arm went for nothing, and I had been promoted out of another transfer. My later consolation was that these guys went to new tin cans which caught hell in the battle for Leyte, and Okinawa.

My Boot Camp buddy, Scotty Harris was still second class, and he was transferred to Gunnery School in Washington D.C. The next time I would see him would be in Yokosuka Japan in 1961. After the war he went out, and back to college on the GI Bill, getting a Commission in the Reserve.

We both retired with the Grade of Commander, and it was a far cry from the boots we were when we went aboard *Lamson* on 12 February 1942 with other members of Company 41-84.

No sooner had the school boys left the ship than we got underway for Ulithi Atoll, screening several Fleet Tugs that were towing floating dry docks, barges, and all the other gear that went into a forward base. Ulithi was closer to the Philippines, and Japan, and we were moving forward to attack both.

14 OCTOBER 1944. SATURDAY. When we dropped our convoy off at Ulithi, we were ordered alongside, just like 1942 in Espiritu Santo, for a short 'voyage repair' availability, and some ice cream. While we were in port, Task Force 38 was striking Formosa, and destroyed nearly 500 Japanese planes.

18 OCTOBER 1944. WEDNESDAY. The rest did not last long, and at noon we were underway in company with COMDESRON Five headed for Hollandia, New Guinea. CDS5, and CDD 9 was in *Flusser*, and *Lamson*, *Drayton*, and *Shaw* followed. Astern of SHAW was CDD 10 in *Smith* with *Mahan*, *Reid*, and *Conyingham* bringing up the rear. The Old Man was not going to lose time, and we were making 19 - 20 knots.

19 OCTOBER 1944. THURSDAY. It was shortly before 2400 when we crossed the Equator at 140°. E. In anticipation of this the afternoon had been set aside for a ceremonial welcome of the Court of Davey Jones. There were a lot of pollywogs on board, but they were outnumbered by the Shell Backs so when Davey Jones came aboard with his Royal Court he announced that there was to be an initiation of all of the scum on board into his exalted realm of the deep.

The Electricians were able to provide a megger for the hot seat, and the Fire Room provided the "Royal Baby" in the person of "McFoul Dilworth" of Hollywood fame, and obese frame. He had a hairy belly that was liberally smeared with grease, and the lowly Pollywogs had to start by kissing his navel as they paid their respects to the Royal Couple. Next they were entertained at dinner in a long canvas chute that had been filled with garbage.

A fire hose at the exit kept the entrance, and the fine food courses, stirred up in the faces of the unworthy ones as they crawled toward daylight, and the nozzle. Many paddles were used, and the day was just right for the ceremonies--bright, hot, breathless, and a glass-like sea.

ENS Wendell Johnson was the most fair of the officers in the Wardroom, and he was selected to be the lookout during the ceremonies. He was fitted out in a set of oilskins, and took his station on the Whistle Platform. He was provided with a 4 x 4 shore so he could stay steady at that height on the small grating that was surrounded by a low safety rail. He did get a little red in the face, acting as lookout for the Royal Party, but took it in good spirits. In fact everybody took the hazing well, and except for a little sunburn there were no casualties, and the whole crew was composed of Shellbacks once again.

20 OCTOBER 1944. FRIDAY. It was almost 1130 when the Squadron anchored in Hollandia. The overcast skies and rain did not make our return to New Guinea any more pleasant than it had been in the fall of 1943. What made it worse was the fact that the General did not welcome us, for he was up at Leyte making his famous walks through the surf.

Mahan, Lamson, Flusser, and *Smith* drew the honor of taking the first re-supply convoy mission to Leyte Gulf where the troops needed reinforcements, and supplies, very badly. The landings in the vicinity of Tacloban, Leyte began on the morning of the 20th, and the order to "Deploy" was given at 0645. The Battle of Leyte Gulf had begun.

The weather cleared a bit in the afternoon, and Kay Keyser's band was being broadcast over the airwaves. The E Division. Workshop was amidships, and a stopping off place for everyone passing on the Main Deck. The old Bull Sessions about women continued as before.

Hollandia was better than Buna, or Port Moresby because it was a little cooler, and the rains helped keep the decks cool. the Mail Orderly came back from the beach with several bags of mail so Holiday Routine was sounded, and then Liberty Call. What a miserable scene confronted the Liberty Party when they hit the landing. The place was active, but the mud was deep, and everything blended into the jungle background. There was really no recreation area as there had been in Milne Bay the year before.

Liberty in Hollandia really turned out to be a chance to exchange the confines of the dry ship for a walk in the muddy open spaces. We were able to visit with MacArthur's Women's Auxiliary Army Corps through the barbed wire fence of their recreation compound. The "ladies" were not pleased with the changes that had been thrust upon them since their departure from the civilized world of Brisbane, Australia where the Generals Headquarters had been set up during the New Guinea campaign.

They did look miserable but from our point of view they were white American girls, and it was fun talking to them about the latest rumors and activities from the headquarters. They gave us insight into what was happening at Leyte, and what we could look forward to. Later we wondered who General MacArthur took with him when he moved his headquarters to Tacloban on the 25th. He had been aboard his old Flagship, *U.S.S. Nashville*, during the landings, but the cruiser was needed badly by the Navy, and he moved ashore.

On the 23rd, General MacArthur and Philippine President Osmena visited

Tacloban on Leyte when it was secured, and announced the reestablishment of civil government in the Philippines. Now all they had to do was convince the Japanese to go back home and leave them alone.

Note: 24 - 25 OCTOBER 1944. The Japanese Navy tried to destroy the 28 Liberty Ships that supported the landing in San Pedro Bay between Leyte, and Samar. The Japanese High Command split a very powerful fleet into Central, and Southern Groups. One Task Force, commanded by Admiral Nishimura came up through the Surigao Strait after midnight on 25 October while the Central force under Admiral Kuita came through the Straits of San Bernardino Strait, and down the east side of Samar, attempting a pincer attack on San Pedro Bay. The Battle of Surigao Strait defeated Southern Force, and a group of light carriers, DD and DE caused Admiral Kurita in Yamato *to turn back.*

25 OCTOBER 1944. WEDNESDAY. It was late in the afternoon when we got underway with the Squadron enroute to Kossol Passage in the Palau Island group. We were escorting *SS Yeager.*

General MacArthur had refused to delay his landing even though he knew what type of weather his troops would face. The torrential rains, and mud had hampered operations, on the ground and in the air, so the troops were bogged down. There was not enough steel matting in the world to make dry runways for the aircraft that were so vital to the ground operation.

It was a good thing that the runway at Tacloban was operational during the Battle of Samar, for aircraft from the light carrier forces had to use it. Ships in San Pedro Bay were at the mercy of Japanese aircraft operating from better bases on Luzon, Panay, Leyte, and several other islands. The Infantry suffered, and our turn was not too far away.

The Japanese Army had spent three years preparing their defenses. They were well dug in, and well supplied. Their naval and air forces attacked frequently from as far north as Manila, and they were giving us a bad time. Gen. MacArthur had returned as promised, but there was considerable loss of American lives and much worry, attached to his political adventure.

26 OCTOBER 1944. The Squadron crossed the equator at about 0700 at 138° East.

27 OCTOBER 1944. FRIDAY. *Flusser, Smith, Mahan,* and *Drayton* left the formation just off the Kossol Passage in the Palau Islands to escort Echelon L-6 onwards to Leyte Gulf; nearly 450 miles to the west. On the 28th we joined the group about half way to Leyte.

29 OCTOBER 1944. SUNDAY. The Battle of Samar was long over when we entered San Pedro Bay with the reinforcements, and the supplies that were badly needed by the troops on the beach.

On the way into the bay we passed a 2100 ton destroyer that had been badly damaged. It was down by the stern with about a foot of freeboard aft. This was going to become a common sight before much longer. It could have been one of the cans that survived the Battle of Samar against the Japanese heavies.

1332: Condition red on the beach. The convoy was turned over to the Army, and our Division was instructed to anchor in San Pedro Bay, and provide anti-aircraft coverage for the assembled ships in the anchorage. By 1530 the hook was down in the assigned anchorage, and the watch on the guns was told to keep a sharp eye out for low flying bogies.

The wind came up, freshening to about 65 knots, and the First Lt, and the Anchor Detail stayed on the Fo'c'sle all night long, tending the chain in an effort to keep the anchor on the bottom. Cdr. Noel stayed in his chair on the Bridge, and down below in the Engine Room the throttlemen kept a few turns on the screws, answering the "Turn Indicator" in an effort to take some of the strain off the anchor chain.

30 OCTOBER 1944. MONDAY. At breakfast we were still at anchor.

NOVEMBER 1944. TUESDAY. DESRON 5 reported to Admiral Weyler in Leyte Gulf, and began operating with TASK FORCE 77.1 which included the old battleships rebuilt after the Pearl Harbor debacle. The wagons were those that we worked with in 1942 when Task Force I was made up of the salvaged wagons that survived Pearl Harbor. The *Pennsylvania* (BB38), *U.S.S. Mississippi* (BB41), and *California* (BB-44), were supported by Light Cruisers *Boise* (CL47), and *Nashville* (CL43). *Nashville* had been MacArthur's flagship in New Guinea when we were in his Navy. DESRON 5 ships, *Mahan*, *Drayton*, *Lamson*, *Flusser*, *Reid*, and *Smith*, were supplemented by some new 2100 ton cans from DESRON 60—*Abner Read* (DD526), *Ammen* (DD527), and *Claxton* (DD571).

The November War Diary developed by Captain Noel provided the details of our actions in the Leyte area. At 0800 *Lamson* was underway with *Mahan*, *Flusser*, and *Smith* with orders to rendezvous with a west bound convoy about 100 miles off the mouth of Leyte Gulf entrance. From 0900 until almost 1100 enemy aircraft were in sight, and planes were taken under fire by *Mahan* and *Flusser*, for they were out of our range.

In addition to the American forces we were in company with *HMAS Shropshire*, DESRON 60, and an old destroyer buddy from ANZAC Squadron days in 1942; *HMAS Arunta* . The main body was under attack, and to the north the vessels in San Pedro Bay were under air attack also. Our job was to provide AA protection for the supply ships in the Bay, alternating with a patrol between two islands--The Surigao Straits-- a route for submarine or surface penetration of Leyte Gulf. We were currently in an Anti Aircraft screen, and at General Quarters almost constantly.

Heavy Kamikaze attacks began early in the morning, and *Ammen, Claxton, Killen,* and *Anderson* were hit by Kamikaze aircraft, or bombs, and badly damaged. The Japanese had recovered control of the air. At 1115 DesRon 5 was ordered back to the Main Body to rejoin the screen, replacing the cans hit by the suicide planes during the morning.

At 1336 the task group received a surprise attack by diving Kamikaze Vals. *Abner Read* was standing by *Claxton,* and was hit amidships, sinking almost immediately. CAP was very light, and at times there were no friendly fighters overhead. Task Force 38 was being recalled to suppress the Japanese aircraft staging on Luzon.

Air attacks were the main concern, but later in the afternoon reports came in from our scouting aircraft that an enemy force of three battleships, four cruisers, and ten destroyers were about 300 miles west of the Surigao Straits on an easterly course. Task Group 77.1 deployed in a semi-circle around the northern entrance to Surigao Straits, and patrolled all night.

3 NOVEMBER 1944. THURSDAY. On patrol off Desolation Point, Leyte Gulf. This patrol area was aptly named, for we were all by ourselves steaming slowly back and forth between two points of land; a real sitting duck. Other cans had been hit on this very quiet patrol.

I was celebrating my 22nd Birthday, and the only present I'd have liked was a pair of old coveralls that I kept in the car. Now that my heat rash was giving me the works I could really have used them. The older and lighter they were the more comfortable they'd be down in the Engine Room. Our patrol continued quietly through the, and on the we were relieved and went into Leyte Gulf to fuel. There was an alert about sundown, but we managed to get some sleep in our bunks, and that was a welcome change. Ammunition was replenished on the run, for we were scheduled to go back on AS patrol and relieve *Mahan* as a RADAR picket ship about 15 miles out of Leyte Gulf.

7 NOVEMBER 1944. MONDAY. The Japanese used dawn and dusk for their main Kamikaze attacks, and one dawn we went to General Quarters when a lone aircraft was penetrating the formation. All the ships in the screen had opened up on it, but the pilot was about masthead high, and skated out the other side without doing any damage. Our gunners did all the damage, killing many on our own ships, including *Honolulu.* She had taken an airborne torpedo and then one of the fleets AA shells hit her adding 5 dead and 11 wounded to the casualty list. *Lindenwald* took a 5" burst and lost 7 men.

Most of the day was spent with the Task Force in Leyte Gulf, but we had been ordered back to our lonesome patrol station, and by 2000 we were 15 miles off the Leyte Entrance where we relieved *Mahan* as radar picket on station 'Echo'. A warning of an approaching typhoon was received. The weather looked bad, but everything was running smoothly when I turned in that evening, and my bunk was very cool and inviting. After being asleep for a few hours I was awakened by a feel that we were underway, for the ship was pitching and rolling quite heavily. *Lamson* stayed on station until the wind increased to a velocity of 70 - 80 knots, and the Captain decided to seek shelter in the lee of Dinagat Island.

The one good thing about the storms was the fact that the Japanese aircraft stayed on the ground and we got some sleep. When the weather cleared we were at Air Defense and GQ much of the time. If we were not at AA station in the Gulf we were assigned to the lonesome patrol of the straits, and still subject to attack. We lived and slept in our clothes in a continuous state of readiness with all the guns manned by a skeleton crew that would be ready to open fire instantly. The crew slept in shifts, and as close to GQ stations as men could get with comfort. By noon on the 9th the storm had passed, and we were back on station again with the SG radar giving phenomenal ranges, tracking the Task Force past 75,000 yards, and cans at 60,000 yards.

10 NOVEMBER 1944. FRIDAY. About mid afternoon *U.S.S. Smith* relieved us, and we went back to the main body to rejoin the screen.

11 NOVEMBER 1944. SATURDAY. The Task Group began fueling at 0800, and we got our drink at noon, just about chow down, and resumed our screen position again by about 1700.

2000 - General Quarters because of numerous bogies in the area. Low flying attacks threatened, but nothing happened. The enemy planes seemed to be so close that we could hear their engines, and were able to make about 50% of the initial contact reports to the Flag.

No attacks were actually made, but we stayed at GQ a lot. Some ships opened up on the low flying aircraft, but they were some distance away.

13 NOVEMBER 1944. SUNDAY. *Lamson* was again ordered to relieve a can on the northern sector of the entrance patrol. Three DD were strung out over the 10 miles between Homohon and Dinagat Islands. After dark an enemy attack sent us to GQ again. A force of 15 or more aircraft dropped flares, and attacked transports at the entrance to the gulf.

14 NOVEMBER 1944. MONDAY. In between Battle Station Alerts the routine work was done. One of the Ward Room Mess Attendants brought in a toaster, and there were always fans to keep the shop cluttered up along with the batteries that were on charge.

We continued our patrol until about noon when the *HMAS Warramunga*, another ANZAC can, relieved us, and we moved back to Station "E" 15 miles ESE of the entrance. Mid afternoon saw us back on our old station, and at dusk the SC picked up a bogie 40 miles NE, target angle zero. At 10 miles we managed to duck into a rain squall, while the bogie went on into the bay. Reports were made to CTG 77.1.

This patrol was held through the 15th, and 16th until relieved about 1400 by verbal orders from CTG 77.1, directing *Lamson* to report to CTG 78.2 in San Pedro Bay. On station at 2130 after a 25 knot run. Condition red, and much action on the beach. Bogies close aboard, but we stayed quiet, for it was very dark, and we did not want to draw any fire.

17 NOVEMBER 1944. THURSDAY. We stayed at anchor all day, and rain and low visibility helped us get a little rest. Our provisions were very low.

NOTE: MacArthur was in trouble on the beach, and sent in another Division. The Quartermasters had not planned for the larger numbers, and ran out of rations. At the same time we also ran out of food. Ensign Ehinger, the Supply Officer, and Stew LaRue ran around the harbor in the whaleboat picking up a case of this and a can of that wherever they could find food. We tried to beg from the Quartermaster Corps, even though we knew that they were on short rations on the beach. We had not been on such short rations since we were down to noodles in New Guinea over a year ago.

18 NOVEMBER 1944. FRIDAY. Another day at anchor in the screen. This was a hot one for we were at GQ from dawn until dusk. There was heavy enemy action against the airfield on the beach at Tacloban, and kamikaze attacks on the transports and the screen. One headed for us, but turned toward *Flusser*, missing her port side by about 15 feet. At dusk enemy aircraft strafed the Tacloban field again, but no attacks were made against the anchorage.

19 NOVEMBER 1944. SATURDAY. Up and away again at dawn. Three suicide planes, 3,000 to 5,000 yards on the port beam began low level glides on 3 Liberty ships. Two missed.

In the afternoon we fueled ship, and returned to the anchorage to play sitting duck some more, staying at GQ most of the day although we were not directly attacked. About 1600 Tacloban reported 19 planes coming in from the north, but the fighters got to them first, and we were not bothered, for they did not get over the water. About 1630 COMDESRON 5 ordered us underway with *Flusser* and *Smith* to rendezvous with LST Group 42 in the Southern Transport Area. Organized TG 76.5, and got underway for Hollandia with the LST convoy.

20 NOVEMBER 1944. SUNDAY. We were given some relief from the grind when we were sent back to Hollandia with an empty cargo ship convoy where the ships were reloaded quickly and turned around for the trip back to Leyte Gulf. The war in Europe still had priority, and Nimitz and MacArthur had to make do with a very limited sea lift capability. We were able to replenish our own stores, and at least would have something to eat.

21 NOVEMBER 1944. MONDAY. The convoy was attacked by two low flying Lillys making glide bomb runs. The first plane dropped its bomb, and missed, while the second unloaded only to be shot down by crossfire from the LSTs. At 1200 *Lamson, Flusser* and *Smith* left the convoy and headed for Humbolt Bay, New Guinea at 20 knots.

23 NOVEMBER 1944. WEDNESDAY. At 0700 we entered Humbolt Bay, fueled, and moored alongside *U.S.S. Smith*. We had been looking for the Mail Signal everyday telling us to come and get it, but so far it had been no dice. At least we had our hopes nearer fulfillment than at any time of late, and every body was happier than usual. The whole crew looked forward to securing for Thanksgiving Day.

24 - 26 NOVEMBER 1944. Moored in nest while being fitted out as a fighter director ship. Left to right were *Flusser, Lamson, Smith, LST 667, AD-G3, AD-H3, ARD-12,* and *U.S.S. Drayton*. With the fighter director equipment came two Army officers. Lt. Judae, and Second Lt. Fink were Army Air Corps officers.

27 NOVEMBER 1944. SUNDAY. We had looked at the bottom of the barrel again, and had been drinking our coffee black and straight, but we'd get a good chow on Thursday after all. This meal did not turn out as elaborately as the one I remembered that Thanksgiving in 1943 in Milne Bay. Then there had been Liberty in the rain and McShane and I didn't seem to mind at all; and all of that was on top of a delicious ham dinner. Lt. Adams and another couple of officers were able to get a Jeep, and a .45 Pistol, and found some dates.

0736. Underway with *Flusser, Drayton, Mahan, Smith,* and *Coughlan* headed for Leyte Gulf again with reinforcements for the troops on Leyte. The holiday ended just as soon as the transports and cargo ships were full, and before we knew it, Tacloban was in sight once again, and we were back on station.

Ship's maintenance and repair did not quit because of General Quarters. On Saturday a pump on the After Station seized up. As is usual it was right down in the bottom and back in a corner under a ladder. It was well bolted to a half dozen big pipes and secured firmly to the foundation. It took three of us to get it to the topside where a good days work followed. Seems like the bearings were worn out so after a few preliminaries we replaced them and juggled the motor, with chain falls large enough to pull up the bottom, back to its original resting place. All of this plus one other motor gave us a busy two days, and we were glad that no attacks had come while we were working on them.

X-mas packages were coming on board and all of us were really waiting for the mail. There was a rumor that we had about 36 sacks waiting for us some place.

30 NOVEMBER 1944. WEDNESDAY. En route to San Pedro Bay, and at 0810 the SC-3 picked up a low flying bogie. It turned out to be a Jill, and made a torpedo run on *Flusser*. GQ, and we opened fire only to check when *Flusser* got in the way. 1200, entered Leyte Gulf, and at 1500 anchored again in San Pedro Bay, and just in time for pay day.

The stragglers were going down for payday, but since I still had 15 rags I did not draw any more money. I had $284.00 on the books which the Ensign Ehinger, our lanky Disbursing Officer, wanted me to convert to War Bonds. I'd let it ride until I had to get a jeep to cart it off in. Another two weeks and I'd be making 5% more.

1 DECEMBER 1944. THURSDAY. After long weeks of waiting we finally caught up with about 40 sacks of mail and although most of the packages were rather sad it was a hectic and enjoyable time while everything was being sorted and distributed.

September and October letters were in the bundle that I received. We missed, or rather were passed, by this stuff so it was a bit old. There is plenty of bait and fruit cake aboard now though most of it was in pretty sad shape due to the general abuse by man and the elements.

Note: As noted, Lamson had been fitted out as a Fighter Director Ship and on 4 December we were sent with a landing force of troops, vehicles and ammunition to a friendly beach north of Bay to assist with the air support for the operation. It was a night landing, and by 0315 on the 5th the force began to withdraw. It was another trip through the Surigao Straits to San Pedro Bay.

5 DECEMBER 1944. TUESDAY. The formation came under heavy air attacks during the daylight in the Surigao Strait, and *Drayton* was slightly damaged while *Mugford* was severely damaged by Kamikaze aircraft. One Kamikaze dove into an LSM. The Japanese were beginning to get desperate, and our unit was feeling the heat.

6 DECEMBER 1944. WEDNESDAY. General MacArthur was having trouble moving his troops through the mud, and the Japanese Army was dug in on the hillsides on the inland route that he had chosen so he decided to land the 77th Division at Ormoc to leapfrog the heavily entrenched enemy in the Leyte battle area, and to support the forces at Bay.

The Japanese had been using Ormoc as a landing point for their reinforcements. TF 38 had been attacking the Japanese convoys from Manila at every opportunity, but weather allowed a lot of support to get through.

LT(j.g.) Weeks was sent to *LST 464* for hospitalization, and we took on two Army Air Control Officers. Several other men were transferred prior to our getting underway with Amphibious Group 9, lifting the Division with nothing larger than a DD transport. At least the weather stayed good, and the sea was like glass as we rounded the cape at night, steaming toward Ormoc.

7 DECEMBER 1944. THURSDAY. The landing was successful and *Lamson* provided AA and shore fire support but air resistance increased during the morning and *Ward*, and *Mahan* were hit by Kamikaze aircraft, and ordered sunk. *Cooper* was also hit and sunk.

In the afternoon, the group departed Ormoc with *Lamson* bringing up the rear. The Force was attacked from the air, and the talker on the 1JV circuit on the Bridge told Hylton and me that an LCI was hit.

We had been dogged in since daylight when the landing started, and I was ready for some fresh air so I called Amsler, one of the Repair Party electricians, to come down and relieve me.

I got topside just as a twin engine bomber swept in from the starboard side astern. The guns were making a hell of a racket, and the CO was twisting to bring everything to bear when a 40mm round took out the plane's right engine, and it dropped a bomb off the stern and wheeled into the sea. I could see the two men in the cockpit as it went by. I had been caught in the stampede as the Repair Party ran from the stern, and I vowed to go aft if they went forward to stay out of the way the next time.

A few minutes later a Val piloted by another kamikaze pilot who really knew how to fly came in from astern with guns blazing. I headed forward along the port side, as bullets went into the water to my left, causing me to hit the deck and roll in under the uptakes of #2 Fire Room. Another member of the Repair Party landed on my back just as the plane hit the superstructure and exploded. We both got up shaky, and scared as hell, and I went back to the shop after taking a quick look at the carnage just forward of the blower shield.

The Forward Repair Party, and people from the Fire Rooms, had taken bomb fragments, and nobody was moving. I did not investigate further, and figured everyone was dead. I was badly shaken, and headed for the Electrical Shop to get oriented again. I could see that people were going over the side, and had no idea what the situation was. Hebard was not around, having gone over the side, in fact the midships area was deserted.

I could feel the ship slow down, and noticed that the guns had been put out of action aft, and everything was very quiet; with the exception of the noise of the fire. The #2 stack was plugged by the wing where he hit first and the Watertender had shut the boilers down at the first hint of a flare back. We were almost dead in the water by the time I got to the shop. People were going over the side, and I took off the heavy army shoes that we had been issued, and went to starboard rail outboard of the shop where Sivcovich was looking down at the water. We could not bring ourselves to dive in, despite the numbers in the water.

USS Lamson (DD-367) afire off Ormoc, Leyte, on 7 December 1944, after she was hit by a Kamikaze. The tug assisting with firefighting is USS ATR-31. (Official U.S. Navy Photograph, National Archives)

Crewmen of USS Lamson (DD-367) swimming to USS Flusser (DD-368) to be rescued, 7 December 1944. (Official U.S. Navy Photograph, now in the collections of the National Archives)

Lamson was on an even keel, and burning above the galley passage, but seemed to be a safe haven for the moment. There were people on the Fo'c'sle heaving ammunition over, and some were on the fantail with wounded so I put my shoes back on and dropped into the Engine Room and lit off the Emergency Diesel and put power on the Submersible Pump outlets on the Main Deck so we could get some water on the fire above the fuel tanks, and the Galley Passage.

Knobby Walsh came up to help me with a pump which we dropped over, hoping to attack the fire in the Galley Passage, and keep it away from the fuel tanks. The pump ran for a short time, and then shorted out and blew the Main Board off the line. I started the process again with another pump, and the same thing happened so we gave up on that tack, and in our excitement and confusion decided to go with CO_2 extinguisher into the passageway, and smother a smoldering fire in the cable run. The hoses on the extinguisher were rotten from the tropics, and blew off. We threw the bottles into the burning Laundry, and headed for the after Repair Locker and a gasoline Handy Billy. About the time we had it lit off, the accompanying support tug, ATF-31 came alongside and threw salt water all over us, killing the gasoline engine, and soaking us as she put the fire out in the superstructure.

Captain Noel had gone overboard, in a perfect swan dive from the bridge, because of the flames around the Bridge, and was picked up by *Flusser*, and persuaded the Commodore not to sink the ship, so the tug had been ordered to our rescue. Meanwhile, Knobby and I had experienced frustration, and were called back to the fantail. The ATF came up, and a stage went over. The wounded had been transferred, and we walked from *Lamson* to the tug, joining a real crowd of survivors that was herded below decks, and out of the way of the small gun crew topside.

LT(j.g.) Hixenbaugh, and a line handling party in *Flusser's* boat, was able to get a line to the bow, and *Lamson* was taken in tow as Japanese air attacks continued. It was a very shaky experience being packed below while that little 3" popped away topside.

We heard that Lt. Behan had been killed on the Bridge, and that there were many casualties among those that had been in spaces in the superstructure, Fire Control platform, and on the after gun mounts. Later 17 were reported Killed In Action, and MM3/C Holewa's body was never found. Nobody got out of Number One Fire Room, and the forward repair party had been wiped out. We were a scared and miserable bunch.

After dark there was a request for volunteers to go back to *Lamson* and get the rudder amidships and begin the clean up, as well as check on casualties. I wanted off the tug badly, and as a leading electrician elected to go back. Captain Noel, Lt. j.g. Hixenbaugh, Lt. Burkhart, Rackley, EM2/C,

S1C(RM) Pericle, CMM "Red" Waite, and I made up the party that got into that dark whaleboat, and returned to the ship, and made it easier to tow.

A previous trip had been made to the ship in the *Flusser's* whaleboat, but they were cut short by an attack, and the *Flusser* wanted her boat back. The CO's report said there were six that returned, and there may have been one more.

The Captain's cabin had been burned out, but he was able to scrounge up a bottle of Listerine that had been contaminated by brandy; which he shared with us. While the rest of us went to the CPO quarters he had a sack taken to #1 Gun Shelter, and we secured until dawn, spending a restless night with the knowledge that there were at least 16 bodies in the wreckage.

At first light we ate what was available in the Chief's Mess and Wardroom, and got a good look at the mess topside. The first thing that we did was pick up the bodies and lay them out in mattress covers on the fantail. I went up the starboard ladder to the superstructure with a mattress cover, and picked up a body. I was able to identify TM3C Wade by his name in his web belt. Several others in the RADAR Transmitter Room were in about the same shape, and we were all numb after that chore was completed.

The tug towed *Lamson* to Tacloban, and the bodies were removed to the cemetery on the beach. From there the ship was sent alongside *U.S.S. Gilliam* (APA-57), and the crew was billeted, and a clean up operation began. Since I was able to get power to the after compartments I chose to stay aboard, enjoying my own sack and fan.

My job was to get the Electrical System back together so we could get power to the living and Engineering spaces. The worst part was working in #1 Fire Room while Peavy and his seamen tried to get the casualties out. A Burner had to be used to open the main deck hatch to Number 1 Fire Room. The air lock was impassable because there was about 12 foot of water in the boiler room. The bomb fragments that had wiped out the Forward Repair Party, including my man, Sam Tinsley EM3/C, went through the Main Deck, opening the steam lines on the port side, killing the Firemen on duty, and then on through the bottom, flooding the space.

Topside the Deck Force tried to clean up the dried blood that covered the port side of the Main Deck, and they kept pouring water on me through the bomb holes in the deck, and I had to rig a tent over me, and the damaged wire runs on the port side, and continued my splicing while CBM Peavy and his hapless crew continued to gag, and throw up over their miserable job, but they got the men out, and I continued with my splicing.

Underwater welders patched the holes in the hull and the boiler room was pumped dry. The transport had plenty of lifting capacity, and #1 stack was cut loose, and heaved overboard, along with the top portion, and wing parts, from #2 smoke pipe. Just as soon as # 2 stack was cleared; boilers three and four were lit off, and the main generator was put back on the line. It was then that E Division was able to evaluate the real extent of the damage to the wiring system. It was monumental, but everything that we needed to steam, including the compass, and repeater system aft, was operational

The Fire Control Director was deemed of value and salvageable so it was lifted off it's mount and secured backwards on # 1 uptakes. The ship began to look even more weird.

The dead had been buried at the military cemetery at Tacloban, and the 49 injured were sent first to the *U.S.S. Mercy*, where two more died, and then on to the U.S. Navy Base Hospital #17 at Hollandia for further treatment of their wounds.

The Personnel Roster of 1 December 1944 listed an allowance of 235 men, but an on board count of 246 in the crew, and 23 officers in the Ward Room. The Recapitulation Sheet noted the following:

"On 7 December 1944 the Ship's Office was completely gutted by a fire resulting from enemy action. All Personnel reports were destroyed, except a few muster cards. On 1 December 1944 there were 246 men on board; included in the attached report of changes. On 7 December 1944, 17 men were killed in action; on 8 December 2 men died from wounds received in action and 49 men were transferred to *U.S.S. Mercy* for further transfer, leaving a total of 172 men on board. There were 16 Officers on board for a total of 188 people."

11 DECEMBER 1944. MONDAY. The living spaces were OK and *Lamson* was ready to receive the crew again, and the men returned to their own bunks gladly. We were just about ready to get underway with a jury rigged Secondary Con, forward lookout station, and emergency radio/radar system.

15 DECEMBER 1944. FRIDAY. #3 boiler was lit off, and #4 went on the line on the 12 - 16 as we prepared to get underway.

1409. It was a strange looking ship that departed Leyte Gulf, with the Captain at the Con, on the jury rigged bridge aft, for the long voyage to the States. We had an escort assignment with a convoy headed for Hollandia, but when the merchantmen dropped at the Kossol Channel we kicked it up to 16 kts. The jury rigged Division of Destroyers were *U.S.S. Lamson*, *U.S.S. Liddle*, *U.S.S. Orange*, and *U.S.S. Van Buren*, and we were headed for Seeadler Harbor at Manus in the Admiralty Islands for more extensive repair work.

21 DECEMBER 1944. THURSDAY. The formation arrived at Manus, and *Lamson* tied up outboard of *U.S.S. Charrette* (DD581) which was

alongside *U.S.S. Sierra* (AD-18). COMSERVRON 10 was S.O.P.A. in *Sierra*. The plant was shut down, and we began receiving service from the tender. The electricians had it easy, for there was just one ship across which to pull that heavy shore power cable.

Mail was waiting for us, and my coveralls arrived from home just in time. Additional electrical, and machinery repairs were made in an effort to get the ship ready for the long haul to Pearl. The director was heavily secured to the uptakes from #1 fire room so it would weather any storms that might come along.

24 DECEMBER 1944. SUNDAY. Lt. j.g. Weeks, DuBay, Kosven, Bracci, Gotchal, Gottbrath, Sherman, Clancy, Aellig, Humphrey and Davis came back from the Hospital. It was a good reunion, and a great present on Christmas Eve.

The lights were back on in the forward spaces, and there was a busy scene, for some of the tables were occupied by card players, others by letter writers, and some men were even studying for advancement. It had been a restful evening with a movie, and no fear of sudden interruption. The crew was living on board, but the galley had been burned out, and the cooks had it easy, for we were eating on board the Repair Ship. It gave us a welcome change from the canned beans and spam that we had eaten on the way from Leyte.

26 DECEMBER 1944. TUESDAY. *Charrette* was ready to get underway so we had to break the service connections with the tender, but we were then directly alongside so it was easier to get to the gedunk stand. *Claxton* (DD571), another 1 November Kamikaze casualty, was outboard of *Lamson*.

Ship's Force had continued with what cleanup work could be done, and the repair ship had undertaken the heavier repairs. It had been a good Christmas alongside, and my only problem was a sprained ankle. We were all anxious to get underway for the Navy Yard. #2 Fire Room was lit off on the 04-08, and the Special Sea Detail was set at 0745, and at 0803 we moved from alongside *Sierra* to anchorage E-15, dropping the hook at 0809.

28 DECEMBER 1944. THURSDAY. S1C Atkins came back aboard, having escaped from the Navy Base Hospital #17. He was glad to be back after a hectic time in transit, and he had been afraid that he would be reassigned to another ship in WestPac.

29 DECEMBER 1944. FRIDAY. *Lamson* was underway again in company with *U.S.S. Iowa* (BB-61) with COMBATDIV 7 as OTC; *U.S.S. Killen*, and *U.S.S. Caldwell*. Base course was 066, and the speed of advance was 18 knots. The canvas on the jury rigged bridge was really flapping. A sailing

report on 29 December 1944 listed the Officers on board, and a copy was sent to *U.S.S. Iowa*, BUPERS (Bureau of Naval Personnel), and COMDESPAC inter alia.

30 DECEMBER 1944. SATURDAY. We were still partially armed, and the Old Man held GQ Drill just to remind us that we were still in the war. Another reminder of our return was the fumigation of the ship to kill the bugs before we hit Honolulu.

31 DECEMBER 1944. SUNDAY. We were now on Base Course 076 zigzagging to foil submarines, and doing 19.5 knots. With a reduced magazine load #2 Fire Room could handle the load nicely. There were now 184 enlisted, and 16 Officers, on board for the return trip; a total of 200 souls. 1944 was over, and we were out of the war for probably six months. I had made it again.

1 JANUARY 1945. MONDAY. Lt. Burkhart had the Conn on the 00 to 04, and his poetic Log entry showed us still on base course 076°, Speed 19. We were 1000 yards astern of *Iowa* and the Task Force was still zig zagging on and off. This small group of cripples, led by *U.S.S. Iowa*, included *U.S.S. Caldwell* (DD605) that had taken a Kamikaze on 12 December, and *U.S.S. Killen* (DD593) which had been bombed on 1 November. *Killen's* sonar was operational, and she was designated the Screen Commander.

The force slowed down, and changed course to fuel. *Lamson* went alongside *Iowa's* starboard side at 0858 and took on 50,000 gallons of black oil before securing an hour later. We were getting some of our hot meals from *Iowa* by highline, which gave the deck force and the OOD plenty to worry about, but we got a change of rations so it was worth the fuss. By noon the force was back on course, and zig zagging at 19 knots, once more.

5 JANUARY 1945. FRIDAY. The Task Force was gradually turning north, for we were getting close to Oahu. Coming in from the south you sail almost due north to get to the Pearl Harbor channel.

6 JANUARY 1945. SATURDAY. By 0600 we had dropped to 15 knots, and were heading 000T. At 1040 we passed the entrance buoys, following *Iowa* into port with *Killen* and *Caldwell* astern. 1135 moored to buoys in Anchorage X-17. It was good to be back in a cool climate again.

On the 12-16 Lt j.g. Adams and seven other casualties, Acker, Clark, Clifford, Grimm, Hogan, Johnson, and Kilgore returned to the ship from the Base Hospital, having been released on Dec. 27th.

We were ordered to shift berths, going alongside *Caldwell* in X-19, and took on over 98,000 gallons of black oil from a YO. We were not going to be in Pearl very long. *U.S.S. Haraden* (DD585) was in the nest with *Caldwell*, *Killen* and *Lamson*, making a Division of four cripples. She had been hit by Kamikaze while escorting "Jeep" carriers in the Sulu Sea on 13 December

1944. She lost #1 stack, and the forward machinery spaces, and would go back to Bremerton with us.

Several seamen were sent to other destroyers and destroyer escorts needing replacements, and we got a S2C named Wages. MoMM1/C DuBay was sent to *U.S.S. Elder* (DE264), and did not come back with us. That was a blow.

7 JANUARY 1945. SUNDAY. Adm. Ainsworth, COMDESPAC authorized unlimited beer for the crews of the four tin cans. We had time to work a few kinks out of our legs, and enjoy the Recreation center, and that was about the extent of it.

9 JANUARY 1945. TUESDAY. The Special Sea Detail was called away early, but nobody cared, for we were underway for the States just after 0630 with the Skipper, and Lt j.g. Apple on the bridge. *Lamson*, with 5 enlisted passengers, and *Haraden* sailed together for the Puget Sound Naval Ship Yard at Bremerton, Washington.

All of us had been looking forward to Mare Island, because most of the friends and families were either in the Bay area, Los Angeles, or San Diego. It was a disappointment to head for Bremerton. As the weather cooled we were glad to have the warm engine room available, and the poor guys topside in those jury rigged shelters really began to take a beating. My two boot camp wool blankets just barely kept me warm at night.

14 JANUARY 1945. SUNDAY. It was a misty morning when we steamed into the Straits of San Juan de Fuca, passing the entrance lightship abeam to starboard at 1024. By 1755 we were anchored off Port Townsend awaiting orders to go to the Naval Ammunition Depot. At 1849 the ship was alongside the pier at Indian Island, Hadlock, Washington where the depth charges were removed. This was finished by 1941 and we were underway again for the Ship Yard.

15 JANUARY 1945. MONDAY. On the mid we moored alongside a lighter off Pier 5, Puget Sound Navy Yard with *Haraden* on our starboard side. *U.S.S. Nashville*, our New Guinea leader and General MacArthur's former flagship, was SOPA and had beaten us back to the yard. She had been bombed on 13 December enroute to Mindoro, and was badly damaged amidships but had been able to sail directly to the yard.

The ammunition that we had carried back was off loaded by 0750, and by mid morning the barge with the ammunition was removed from alongside, and replaced with one that would take the torpedoes to Torpedo Station Keyport, Washington. We had returned with six fish, and eleven warheads.

The first man off the ship was J.D. Uzzell, GM3C on 20 days leave because of a humanitarian situation. By 1655 all the ammunition had been removed from the magazines, and we took on a pilot, and were moored port side to

Pier 5 with *Haraden* outboard. It had been a long day.

Liberty call was sounded, and my first stop outside the Navy Yard gate was a State of Washington liquor store. The State had a monopoly on the sale of wine and spirits so I bought a bottle of whiskey, and caught the Seattle bound ferry that started in Port Orchard Bay, and spent an hour winding it's way through the Rich Passage, and on around Duwamish Head, stopping at the foot of Marion St. and First.

I got wind of a dance hall nearby, and with my bottle tucked into my Peacoat I headed for the dance, and girls. I had to check the bottle at the door, but that was not a problem. Imagine my surprise, when I got into the "sailor" packed hall to run into RM1C Satterwhite. He was in trouble with two girls at his side. It turned out they were inseparable, and when I told him that I had a bottle of whiskey; he thought that we had it made. After a few dances we picked up the bottle, and cast off with the two lovelies to find a place where we could get a bite to eat, and a "Setup." The girls knew just the spot where we could get the ice, mixer, and still enjoy a dance floor.

We were pleased with the appearance of the joint, and found a booth, ordered the mixer, and then I noticed that there were four eight ounce water glasses included. One of the "Ladies" volunteered to pour, and she filled the four glasses to the rim, and then they both said "Bottoms Up," or "Chug a Lug," and down the hatch went my booze without any hesitation. This was on an empty stomach, and much unexpected by both Satterwhite, and myself; innocents that we were.

We got up to dance, and I went to my knees when the booze hit my insides, but not for long. We got back to the booth, and the girls announced that they had to go home and relieve the "Baby Sitter." We had been had.

The evening was not completely shot because we did get half the bottle, and some chow as well as a few dances, but we were not about to go back to Bremerton. The Olympia Hotel was not far away and we checked in for the night. The Desk Clerk questioned us closely about any girls that we might have lurking in the shadows. The City of Seattle was being very strict about unmarried cohabitation, and venereal disease. We assured him that we were pure as the driven salt spray, and were after a good bed off the ship. I was concerned about putting in a call so we could catch the first Ferry back to Bremerton, but Satterwhite said that he knew the Washington State Ferry Schedule, and "Not to Worry."

16 JANUARY 1945. TUESDAY. We slept well, and the next morning, after a brisk walk in the fresh air, we arrived at the dock just in time to see the stern of the ferryboat as it headed for Bremerton. We were going to be AWOL, and our leaves were supposed to start this date.

One nice feature of the ferry was the snack bar. We were able to enjoy coffee, and a light breakfast in the hour that it took to get back to the

Bremerton dock. It must have been about 0930 when we crossed the gangway to be confronted by LCDR Lovejoy, our Executive Officer, who had our leave papers in his hand. Satterwhite owned up to his poor memory, and the Commander gave us our leave papers, and we heaved a sigh of relief.

Note: Later, Lamson *and* Haraden *were placed in a dry dock side by side. A former ferry boat moored close by became the* Lamson *living area. I did not move immediately, and left much of my gear in my locker in the Engineer's Compartment.*

I gathered the gear that I would need on leave, and CEM Hebard and I got off on the first liberty party. I remember Hebard coming back from Arkansas with a quart Mason Jar of white lightn'en that was made in an old still. It was very smooth. But that came later.

Just as soon as my leave was authorized; I checked out, and headed for the Seattle Ferry. I was headed for the Railroad Station at Second St. and King for a two day trip in the 'chair car' down the coast to Los Angeles. The train got underway in the afternoon, and I found that I was sharing the bench seat with a pregnant WAVE. She had gotten tired of the Navy, and found that this was an easy way out. She had been discharged, and was headed home.

17 JANUARY 1945. WEDNESDAY. When I got back I found that on the 17th another draft of 42 men came aboard just after we pulled in, and that E Division received another older Reserve; EM3C Frank B. Kuehn. He was also an electrician on the outside, and now I two seniors to contend with. Frank was great to work with..

19 JANUARY 1945. Travel time was included in the time off the ship, and my Leave actually began when I hit Wilmington. It was good to get back home again, even though I had been gone just a little over 7 months.

Some of the leave period was spent in San Francisco with Corrine Roosman, and before I knew it the time was up, and I had to head back to Bremerton, and the *Lamson.* I had been gone a little over three weeks, and had no idea what progress had been made in rebuilding the ship. I knew that a new forward superstructure had been built, and was waiting for us when we arrived at the yard.

12 FEBRUARY 1945. SUNDAY. I was able to fly back to Seattle instead of spending another couple of days on the train, and was able to get a reservation on the United Airlines Mainliner. It flew up the San Joaquin Valley, stopping at Fresno before going on into San Francisco. From there north there were stops at Medford, Oregon, and Portland.

The flight was an hour out of Oakland. Below lay the rivers and drainage facilities of the Sacramento Valley, while on either side I could see the snow capped peaks of the Coast Range and the Sierra Nevada Mountains. The

Mountains were beginning to overshadow the valley, for the sun was just about to drop below the horizon. The flight had been very pleasant; and the food very good. Next to me was a young mother and her 2 yr. old boy. He was a good kid and all little boy, but she had her hands full with him, and I did what I could to help her with the boy.

My seat was amidships, and the flight had been smooth. We were between 5,000 and 6,000 feet with little turbulence. This was the way I liked to end a very good leave, and I got back on board on the Mid Watch so got some sleep.

Note: When Shop 51 surveyed the damage they estimated that 25% of the work would be electrical. Everything in the forward superstructure above the main deck had to be replaced, as well as the cables on the port side of the fire room. The fragments had wiped out over 200 major circuits.

U.S.S. Lamson (DD-367)and U.S.S. Haraden (DD-585)under repair at Puget Sound Naval Yard in 1945. Lamson is wearing Camouflage Measure 31, Design 23d. Haraden's camouflage is Measure 31, Design 3d. (Official U.S. Navy Photograph, National Archives)

16 FEBRUARY 1945. THURSDAY. I did not like the barge where we were berthed and on Tuesday I went to Seattle and found a hotel room. When possible I would take a weekend, or a 48 in the middle of the week,

and go into Seattle to get away from the yard. The Bremerton Ferry left Seattle at 0700, and would take me back once more to a rapidly rising "Mighty L". I got acquainted with the engine room gang on the various ferry boats, and instead of fighting the crowd topside: I would go below where it was warm, and catch a few winks on the angles along the hull.

I'd been pretty much on the go, getting settled again after coming back, and trying to pick up the loose ends around the ship. There was not much to be done on the barge, but lay around, or go down to the dock and catch up on what the yard was doing. I'd become acquainted with the people in Shop 51, and the Superintendent of Ships, and they were a big help in understanding the work being done. The Main Generator gear assembly was being realigned, and I hoped that it would scream more quietly when they were finished with the job.

One trip into Seattle gave me quite a surprise. I was headed for dinner, and a movie so when I walked into a small nice looking restaurant, I took a quick look around, and realized that all of the diners were women. I felt like I was in the YWCA, and very conspicuous, even behind a pillar so I departed, looking for another place to eat.

This time I found a small place that seemed coed, and the hostess seated me with an older man, and a very lovely brunette. It turned out that the girl was his niece, and we traded names, and telephone numbers just in case I got back into town again.

I was ready to go back to Wilmington, and do a lot more of nothing.

19 FEBRUARY 1945. SUNDAY. Admiral Nimitz landed the Marines on Iwo Jima in the Bonin Islands to take the airfields, improving the Army Air Corps bombing position.

23 FEBRUARY 1945. FRIDAY. I carried my Liberty Card, and rated liberty every night, and even that was becoming a problem, because I had no real place to go, and the money that I had saved while overseas was running out. I flew down to San Francisco to see Connie, and another time to Los Angeles, making the United Airlines Ticket Agent in Bremerton wonder how I got the authorization to fly so much.

I was in the United Airlines office, buying a ticket for a Friday evening flight, when Ensign I. N. Johnson showed up. He was supposed to be at a wedding rehearsal in Palos Verdes Estates with his fiancee, Laura Bowers. There were no more seats on the plane, and I gave him mine, since the United Airlines lady said she could put me on a flight first thing Saturday Morning. Neal took off like a shot, and made the flight, but I think that he was late for the practice session. What does a groom need to learn anyway?

24 FEBRUARY 1945. SATURDAY. My old High School friends; Neal and Laura were married, but I did not attend the ceremony, for the UA

flight did not get to LA until afternoon. I was not late for the wedding reception at the Bower's house in Palos Verdes Estates, and there I saw several of my old Banning High School friends again. Mr. Bowers introduced me to Crawford's Scotch, and somebody had to drive me home. I think it was the first time the folks ever saw me drunk.

While the ship was in the yard; Officers and men were being sent to various schools, and Neal got a couple of weeks at the Damage Control School on Treasure Island. He and Laura got an extended Honeymoon at a hotel in San Francisco courtesy of the Navy, for there were no Quarters for him on Treasure Island.

1 MARCH 1945. FRIDAY. The ship was still in Dry Dock #1 with *Haraden* (DD585) moored to port.

2 MARCH 1945. SATURDAY. There were dances at the local USO and fraternal clubs. Many of us joined the Fraternal Order of Eagles so we would have a place to drink and socialize away from the crowd. We would leave the ship, stopping first at the bar on the corner outside the Yard Gate, and catch up on the latest news. Then, after gathering a crowd we would hit a Chinese restaurant that did not mind a dozen sailors clamoring for their rations. From there we would go to the Eagles Club where we could get a drink at the bar.

7 MARCH 1945. THURSDAY. At 0515 the yard workers began to flood the dry dock, and by 0820 we were underway, and by 0830 the ship was moored starboard side to Pier 5. It seemed strange to have to consider the tide again. The gangway would become almost vertical when the tide was out, for there was almost a 12 foot change between high and low tides in Puget Sound.

Everything has been going smoothly and the Yard work makes it look like we'll have a good ship again.

It may have been less trouble to build a new one, but with the hull and engines intact that was probably the trade off. Time was another factor too, for we'd be back in West Pac before a new one could come down the ways. Besides, we had a cadre of well trained crew members on board.

18 MARCH 1945. MONDAY. I had taken some more leave and went back to Wilmington, coming back to the ship late. The trip up was very smooth and I slept most of the way. There had been a four hour weather delay at the Los Angeles Air Port after the folks let me off. At Oakland there was another weather delay. We spent all night in that miserable terminal, and left about 0600 Tuesday morning when the sky cleared. As a result the plane got into Seattle late, and as usual it was raining heavily. I had to phone the ship from the airport, for I would get back ever leave. The matter was dropped.

I tried to traveled light on my trips. I was able to carry my luggage in my pea coat, but at home I had to wash my change of skivvies and socks every morning. Somehow I lost a pair of good wool socks on the way back.

22 MARCH 1945. THURSDAY. I came back to the ship, and discovered that the Captain had written a letter to BUPERS recommending me for Warrant Electrician, and that it had left the ship. I'd taken the physical for the qualifications. Everybody was giving me a lot of kidding about wearing a stripe. Warrant would beat any medals.

Friday was Payday, and I did not have to stay on the barge with the rest of the broke sailors. It was going to be difficult trying to make $60.00 last for two weeks, but I had made $10.00 last for a month so I knew I could do it. There had been a pay raise too.

Scuttlebutt had us sailing from Bremerton to San Diego for Underway Training. We were looking forward to some decent weather again, and from there I could get home easily.

25 MARCH 1945. SUNDAY. Inclining tests had to be run after all the gear was back on board so at 0555 a tug shoved *Lamson* back into #1 dry dock again for a couple of hours of testing, and then took the ship back to Pier 5B.

26 MARCH 1945. TUESDAY. *Lamson* was moored to Pier 5 again, and #3 boiler was on the line for auxiliary purposes. With the Engineering Plant lit off again, and power on the ship we began to stand watches again. I had the Engineering Duty along with the poor guys who had to stand the Quarterdeck Watch. We were probably the only ones on board, except for a skeleton watch in the boiler factory, and engine room.

The superstructure was completed, and much of the electrical and electronic work too. On the Fire Control Director there was a new Mark 28 Fire Control Radar that replaced the heavy Mk. 4. All the latest gadgets had been installed in the modernized Combat Information Center. The electrical system had not been changed that much, for Mare Island had brought us up to date with the new Interior Communications technology.

The weather was improving, and it had been a nice sunny day. It was warm enough to go in shirt sleeves, for there was no driving wind for a change. Since there was steam up I was able to test the Main Generators. For about half an hour I had those two machines going through all the tricks I could think of. When the lights would go out and the breakers crash I'd be grinning madly. It was good to have them come into parallel synchronism and hum in a high scream that was somewhat less than when we came into the Yard. I needed the practice too.

Borrell and Amsler, another of the electrical gang, were in the hospital so the work was piling up on me, and Commander Noel, was bypassing Ensign Phelan, the Assistant Chief Engineer, and staying on my back. I had Ensign Gutelle, a Merchant Marine Engineering Officer conversion, to deal with too, for he had reported on board for duty, and was trying to get acquainted with the plant.

The crew was getting ready to move off the barge, and back into the refurbished Crews Compartments. New 6 inch thick mattresses were placed on all the bunks, with green fire proof covers, but the planners did not think of the tropical heat, and the sweat that would saturate them quickly. In hot weather they would be too warm because one would sink into the mattress. They would be impossible to drape over a life line at "Air Bedding."

The yard painted the Electrical Work Shop for me and it was cleaner than I'd seen it in months. There seemed to be more room in it, for I had been able to get Shop 51 to rearrange the Battery Charging Switchboards.

31 MARCH 1945. SATURDAY. The work on the ship was nearly finished. Some of the Yard Workers were being sent to other ships in the Yard. At quitting time, more than one came up and wished me luck as he went over the gangway. A couple of them were swell guys. It was with regret that I shook hands, thanking them for their work, and said, "So Long."

A few of us put the new Laundry back in commission, and really had a time testing the new equipment. We washed all the clothes we could find. Everything from skivvies to blankets. What an improvement over that junk we had lived with for so long. Mare Island did not replace the Laundry in 1944 so we had no qualms when it was burned out.

1 APRIL 1945. SUNDAY. Moored port side to Pier 5, and receiving water from the dock. #3 boiler was still lit off. After Quarters for Muster EM2C Borrell came back from the hospital. I needed him badly.

Test ammunition and depth charges came aboard for our sea trial, and after lunch we shifted from #3 to #2 boiler, and began to get ready for our trial run with a General Quarters Drill.

At 1500 there was a formal parade of the crew on the dock, and the Captain conducted a Personnel Inspection. The Commandant of the Ship Yard joined us and 5 men were awarded Purple Hearts for their wounds. At 1645 all was over when the Commandant left the ship. I must have been on leave, or down below, for I do not remember the ceremony. CMM "Red" Waite was promoted to Warrant Machinist, and was standing deck watches. He got a few laughs from his old shipmates too, but would leave the ship within the week, for there was no billet for him on the tin can.

2 APRIL 1945. MONDAY. On the 08-12 we began Dock Trials, turning

over the engines and checking out the plant. This only took 45 minutes. The Bosun's Mate of the Watch sounded Quarters for Muster twice; once at 0800, and again after lunch at 1245. The Old Man wanted all the new men to know where they belonged.

3 APRIL 1945. TUESDAY. All the boilers were lit off, placing both fire rooms on the line, and we left Pier 5 at 0750 for our sea trials. The last few hectic weeks had been completely taken up with the final testing of the work that had been done by the yard, and now they would prove that everything worked. The Bremerton Yard workers were on board, and the Official Photographers were going along in a launch to prove that we could steam on our own. The "Atlantic Fleet" new paint job was haze gray over a dark blue stripe from the water line to the main deck. The ship was almost beautiful.

Lamson was scheduled for a full power run, and hull tests, but first came the degaussing range, and about 1030 the Bridge rang up 'All Ahead Full,' and then 'Flank,' and we ran for a half hour due west, then wheeled back down the course at 090 degrees making the maximum of 342 RPM and heading out to sea. On smooth water it was really exciting to run at flank.

Captain Noel let us finish lunch, and then we went to General Quarters in preparation for the gunnery drills with a tug and target. By 1440 the full power run was ended and I was down in my old familiar I.C. Room, dogged in as before.

1518 - Fired a full pattern of 9 depth charges, including two 600 pound charges off the fantail, at minimum settings. I was sitting on a bucket watching the meters when the first one exploded, and everything went off the line. The Main Board tripped, and I went straight up in the air, banging my head on a beam.

I'd no sooner gotten it all back on line than the second went off. This time I saved my head, but what a shaking we got, for the channel was not very deep, and it was different than dropping them in the open sea.

That ended the trials, and by 1800 we were back at Pier 5 so the Yard birds could go home. The engineering plant was secured, and we took steam from the dock, but ran the generators so I had to keep a generator watch set. Except for a few minor details, things were going fairly smoothly. Trying to get every box and item back in its place and the spares sorted and stowed and ready for sea was work.

With so many changes to the electrical system every one needed an Electrician to do an odd job, or explain how something worked. Naturally the operators thought that their problems were important, but compared with the major work schedule; they were trivial, and the Leading Petty Officers should have been called. Chief Hebard had turned the details over to Rackley and me so he stayed in the Chief's Quarters. I was the senior

First Class, and now in charge of the watch bills, and work assignments. I looked back on the easy going days when all I had to do was take care of the I.C. Room, and was more free and easy. The gang lacked experience, and a couple of more Second Class would have been welcome. I was finding more wrinkles and less hair than I thought normal for a 22 year old. The lady that I met in a First Street establishment may have had a part in this condition.

4 APRIL 1945. WEDNESDAY. The ammunition barges came alongside again, and this time we loaded for WestPac. We had lost the main deck torpedo tubes, port and starboard, and only took on four fish.

6 APRIL 1945. FRIDAY. I had problems, but they mounted when Amsler got sick and had to go to the Hospital.

11 APRIL 1945. WEDNESDAY. An inspection party from Training Command came aboard in the morning, and decided that we were fit to return to duty, for in the afternoon we got underway for San Diego. There was a problem in the Engine Room so we did not get very far when we had to return to the Navy Yard for more engine repairs. By 1845 we were back at Pier 5 in the yard.

I finally got around to calling the young lady who I had met in the restaurant with her uncle, and we went to a movie. We were getting the bad news from Okinawa, and I was pessimistic about the rest of the war, for the Kamikaze pilots were knocking tin cans off like they were in a shooting gallery. Too bad that we would never see each other again, for she was lovely.

12 APRIL 1945. THURSDAY. President Roosevelt's death put a hush on everything, and in addition there was a delay in out departure because of problems that developed during the Sea Trials.

13 APRIL 1945. FRIDAY. I got a break when Amsler returned from the hospital. In preparation for our super inspection that was to come we had a personnel and material inspection Tuesday that really stirred up a hornet's nest. More guys were restricted last night because uniform, or haircut deficiencies. Fortunately I was down on the Main Board out of the cold and the storm of a busy Commander Noel.

Now, the paper work was being sprung on me. There were Logs to start, watch bills and work lists, and jobs to inspect as the Job Orders were presented by the shops for signature of completion.-and on into the night. There were seven working Electrician's Mates now, Lichlyter, Rackley, Borrell, Kozlowski, Kuehn, Adamson and Amsler. There were some strikers: Ferris, Hargarther, and Hoffman, but we were still short handed from our normal crew. Chief Hebard was on call, and had a General Quarters station; otherwise the gang was mine, and I got called by the Captain, and the Engineering Officer if there were any problems..

It was what I imagined a peacetime ship would be like. The Duty Section worked far into the night on the small stuff, and during the day the crew and the yard force worked to correct the problems that had appeared in the main electrical plant, during the sea trials.

The *Lamson's* colors still flew at half mast, because of the death of the President, and the general reaction aboard was one of regret, and every one wondered about the capability of President Truman, for his reputation as Vice President had been poor.

15 APRIL 1945. SUNDAY. At last the yard period was over, and *Lamson* was underway once more for San Diego, California, and the duty with the Under way Training Group.

Their was a brief stop at Indian Island to receive depth charges, and then we were underway again By 2000 the ship was outbound at the mouth of Puget Sound.

Behind were lots of good memories, such as the parties at Port Orchard where the married Johns lived. We would miss the cozy bar and dance floor of the Eagles Club, and a fine Chinese restaurant where we all ordered differently and shared the feast; but not the Marine guards patting us for bottles, or Lt. Lovejoy, the XO, standing on the Quarterdeck with my Leave Papers when Satterwhite assured me he knew the ferry schedule, and we were an hour Over Leave.

There were also the Seattle - Bremerton ferry rides, and a little sleep in their engine rooms, after an evening with the friendly girls of Seattle. Then, there had been the United Airline Flights to LA & SF. What a liberty port this had been, for I'd gone through over $700 bucks on transportation, fun and frolic.

19 APRIL 1945. THURSDAY. At 0800 we were south of San Clemente Island. The cruise down the coast from Bremerton had been uneventful, and gave the crew a chance to get acquainted with the new equipment installations, and test all of the new gear under actual steaming conditions. Cdr. Noel exercised the crew at General Quarters frequently, and it was a short trip.

Upon our arrival at San Diego the Skipper was directed to anchor out in the channel, for all we were going to do was fuel ship and get underway the next day. With the Kamikaze battles in the Pacific, especially at Okinawa, knocking destroyers out as fast as they could be built; *Lamson* was ordered back to sea with no formal training in San Diego. Despite restrictions on travel outside the San Diego area; Neal, myself and a couple of others went to Wilmington for a brief visit, and my Dad drove us back to San Diego, pushing the '36 Pontiac hard, the morning of the 20th, and we were underway for Pearl Harbor again. Commander Noel heard of our jaunt, and was curious to know how it was done, and was not in the least put out.

20 APRIL 1945. FRIDAY. After lunch WESTPAC called, and we were headed for Pearl Harbor again with only 3 men absent, and who missed the ship's sailing. *Lamson* was OTC of CTU 6.11.47, and had *U.S.S. Conner* (DD-582) for company.

23 APRIL 1945. MONDAY. With all the green hands on board there was a pressing need to drill at every chance. The two 1200 KW generators still made as much noise as ever, and the workload and watches added to the misery after the easy going in port period.

I was in my bunk one morning when there was a boiler failure, and the generator tripped off the line. I ended up on the Main Board in my skivvies, getting the plant back on the line. From my bunk I could tell when things did not sound right. The casualties helped train the crew under realistic conditions though. The Division was still short handed, but Adamson and Amsler would be making Third before too much longer, and I could take on some more strikers. The Chief came topside once in awhile, and that helped stimulate the group to greater effort.

26 APRIL 1945. THURSDAY . Back into Pearl Harbor again, and there did not seem to be many changes. We were back at a buoy so everyone stayed aboard until the Liberty Launch came alongside. The Watch Bill was 4 on and 12 off, with a normal work day. I got the word that we would take on a striker, and this time I was looking for somebody out of the Black Gang, but I can't place the man.

One of the Second Class POs got plastered, and started acting up in the boat on the way back to the ship. A couple of guys heaved him over the side of the whale boat and held on to his feet, filling him with murky saltwater; before they hauled him in again. When he got back on board he was still out of his mind, and began to run around the Quarter Deck in his skivvies instead of turning in and leaving everybody alone. The watch was not boring with such activities to spice up a normally dull routine.

27 - 28 APRIL 1945. were spent off Kahoolawe for shore bombardment drills, then back to Middle Loch.

29 APRIL 1945. SUNDAY. I rated liberty so I went to the Base in dungarees, and ate ice cream until I was about to bust and then came back and just took in the slack. Those of us who were on board in the fall of 1944 knew what was ahead of us, and hoped the crew would be able to develop into a team before we returned to the war zone.

The war in Europe was winding down. The Russian Army was in Berlin, and Hitler had committed suicide outside his bunker. Now the emphasis would turn to the Pacific, and the attack on the Japanese homeland. The old hands had some bad memories of Japanese dedication to the Emperor, and did not relish another suicide mission, for we were outfitted as a radar picket, and had read what the Kikusui (Floating Chrysanthemums) were doing to the outlying picket cans off Okinawa. The new men were too green and gung ho to care, and in their innocence were eager to get out there.

30 APRIL 1945. MONDAY. It was early in the morning when we fell in with *U.S.S. Bell* (DD-587) and *U.S.S. Wadleigh* (DD-689) for some intensive anti-aircraft exercises that lasted all day, and into the night.

We got the word that the Kamikaze pilots were being trained in night attack, either under flares, or by moonlight. There was no escape for the tin cans on picket duty, unless the weather turned bad.

SURRENDER, OCCUPATION AND DEMOBILIZATION
1 SEPTEMBER - 31 DECEMBER 1945

1 SEPTEMBER 1945. SATURDAY. Borrell made EM1/C, and my Striker, Roger Trial, was advanced to Fireman First. The Report of Changes submitted to the Bureau of Naval Personnel showed that *Lamson* had 223 enlisted men on board, and there were 23 Officers in the Ward Room, making their berthing a little cramped, for there had been eleven officers on board when the war began.

00 - 08. Time Zone KING (-10). Attached under temporary orders to TF 94, Vice Admiral J.H. Hoover, USN, Commander U.S. Navy Marianas. Assigned to ComTask Unit 94.7.3 with Captain H.P. Smith COMDESRON 4 in *U.S.S. Dunlap* (DD-384). Steaming singly enroute from Iwo Jima to Bonin Islands patrol station IAW CTF 94.7.3 310503, August 1945.

2 SEPTEMBER 1945. SUNDAY. The formal Japanese surrender took place on *U.S.S. Missouri (*BB 63) in Tokyo Bay. We felt that we should have been there too because of the time we had put into the battle. Instead, we were on our Patrol station. 0912 Expended 160 rounds 20mm H.E.I. and 80 rounds 20mm H.E.T. sinking a partly submerged airplane. At 1130 we heard the official word, and the ceremony from Japan on the radio, but our little patrol of a few highly fortified islands was vital, and all of us were wondering when it would all end, and what would happen next.

The Bonin Islands were rugged bits of land, and one wondered just how the living had been under our blockade. Whenever we'd come in close all the glasses available were in use for a closer look at the beach. It looked very quiet except for a few wisps of smoke here and there. A pair of tall radio towers made an excellent landmark. Even the sea was quiet, and its smoothness reflected the heat of the sun into a clear sky.

It was Sunday, and holiday routine, so the ship was quiet too except for the normal underway noises and now the slap, slap of a punching bag in a spot of shade, and cool breeze. Even our speed was enough to slow a person down, for we were just cruising slowly along, around and around on our assigned patrol station.

I felt so lazy I could hardly keep my eyes open. I had all night in, and since it was Sunday I laid in until about 0900 yet every Sunday afternoon seems the same. Maybe it was the warmth combined with the noon meal, but whatever it was the trick was complete. Ho-hum!

Nine 44 Point men left the ship the other day; headed home. Now the Navy was trying to recruit from the Reserves to the Regular Navy in a few critical Rates. Not much success on here though. One or two guys are signing up, for the Navy is starting to give more "Shipping Over Leave," and more guys would leave for that. They Shipped Over before the war began, and didn't get their leaves at that time due to the Emergency and then the War.

Some of the officers volunteered to teach classes if enough guys put in for something. About all I had in mind was Calculus, and if I can get a start on that I may be ahead in the long run. I hope so anyway. On here studying by yourself was a problem, but I'd been brushing up on my Algebra again and it hadn't been so bad for I'd been able to use the CPO Quarters, or the Ship's Office for studying.

3 SEPTEMBER 1945. MONDAY. 00 - 04. Steaming singly, patrolling the Bonin Islands.

0525 CIC reported contacts bearing 252 deg. 26,000 yards. Identified as *U.S.S. Dunlap* (DD384) and *U.S.S. Case* (DD-370). Changed course to 000° (t), C/S 12 1/2 kts. and steamed to a point two miles east of Tatsumi Wan, ChiChi Jima.

08 - 12 Steaming as before. 0835 C/C to 295°. C/S 20 knots. 0840 C/C 305°. Speed 14 1/2 knots. All hands to general quarters. Commenced patrolling northeast of Tatsumi Wan, ChiChi Jima while articles of surrender were signed. Commodore MacGruder met with Lt. Gen. Tachibana, who came out from the island with some of his staff, boarding *Dunlap* where the surrender was accepted at 0905. The patrol was resumed at 1133, and the afternoon routine was broken by gunnery and casualty power drills.

1155 Maneuvering to investigate object in the water.

1212 Picked up belly tank and resumed patrol. 1515 General Quarters for drill. 1528 Gunnery and casualty power drills, including hand steering. 1552 Secured from all drills. 1556 Secured from General Quarters.

4 SEPTEMBER 1945. TUESDAY. 00 - 24. Steaming as before. Official censorship was lifted, and the crew was able to write home with quite an air of relief, for after writing just what we wished, we could seal and post our little missives in absolute assurance of privacy, and the *Lamson* cancellation stamp was used again. Even though Neal had censored my letters, I'd censored them myself to keep his trust even though I had the privacy.

We had little to do except our circular patrol. Twelve hours from one point to another at about 12 knots; it was not arduous. That had been the extent of our duties for the past four months. At least then we could watch the B-29 flights. There those that were crippled that would wheel into Iwo after a raid, and one afternoon one was shot down by our own fighters after the crew had bailed out over the Island. The bomber was too badly damaged to come in safely so it was disposed of safely.

Lt. (j.g.) Saul, the Gunnery Officer began the first Calculus Class. How far we would be able to go I didn't know, but it looked interesting. If we stayed out for another three months I might learn something yet, for I was taking more time to hit the books, and review my math. Scuttlebutt ran that we'd be out of commission within 6 months, but only the Navy Dept. can say for sure. The engine house sounded like a rock factory after the past hard running years.

5 SEPTEMBER 1945. WEDNESDAY. 00 - 08. Steaming as before. 0600 Set course to return to Iwo Jima.

08 - 24. 1324 Moored alongside *U.S.S. Flambeau* (IX-192) in NW anchorage of Iwo Jima for fueling. 1515: Fueling completed. Underway to assigned anchorage. 1513: Anchored in NW anchorage, Iwo Jima.

Detached this date from Temporary Duty with CTF 94, and reported by dispatch to Fifth Fleet, Admiral R.A. Spruance, USN COMFIFTH Fleet in *U.S.S. New Jersey* (BB-62) for duty.

6 SEPTEMBER 1945. THURSDAY. 00 - 16. Anchored as before. Underway for Okinawa, Ryukyu Islands, IAW COMFIFTH Flt msg. 050115 Sept. Steaming in company with *U.S.S. Helm* (DD388). CO *U.S.S. Lamson* is OTC.

Lamson was steaming to Okinawa to rejoin DESRON 5 and Fifth Fleet which was staging for the occupation of Japan. It was really strange having the lights on all the time in the mess halls when we were underway. Studying down there was impossible.

Several men left for discharge, or leave including CMM McPhee, CWT Rusek, CWT Peters, and MM1C Wiers. I inherited a radio out of the deal. It was the one in the shop, but the owner was one of the Chiefs leaving so he gave it to me.

7 SEPTEMBER 1945. FRIDAY. 00 - 04. Steaming as before.

1015: Gunnery exercises completed. Expended 40 mm and 5"/38.

8 SEPTEMBER 1945. SATURDAY. 00 - 04. Steaming as before.

08 - 24. Arrived Buckner Bay, Okinawa. Went alonside *U.S.S. Cimmaron* (AO-22) for fueling. Completed fueling; proceeding to anchorage. 1437: Anchored in berth ComCruDiv 13 in *U.S.S. Santa Fe* (CL-60) is S.O.P.A.

After arriving at Okinawa *Lamson* was directed to anchor in berth Love 116, Buckner Bay in 11 fathoms of water. (Nakagasuka Wan is the Japanese name of the bay, but General Buckner was killed just before Okinawa fell, and so honored). SOPA was COMSERVDIV 104 in *U.S.S. Hamul* (AD-

20).

NOTE: I would serve in Hamul with COMDESRON THREE 13 years later.

When they lowered the points for discharge, more men would get off. We could afford to get rid of another fifty with no strain unless there were too many Engineering Department losses. As far as Seamen and Gunners Mates go they were now in excess, but it took the same number of men in the Black Gang to fill out a standard 3 section Watch Bill. I sure hated the thought of going back on 4 on and 4 off again. New Guinea, and those watches in the I.C. Room had given me my fill of that. A reduction in crew would make living a lot more comfortable, for when we left Puget Sound there were about 170 on board, until we got to Pearl Harbor, and more men came aboard. Now the Ship seemed deserted.

9 SEPTEMBER 1945. SUNDAY. Anchored as before. As the day was a Sunday it started off as usual with Quarters for Muster. Except for one repair job there was nothing to do. About 1000 the Engineer wanted a man to go to the U.S.S. Hamul (AD20) on an errand so I volunteered to take care of the job, and that is how the adventure started.

The trip to the tender was uneventful and the business was dispatched quickly. I ran into another sailor trying to get ashore too, and he and I started bumming our way to the beach where he had a brother-in-law in the Army Air Corps.

As we stood on the float we saw a guy with mud on his boots so we asked him for a lift, and after finding out that he'd be on business on the way in, we took a chance and got aboard. His business was towing a barge to another repair ship. Well, we towed slowly to the Repair Ship where we waited in the boiling sun for half an hour after helping get the boat hoisted out of the water. Both of us were a little disgusted, and had about given up hope of ever getting to the beach, which was about a mile away, when a whaleboat came by headed for the landing. We hailed him, and lo and behold he came alongside and took us off on another leg of our journey into the unknown to find the brother-in-law.

The Island of Okinawa is made up of low hills and smooth valleys, and it was covered with a heavy grass which gave it a deceivingly cool and inviting appearance. It reminded me of the hills up around the Napa area above San Francisco. It seemed warmer here than around Iwo because of the latitude, and the harbor enclosure.

Well, we were on the beach at last! We headed for the highway, and as our fast pace was set I could feel the lack of anything in my stomach. In fact I was starving. We hit the highway at Yonabaru and started in the prescribed manner--thumb up and out. This soon netted us a ride in a truck and in a direction which we didn't know, but we were moving sitting down and that was the main thing. After riding for about 3 miles we spotted a tree of

124

direction signs-Naha, Shuri, Yonabaru, etcetera, etcetera, and an Army Information Post.

Since we needed info, and badly, we disembarked and found out that the Information Post wasn't very well informed so we went back to the highway and proceeded as before, picking up another truck which took us out Route 44 past an old rail bed, truck wreckage, a Sherman tank (upside down), thatched and tile roofed houses in varied stages of wreckage, through low grass-filled valleys, up and around smooth, grassy rolling hills past the Naha River, and finally into the wrecked City of Naha itself. All of this took about 10 or 15 minutes from one side of the island to the other.

We got off at the Railroad Depot which consisted of a concrete shell, and another Information Post that didn't do us any good either. From there we were directed to the Red Cross where we found a phone-- and dinner-two Hershey bars. The telephone was of the field variety and after cranking on it vigorously and yelling "Moscow" into the transmitter and telling them what you wanted they (Moscow) would connect your number and from there on you were strictly on your own.

The extensions were sad and after a half hour of yelling "Hello!" and a fast little talk, repeated by the same, you hung up muttering things to yourself that wouldn't be considered nice in mixed company. The two of us did all that, drank some hot, muddy water, ate our bars and took off again. This time for home, for our hopes of finding the brother-in-law were nil.

We hoofed it back to Naha, looked the place over and concluded that it would be a long time before they used the place again, for shells had pretty well done it in. On the way in we had the opportunity to whistle at a few of the native stock. A guy will do most anything out here. We even got a wave out of them as we went by in the truck. They were safe from marauding sailors, for we were moving away rapidly. Just after that a Navy nurse went by in a jeep, and she was quite an eye full.

When we were starting back we passed the rail yard again, and I had never seen such a set up outside of the Carnival, or Pike, where there were some midget trains. These were demolished and all the tracks, which were quite small, were ripped up. There were several passenger cars and one box car in the wreckage. Camera fans were very busy around the Depot and all over the Island in fact.

Next, we were able to bum a ride in a Jeep back to Yonabaru, and the dock where we begged a ride back out to the anchorage. While on our way out we happened to run into a cloudburst and did we get soaked. We took saltwater over, and the rain washed it down. We were sunburned also, but it had been good to get ashore. It also felt good to get back aboard and eat a good meal--cold cuts, cheese, bread, a coke and ice cream. Then, there was a hot shower, clean clothes and a letter home. The movie started shortly thereafter, and made the day.

13 SEPTEMBER 1945. THURSDAY. *Lamson* was anchored near two hospital ships and it was considered great sport to watch the nurses on deck-Long Glass Liberty it was called. There was a challenge to keep busy. In fact we were just doing enough to keep the edges clean. A liberty party got over for a few beers every day, but even though today was my day to go ashore; I stayed aboard and did a little patchwork on a shirt that has been on its last legs for some time. I rationalized that I'd need every penny I could save so was getting mighty tight. A month ago the shirt would have been thrown away.

CQM McRae left Wednesday. We were losing a few more men each week now so it would not be too much longer before the crew would be down to a comfortable size. Right now though, everybody that had over 40 Points was giving it hell to go home.

Most of the sailors had not been aboard two years so there would be quite a few left even though the Reserves such as Matsushige who was in my Boot Company would be gone. Regular Navy Petty Officers got off on Shipping Over leaves so there were openings for advancement in rate.

One of the boilers had sprung big leaks and everyone was concerned that we would miss the occupation movement. We were slated for a couple of operations up around Nagasaki, Japan. The engine house bunch had been 'turning to' plenty on the Auxiliary Plant so we could get underway if necessary, and now the boilermakers were catching hell too. This old baby was on her last lap as far as most of us were concerned, and we were almost 7,000 miles from home.

15 SEPTEMBER 1945. SATURDAY. 00 - 04. Anchored in berth Love 116, Buckner Bay, Okinawa in 11 fathoms of water with 45 fathoms of chain on deck. Boiler #4 in use for auxiliary purposes. Ships present: various units of the U.S. Pacific Fleet with ComServDiv 104 in *U.S.S. Hamul* (AD-20) S.O.P.A.

16 SEPTEMBER 1945. SUNDAY. The weather had been cooler, and the sky was overcast with a very brisk wind whipping up the white caps on the open bay. It felt like a typhoon was coming in. The ship was still anchored in berth Love 116 when we got a voice message to get out of the harbor. This holiday routine would be badly interrupted. People scheduled to leave the ship today would thank their lucky stars when they got off after our return to port.

00 - 08. Anchored as before. 0100 Barometer falling 0.03 inches per hour. Wind is Force 4, coming from the Southeast. 0500 Wind increased to Force 6. 0615 Lighted fires under boiler #3. 0725 IAW voice msg, weighed anchor to get underway in preparation for riding out approaching typhoon. Barometer steady at 29.69"

0731: Due to difficulty of bringing bow into the wind from, and being set down on the beach, we let go the anchor with five knots way, in eight fathoms of water.

NOTE:Drifted broadside through anchored merchant fleet due to lack of maneuvering room.

Veered to 60 fathoms of chain on deck. 0749: Commenced hauling in the anchor, keeping the bow into the wind with full rudder, and main engines.0756: Underway on course 0850. Speed 10 knots, clearing Yonabaru Bay. (Nakagasuku Wan, or Buckner Bay.)

08 - 12. Steaming as before. 0805: Maneuvering with difficulty on various courses and various speeds to keep headed into the swell, and avoiding anchored vessels.

The deck log shows that we dropped the hook once, but I recall being carried through the anchorage twice before getting the ship under control. Finally, 60 fathoms of chain was veered, and using main engines, the Captain managed to get the bow into the wind while hauling in the anchor.

0800. There were some tense moments, but control was gained without a collision, and a speed of 10 knots attained as we made our dash for the harbor opening. 0807: In channel, and clear of the anchorage berths. Set course 085^0, speed 10 kts.

0850. Commenced maneuvering at various courses and speeds to keep safe position in mass sortie from the harbor. 0901: Passed through anti-submarine net entrance gate. Heavy seas from the Southeast. Ship rolling to 47° while beating to Southeast.

The sight of the whole Fifth Fleet fighting its way out of the harbor through that narrow net opening, and against the heavy swells was a new and chilling experience. The visible reefs were tearing the giant waves to shreds as we went out alongside a jeep carrier, and on the roll I could see the bilge keel, and then the tie downs on the flight deck. A DE astern of us was tossing her sonar dome out of the water, and there was breathtaking confusion as the skippers fought to maintain control over their ships.

The skipper of *U.S.S. Coghlan* (DD 606) took command of the destroyers, and directed that *Lamson* take station 309^0 on CTF55.1 in *U.S.S. Santa Fe* CL60). It was almost 1030 before we could battle our way into position while the hastily formed 3 cruiser TASK FORCE 55, of *U.S.S. Santa Fe, Miami,* and *Biloxi,* fell into a column and began to maneuver on a base course to the west at 10 knots in an attempt to get away from the center of the typhoon.

1025. On station. Set Fleet Course 240^0, and fleet speed 10 knots. Wind and sea running from 090^0. 1033 C/S to 5.5 kts to form screen 3000 yards on starboard side of three cruisers in column. *U.S.S. Santa Fe* is the guide with CTF 55 embarked. Destroyers in column, distance 1,000 yds. From Van to rear; *U.S.S. Coghlan* (DD-606), *U.S.S. Helm* (DD-388), *U.S.S. Bagley* (DD-386), and *U.S.S. Lamson* (DD-367).

1100. Barometer still falling at 0.03" per hour.1120: Changed fleet course to 230 degrees(t). 1127: Took station #3 in column. 1140: Took station #4 in column.

12 - 16. Steaming as before. 1200 Changed Speed to 10 knots. 1230: Barometer falling rapidly, increasing to 0.08" per hour. Wind now estimated to be Force 9 out of 050^0. Very heavy seas running from the east. 1255 C/C to 180^0 by turn movement.

1328. Changed course to 230^0 by turn movement. 1332: C/S to 13 knots. 1401: Changed speed to 15 kts. 1500: Winds now estimated to be between 50 and 60 knots with gusts to 70 knots. Rain squalls coming out of 030^0(t). Very heavy seas running from 060^0 (T).

1532. Ordered out of formation to search for man overboard from *U.S.S. Miami.*

Changed course to 158^0. Attempted to increase speed to 27 knots while running into storm.

1533. Lost all steam, and power due to the entering of water into the boilers through the uptakes in # 2 Fire room. A minute after going to flank *Lamson* rolled into a breaker, and took water down the stacks, or through the blower uptakes, putting the fires out under #3, and #4 boilers. A roll of 57 degrees was noted. Now, the ship was in irons, and dead in that raging water with swells that looked to be masthead height all around us. Would we sacrifice hundreds to save one man?

NOTE: War Diary Summary. 1535 an unusually heavy sea breaking across the main deck forced the breeches of number two stack, and entered the fire boxes, extinguishing the fires in boilers # 3, and #4, causing the loss of all power. Boiler #1 already being inoperative, boiler #2 was lighted off as soon as possible. (Emergency Generator started when Main Board lost power. Emergency Power restored to ship.)

The log shows that we discontinued the search for the man at 1642, and that it was 1705 before steam and power were regained. Course changes, and gradual increases in speed to 18 knots brought us back into formation at 1817, and back on station at 1853. Over three hours had elapsed since we answered that distress signal.

When the flank bell was answered I was in the Electric Shop trying to stay comfortable, and be near the phone. I could hear the Forced Draft Blowers pick up speed, and felt the ship shudder as we pulled out of formation, and when everything went dead I dropped down the Engine Room hatch in the Main Deck. The new Emergency Diesel came on automatically, and I hit the Main Board, and the Watch Stander and I got the Emergency Board energized, and had power and lights in the Engine Room and Number Two Fire room as well as the other spaces requiring Emergency Power. (I thought that

CMM Sessions was involved, but he said some clown opened the fo'c'sle hatch into the CPO quarters, and washed him out of his bunk.)

After getting everything on line I stuck my head out of the Engine Room Hatch and observed that the whole life jacket clad crew appeared to be stuck to the topside, and hanging on for dear life as we wallowed at the bottom of that deep trough. The waves looked like they completely covered us in a tunnel of water. There was little water on the deck, but the wind driven froth at the tops of the surrounding waves was going crazy.

It seemed that we were down but a short time, and when I read the log, and found that we were out from 1533 to 1602, I could not believe it. The new skipper had himself a real casualty drill this time. I guess this blow was tame compared to typhoons Cobra and Viper that gave Task Force 38 such a bad mauling. I don't see how we made out at all shaking like we did. It was sure a relief when the Throttlemen poured the steam to the turbines, and the Main Generators began to scream again.

16 - 18. Steaming as before. 1602: Steerage way regained. 1642: Secured from search for man overboard. 1705: Regained full boiler power on boilers #3, and #4. Normal power restored.

1713. Changed speed to 13 knots, commenced to rejoin the formation. 1721: C/S to 16 knots, and C/C to 225^0. 1727: Increased speed to 18 knots.

18 - 20. Steaming as before. 1800: Barometer ceases to drop at 29.10 inches of Mercury. Wind still Force 12 (over 70 mph.) and shifted to 330^0(T). Sea now running in from the North. 1817: Rejoined formation, and changed course to 220^0. (T). 1853: On Station. Reduced speed to 13 knots. 1907: Flag signaled change in base course to 180^0. 1915: Changed base course to 160^0. Barometer rising slowly. As the wind continued to veer to the westward, and then to the southward, formation courses were altered to the eastward, and then to the northward.

Nobody on board *Lamson* was lost, but several were hurt by the seas coming aboard after the casualty. All those not on watch weathered the storm in their bunks, for topside was too dangerous. Lifelines were strung inboard to enable the Watch Standers to get about, and the cooks served sandwiches to those who braved the Main Deck. The Shop was amidships, and I could come and go to my bunk through the Engine Room, but dodged the waves when making the Mess Hall, and I.C. Room.

17 SEPTEMBER 1945. MONDAY. 00 - 04. Steaming as before, riding out typhoon with Task Force 55 in two columns.

Port-- U.S.S. *Santa Fe* (CL-60), U.S.S. *Biloxi* (CL-80), U.S.S. *Miami* (CL-89).

Starboard--U.S.S. *Coghlan* (DD-606), U.S.S. *Helm* (DD-388), U.S.S. *Bagley* (DD-386), U.S.S. *Baldwin* (DD-624), U.S.S. *Lamson* (DD-367). Course 060^0(T). Speed 13 knots. Boilers #3 & #4 in use, and boosting steam on boiler #2. Conditions 2 MIKE and BRAVO set with running lights bright.

04 - 08. Steaming on various courses and speeds with TF55 to avoid typhoon.

08 – 12: Steaming as before. 0800 Position 25⁰. 18'N. 128⁰. 26' E. Formation returning to port. 1207: SG Radar contact on Okinawa 308 ⁰· 28 miles. 1235 C/C ⁰00. 1320 C/C 320⁰. 1327: *U.S.S. Biloxi* and *U.S.S. Coghlan* left formation for other duty. 1337: Set the Special Sea Detail, Captain at the Conn, Navigator on the Bridge. 1340: Steaming on various courses and speeds entering Buckner Bay. 1535: Began approach on *U.S.S. IX 188* in Berth 118, for fuel. 1549: Moored port side to *IX-188*, and commenced fueling.

16 - 20. Moored as before. 1746: Completed fueling ship, having received 45,898 gallons of fuel oil. Draft forward 12.6 ft., aft 13.6 ft. 1749: Underway. 1812: Anchored in berth Love 148, Buckner Bay, Okinawa in 9 1/2 fathoms of water with 45 fathoms of chain on deck.1820: let fires die out under # 3 boiler. Lighted fires under #2 boiler. 2030: Let fires die out under No. 4 boiler, using #2 for auxiliary purposes.

18 SEPTEMBER 1945. TUESDAY. 00 - 04. Anchored as before.

1300: Clevenger, H.C. S1C reported on board for transportation to *U.S.S. Flusser*, having been left when *Flusser* got underway.

1735. Transferred draft of 20 men to Receiving Station, Okinawa FFT to nearest West Coast Receiving Station for discharge. The 20 people scheduled to leave on the 16th; including 'Chugie,' and Herrera from Co. 184, Al Shipman, Gartland, Hogan, Humphrey & Jarrell finally were able to leave the ship for Receiving Station Okinawa, and I'll bet with a big sigh of relief after the last 48 hours. CQM McRae, BM1C Verbracken, and S1C Quattlebaum had left on the 12th; the older shipmates were disappearing fast. 2050 Lit off #4 boiler, secured #2.

19 SEPTEMBER 1945. WEDNESDAY. 00 - 04. Anchored as before.

0630: Underway to exit Buckner Bay enroute to Sasebo, Japan. 0746: Maneuvering on various courses and speeds to take station 2288, fleet axis 000deg. Fleet course 40⁰. Speed 16 knots. OTC in *U.S.S. Santa Fe* (CL-60). Ships in company, *U.S.S. Bagley*, *U.S.S. Helm*, *U.S.S. Baldwin*, *U.S.S. Strauss*. (DE-408). 1008: Fleet course and axis changed to 340 ⁰. 1022: Sighted *U.S.S. Mugford* (DD-389) and *U.S.S. Cape Gloucester* (CVE-109) 350 ⁰. relative. 1112: Passed left tangent Yoron Shima to starboard, 14,600 yards. 1133 Fleet course and axis changed to 345 ⁰. Speed 15 kts. 1445 Changed fleet axis and base course to 000⁰. 1445: Passed Tori Shima abeam to starboard, 9 1/2 miles.

CTF 55.1 in *Santa Fe* had regrouped, including *Lamson, Baldwin, Bagley, Helm*, and *Strauss*; and were underway for Sasebo, Kyushu, Japan. We were all looking forward to cooler temperatures, and sheltered harbors. The fruits of three and a half years of war were soon to be in our grasp; especially the "enemy women" of whom we had heard much of as relating to their desire, and ability, to please the male of the species.

The first occupation port was to be Sasebo on the southern island of Kyushu. Marines were landed, and the Fifth Fleet covered the unopposed landings while TF 38 stood well out to sea. There had been some concern over the acceptance of the surrender by the Japanese people because of the fanaticism of their soldiers, but Emperor Hirohito had told his people that they had lost the war, and must accept the occupiers without trouble, and that was the end of the fight; except for a few outposts in the jungles.

20 SEPTEMBER 1945. THURSDAY. Steaming in formation with CTF55 in *U.S.S. Santa Fe*. 0135: Radar contact with Kusakaki Shima, 062^0. 27 miles. 0220: Radar contact with Uji Gunto bearing 045^0 27 miles. 0230: Passed Kusakaki Shima 090^0, 20 miles.

0735: Changed course to 000^0. (T). 0847 Signal from the Flag to form column in order: *U.S.S. Strauss.*, *U.S.S. Santa Fe*, *U.S.S. Baldwin*, *U.S.S. Lamson*, *U.S.S. Bagley*, *U.S.S. Helm*.

0851: Changed speed to 20 knots, course 000^0. 0852: Reduced speed to 16 knots.

0900: Commenced exercising crew at General Quarters. 0935: Secured from GQ.

1052: Set the Special Sea Detail for entering Sasebo Harbor. 1159: Moored starboard side to *U.S.S. Baldwin* at buoy #18 Sasebo Harbor, Kyushu, Japan.

Ensign Gutelle had been promoted to LT(j.g.) and he had the deck as we anchored so the Engineers felt they were in good hands. From our anchorage we could see some of the devastation on the beach. There were small craft of every description on the beach, and from what we heard, the island structures had taken a beating too. I inspected the topside, and found that both power and sound powered systems had been saturated. We would stay busy washing the salt out of the system.

22 SEPTEMBER 1945. SATURDAY. 00 - 16. Moored as before.

1500: Underway, proceeding to Terashima Suido for fuel in company with *U.S.S. Baldwin*.

16 - 24. 1720: Moored to *U.S.S. Cossatot* (AO-77) for fueling. 1815: Underway proceeding to anchorage. 1821: Anchored in Terashima Suido anchorage area.

23 SEPTEMBER 1945. SUNDAY. 0800: Underway proceeding to Sasebo inner harbor anchorage. 0944: Moored with *U.S.S. Flusser* (DD-368) at buoy #25, Sasebo, Kyushu, Japan. It was about 1100 when we wound our way through the channel that opened into a beautifully land locked harbor.

Three DD types were moored at buoys, and we went alongside *U.S.S. Baldwin* at Buoy #18. On all sides rose green lush hills terraced in a manner to give the greatest amount of arable land.

The terraces, with their short expanse of green crops, and brown stone holding walls made the hills into many symmetrical patterns that were only broken by sections that were too steep to cultivate.

The dwellings were rather small and all seemed to be gray with gray tile roof, or rice thatch. Those were mostly rural. An occasional Shinto shrine rose sharply against the sky to tell us just where we were in the world of many cultures.

The City of Sasebo was too far away to see clearly, but it appeared to be of fair size and mostly one or two story buildings with the same gray cast. Residential areas rose back up the hills which started right from the water front, and changed to towering mountains within a short distance. Nothing like the L.A. area at all. The lack of life, or movement, was enough to make one believe the place deserted, but through the long glass once in a while people could be seen around the farms.

The Naval Base seemed to be in fair shape although there were three large damaged carriers, painted green, and many smaller craft at remote anchorages. Several very large cranes were in evidence in the dockyard area, and they appeared whole. Damage must have been localized in this area.

The fact that the port was not to be officially occupied until the 21st restricted us to the ship, but we were all eager to see the place squared away for Liberty. The Second Marine Division was given the honor of this occupation of Kyushu because of its heavy participation in the campaign. Before too much longer we would set foot on Japan after almost 4 years of struggle. There were many times when I had good reason to doubt the final outcome, but this was quite a realization after so much misery.

It sure was good to get back to a cool climate again. Sasebo and Los Angeles are at about the same latitude. It was a bit warmer, for the sea injection temperature was 78°, but after the Horse Latitudes it was cool indeed. We broke out the blankets from under our mattresses and sleep was so much better. In fact, I hated to hear the call to roll out now worse than ever before, and usually made breakfast just before they secured at 0800.

Captain Ayer ordered a 'Big Field Day' today and the shop was given a new coat of paint. White with a gray deck and black trim with the black Switchboards and shining copper switches. The ship was about to fall apart, but it was becoming cleaner. 20 more men left, and the rest of the bunks were taken out of the Mess Hall, improving living conditions even more. Now all we needed was Liberty.

27 SEPTEMBER 1945. THURSDAY. Moored fore and aft to buoys with 2 DDs. After a week in Sasebo we were still on board and wondering whether or not we would ever get ashore. The Occupation Forces had been on the beach five days now, probably staking out the territory, posting the "Out of Bounds" signs, and making sure the sailors don't get into their hair.

I was still 3rd in a class of three, in our study of Calculus, but the class gave me something to keep my mind occupied and I was learning a little about it. I had been away from advanced algebra, and trigonometry since 1941.

The mail situation was going from bad to worse. We'd laid in port a week and had not gotten a postcard while the ships on either side had received sacks of mail. Last I heard from the States was around August 30. Nothing from the 'True Love' since 15 August. Our mail, as in 1942, probably toured all of the islands and was now on its second trip to ensure that the packages were smashed, and the letters soaked in saltwater. What a mess.

The monotony was broken by the distribution of the "Spoils of War." The Storekeepers brought straw wrapped bundles of Admiralty China on board. The Japanese Naval Stores were confiscated by the Marines, along with a quantity of Japanese rifles. Each man was given a rifle, and a couple of pieces of the china. I took a teapot, and a serving dish, plus the rifle for my Dad. I could not believe how crude the machine work was on the rifle.

I was called out to join an inspection party headed for three Japanese mine sweepers. We found it very interesting to board the enemy's ships and see how the Japanese sailor lived. We were looking for any damage to equipment, firearms beyond the allowance, and anything out of the ordinary. A Machinist Mate and I with an officer were together, and we had quite a time poking around through the engine rooms of the three ships. They were Diesel powered, and the electrical plant was small 6 and 15 KW generators. Wood cooking stoves that you could not get near without a gas mask, and living quarters that were as barren as an unfurnished house. The berths had no springs, or mattresses, just a board with maybe a mat of straw, or a blanket. The space was dark. There was one light bulb, and it was giving off less light than a candle.

There were many damaged, or unfit, ships and submarines around the anchorage and the three carriers, which were painted green, were not yet finished. The larger looked like quite a ship and was well equipped with radar antennae.

29 SEPTEMBER 1945. SATURDAY. The monotony was further broken by a short trip to Nagasaki. After more than a week in Sasebo we escorted the cruiser U.S.S. *Wichita* (CA-45) and a 2 Star Admiral to Nagasaki where we were the only two ships present. On the way into the harbor we just

lazed along at about 10 knots. and played around the cruiser while her photographer, who was on board *Lamson*, took Official Navy public relations photographs of her.

As we passed *Wichita* on the way out we gave the flag his salute and noticed that everyone topside, except the Line Handling Detail was in Undress Whites with neckerchiefs. They must have been setting up for Personnel Inspection, for a little later the crew was lined up fore and aft and it must have made quite a picture. The photographers on *Wichita* were taking pictures of *Lamson*, which had been painted a dark color; perhaps while we were alongside the tender in Saipan- for some reason.

We entered port of this old shipbuilding, and commercial, city early in the afternoon. The harbor was well protected, and we were moored about half way down the channel pointed out toward the afternoon sun. Off the starboard beam was a large shipyard with medium ways and dry docks plus the usual array of sheds and buildings. There were several large cranes still standing by the ways, plus the shipbuilding ways themselves, and two of the larger buildings appeared to be undamaged.

NOTE: TASK FORCE 38 had worked the Inland Sea Area over about 24-28 July 1945. Army Air Force had it targeted too. All around the edge of the harbor were small shops and warehouses. All of these are damaged to some extent. Some ships were in sight, or rather their pilot houses and masts were, around the various wharves.

The green terraced hills, and their share of gray roofed villages, rose quietly from the edge of the water; and up and down the ridges ran lines on steel towers similar to that of any ski area cable run. Away in the distance was the body of the City, and the waterfront areas were in a shambles; as were areas a block or so back from the docks.

The area of the atomic bomb damage was obscured by low hills, but in the early evening one Section was taken through the 'bomb' area by the Marines that were occupying the City. I hoped to get over on another trip, for they had been given a great opportunity to see what had happened.

I talked to the Photographers Mate from the *Wichita*. He had been the Official Photographer for a Medical Inspection Team and he gave us a few highlights on the set up. They had visited several Hospitals which he said were filthy, and poorly managed. The dead were not taken care of immediately and the general confusion was terrible.

The Inspection Team wanted to see what a geisha house was like, and the local Police had one opened up in about 20 minutes. The girls were very young and quite frightened, crying like mad, but after the initial shock they were polite and friendly serving saki and dancing for the men. That was the extent of their visit, for it was still daylight. I wondered if they were like the natives of the Samoan and Fiji Islands. No sex in the daytime.

As we pulled out of Sasebo, there was mail at the Fleet Post Office, but as usual we had to leave before we found out about it. Now it would probably be some time before it catches up with us even though we are only 3 hours away by truck.

30 SEPTEMBER 1945. SUNDAY. The crew was down to less than 200 men, and the allowance was still 235. Ted Hoffman made EM3C.

1 OCTOBER 1945. MONDAY. The rain was coming down in torrents, but we got on the beach nevertheless. The rain lifted as we stepped out of the boat, and onto the dock we were cautioned to keep our eyes open and our mouths shut. The Marines had provided 3 trucks which were to take us on a tour of Nagasaki.

The rain had stopped, and the tour was very interesting and educational; taking us from the utter destruction of the A-bombed area to the awesome beauty of the back country landscape.

The buildings around the wharves were standing, but they had no window glass and they were mauled about a bit, farther in along the rise the buildings had been hit harder by the concussion and some had been destroyed, but when we entered the area of the main blast the only things standing were some firmly embedded machinery that didn't stand too high and a few concrete or brick foundations. The rest was a seared rubble of mortar, tile and bits of iron. The main blast was confined to a valley area, and must have followed the valley for what seemed a mile or two.

The bomb had exploded over what was plainly an industrial area by the nature of the structures and wreckage, but due to the fact that the houses seemed to be built adjacent to the factories; they were destroyed too. People were digging around for salvage and here and there one might see a crude shanty, or dug out where shelter could be found and, in a few, family life seemed as normal as could be expected. All of this made us realize the terrible consequences of the weapon and its ability to wipe the earth of all structures on the surface of the ground. There were no bomb craters, just the burned hillsides, and bulldozers could only pile the rubble into certain areas. Only where a space was needed did I see any effort to clear the debris-the rest remained where it fell.

Along the roads were a thin trickle of people moving back into Nagasaki. Quite a few were males of all sizes and ages, still in Army Uniform, and returning home probably. Some women were in evidence and three or four were in nice order, and pleasing to the eye.

The main rail center seemed untouched and an excellent narrow gauge train was seen in operation. Street cars were unable to operate, and one of the car shops was demolished while one in the opposite end of town was in good shape. There was no power though, for the distribution lines had been destroyed. It was going to take a lot of work to repair the system.

From the bombed area we went back into town and noticed how closely built every thing was and how flimsy, except for the tile roof, the houses were. All that which was intact was like we'd seen in travel photos for many years. As we toured the town we were called, "Liberty Hounds" by the Island Hopping Second Marine Division men that had been awarded the 'Occupation Duty' here, but we were given salutes by the Japanese children. Snappy salutes, too, with an occasional 'hello,' or 'cigarette?' but there were looks of every emotion from sullen to happy by the people; but on the whole they were expressionless. The kids, plenty of them, seemed to be getting a big kick out of the whole situation; while the elders stood in doorways and watched with mixed emotions while we whizzed by. Everybody was walking even one man who had a horse was walking along side the un-laden animal. A few bicycles were in evidence, but not too many which was surprising. Maybe the Japanese Army had them.

As we left town for the countryside we passed a small dam and its lake. From each side rose the steep tree-covered hills and here and there along the edge were a few beautiful homes. All you could see was a fancy dark tile roof and lots of shrubbery, but you could tell the people were well off by the fancy stonework around the yards.

The Japanese cremated the dead, and the graves, right at the houses, were well kept; beautifully decorated with small shrines, statues, or stones. Small pines and evergreens were in abundance and they make everything cool and green. The Marines even took us through a tunnel that had been used for a factory, and this route took us to the valley on the other side of the hill. Below us stretched a vista that extended to the sea. The terrain was a bit flatter than most we'd seen and the view was beautiful with its multicolored terraces and wet gray roofs of the small communities shining up at us.

Rice and potatoes seemed to be the mainstay and the fields were separated here and there by a row of some red flower that stood out against the green like Christmas decorations. It was a rough ride in spots but on the whole the roads, concrete or asphalt, were as good as many of ours. We returned to the ship tired, but satisfied and ready to on Liberty again if and when the opportunity presented itself. "Join the Navy and See the World" still applied.

NOTE: In return for their hospitality, the Marine Officers were invited to dinner aboard Lamson. *I understand they enjoyed the hot showers as much as the Ward Room meal.*

5 OCTOBER 1945. FRIDAY. We had our usual Friday Personnel Inspection, and topped it off with a trip from Nagasaki to Sasebo. After laying in Nagasaki Harbor for a week our cruiser Admiral had finished his business, and now we were nested in the stream at Sasebo again. As we pulled into port we noticed that Liberty Parties were lined up on deck so

there was Liberty to look forward to even if there was no Mail Call. After the usual delay the word was piped that Liberty would commence, and I broke out my undress whites that had laid dormant for well over a year, for the jumpers still had EM2/C crows on the sleeves.

Neal was in the Liberty Party, too, so after getting some Yen we started hiking, for that was the only way to get around. From the stream Sasebo looked like nothing but a few houses strung along the side of the Mountain, but once on the beach, and looking from a different vantage point, we could see that it was built in a small coastal valley, and on the surrounding foothills.

What was left of the city was exceedingly dirty and run down. The fire bombs did a good job, for there were acres of leveled tile, and brick. The general appearance was that of a fire that had eaten all the woodwork out from under the solid roof, letting it fall, and then a steamroller hired to break up the pieces the fire couldn't touch.

As we walked up the hill on a winding concrete pavement we moved into the residential district and there were the usual few people digging in the wreckage and cleaning up in general. Most just ignored us and we both wondered just what they thought about these clean people looking them over as they toiled through our destruction. Some had a trace of hostility in their eyes, but on the whole it was curiosity, or a blank face. The children, as everywhere, were either shy, or boldly laughing and waving with an occasional word of greeting, or asking for something. "Koneeshewa" seemed to be the main greeting and means "Good Day."

As we proceeded upward we found ourselves in a school that was just being dismissed. There were several other Sailors about and we were drawing quite a bit of attention from students and teachers. As we entered the building we noticed quite a difference from ours. The classrooms seemed to be in two stories around a central opening that probably serves as a gym and auditorium. Everything was made of concrete. As we left we noticed a line of girls and a leader. At various sharp commands they would bow to the school, face left and march off, some in good military step and others in a neat oriental shuffle.

Outside the gate they turned once more and bowed then marched on down the street. We followed, but were stopped by several small boys that tried to teach us the language and give away small snapshots for free. I offered them gum and they all took a stick, but one. Someone must have told him to be careful about taking anything from the Yanks.

We finally made the main drag after walking through quite a bombed out area, and noticed that the Armed Forces were out in force. Small shops that had doorways about 5 ft. tall were crowded and inside was a gesticulating mob trying to get rid of their Yen for a small item that was worthless.

The Yen had value, and you could go ashore with 10 Yen and come back with 9 plus a fistful of Sen. The rate of exchange was 15 Yen to the Dollar, and 100 Sen to the Yen so you can see how confusing it became trying to buy something when the sales person was familiar with the currency, and you were not. I didn't notice any short change deals, but I probably couldn't tell anyway. In one place we bought a counting board (abacus) and some bamboo chop-sticks.

The sales girl was pretty clever with them, but they got all tangled up in my clumsy hands so I bought 20 to take care of breakage. There was little to drink, and no food in the eating places. The Red Light area was strictly Out Of Bounds so we couldn't even walk through it to take a short cut to the Fleet Landing. There were big yellow "Out of Bounds" signs everywhere.

Women on the streets were either old, or appeared very young, and in all of the walk we noticed only one who was dressed neatly and cleanly in bright oriental dress, and she was probably a geisha. The community and the people were drab, but I did not expect much after the punishment these people were given. They had been at war since the '30s, and must have really sacrificed for their Emperor, and the war machine. The people were accustomed to a dictatorial regime though, but the contrast between their state now and before the war must have been very marked. I don't know what these people had before the war, but now they had nothing. Women labored in town, clearing and cleaning up. There was no machine work at all. With the heavy manpower losses the female out here seems to be either a beast of burden or a plaything--more of the former probably. Maybe the neighborhoods, and the homes, provide a different view, but there were not too many left.

Liberty had been authorized for only 3 hours, 1400 to 1700, but we had walked a long time, and my legs were really tired. The exercise was really hard on an idler.

8 OCTOBER 1945. MONDAY. I volunteered for Shore Patrol to relieve the monotony. The day was completely different from any other, and that in itself was enough to make it worthwhile. The Patrol group left the ship about 0900 for the Fleet Landing where we were to be on duty. It turned out that there were ten of us, and our headquarters was an old Customs House with a beat down ramp and a pair of floats made up the Fleet Landing.

The first thing that got our attention was the fact that 10 sandwiches provided by the Cooks would not go very far so we started scouting for more food, and water. The Gyrenes were gnawing on their shoes and a few 'C Rations' and had no spare canteens for water. Their supplies had not caught up with them, and they were living off the land.

The local water supply was contaminated so that was out. We resigned ourselves to hunger until the first Liberty Party hit the Landing about 1230. The ship would send more rations after being notified of our plight. Suddenly one man showed up with a case of C Rations, and the day looked brighter than ever even though it had begun to rain, and I had no rain gear. At least the experience of the day was going to be different, and that is what I wanted.

All we had to do was police the area and take care of boat traffic at the floats. The traffic was very light until Liberty Parties started to come in. Even then it wasn't bad, and by that time we had a pair of thermos jugs, one coffee and one water, plus another 10 beef sandwich packs. We tested the coffee on the Marine M.P. at the intersection out front and when he didn't keel over we decided it was safe and took the rest of it ourselves. That is where the 'C Rations' came in handy. We used the supper units for cups, biscuits as spoons, and had quite a feast. The beans were good and the chicken and vegetable proved to be very palatable so all-in-all we did not starve, or get too thirsty. After the Liberty Parties had been landed there was little to do until later in the afternoon when they started back to the ships.

When Liberty expired there was a big change. Then, for an hour we had one gay time keeping the lads informed, by voice-rasp, hack, cough-of the respective Ship's Boats at the landing. Every body was trying to get in out of the rain, and the building wasn't too big so you can imagine the crush.

Several Shore Patrolmen were on the float yelling the ship's names at us as the boats pulled in, and we in turn would give the crowd the word. After five we had only a few stragglers and we took them with us when our boat came at 1730; and we headed for home a sadder but wiser bunch.

11 OCTOBER 1945. THURSDAY. The Captain had gotten the word to prepare for heavy weather. Typhoon Louise had torn Okinawa up, and was headed toward Kyushu. While tied to the buoys we experienced about 70 knots of wind down the channel. The two outboard ships were turning their screws at 15 rpm to keep the strain off the forward mooring cable. The barometer steadied in the late afternoon at a low of 29.12 inches. After the experience of 16 September I was glad we were in a protected harbor, and secured to the battleship buoys.

13 OCTOBER 1945. SATURDAY. At sea again, and a strange experience, for this was the first time we'd been underway for more that 10 hours since we hit Sasebo in September. We had drawn the assignment of escorting a transport U.S.S. *Fallon* (APA-81) filled with men headed for home and demobilization for a few hundred miles. (Japanese Submarines could still be lurking in the deep, and unaware that the war was over.) The transport was going home, and 100 miles east of Van Deimen Straits *Lamson* turned back

to return to the 'lovely-as-ever' harbor of Sasebo and the easy routine of port life.

There was just enough of a crispness to the air to make a sweater comfortable and the moon was bright enough to throw an orangish light on the smooth water. A few clouds broke the monotony of light once in awhile, but not for long. We passed a north bound convoy of many ships, and coming upon them suddenly was like seeing a brightly lighted beach, for they appeared to be stationary, and varying with the landscape.

When the ship returned to port Liberty was allowed again, but it was still rather limited so I had been over only once with Neal, and then the last time as Shore Patrol. The rest of the time was spent on board watching over the Division, studying, or watching a movie.

The crew was expecting a combined Personnel and Material Inspection, but we were just subjected to the latter because of our sudden departure. The Inspection came off well and we were commended on the fine appearance of the Workshop. The Division was staying in good order, and all was smooth, on the surface at least.

Nine more men left this morning, including 'Knobby' Walsh MM2/C & Tullis TM2/C. They were either bound to the West Coast for discharge, or to the *U.S.S. Beale* (DD471). The crew was now down in the 180's and not feeling it too much yet. It was almost definite that I would be one of the Decommissioning Crew of *Lamson*. It would be only fitting after holding her together for so long, and seeing her through so much, that I help take her out of service. Scuttlebutt had it that the ship would be taken out at the Philadelphia Navy Yard.

Mr. Saul conducted another class in Calculus, and up there on the superstructure the breeze was quite chilly in the late afternoon. Darn near froze before we finished. Some of the work was approaching electrical theory, providing the theory for the application I was familiar with.

17 OCTOBER 1945. WEDNESDAY. Liberty had changed a bit around Sasebo. Now that the Fall of the year is upon us the weather has become cool enough to wear blues. The other morning we had our first big Personnel Inspection in some time and it was in Dress Blue too.

Some of the uniforms were in bad shape with no crows, bad watch marks, wrinkles galore. The Old Man really looked us over. My inspection gear had been properly stowed away so when the old boy stopped in front and looked up and down he said, "Very Good," and then started on the next guy.

Blues on the beach sure took a beating because of the dust which was so thick you needed a gas mask. We were told that Sasebo was only 18% destroyed, but that 18% was certainly well placed, and left a lot of dust. The past few days had really been hot ones for the E Division. The work brought the plant up to snuff again. The two Radar Technicians in Class caught it too so we slowed down a bit on the Calculus class, and I got rusty in a hurry.

20 OCTOBER 1945. SATURDAY. This being Saturday we had the usual, rather this time it was an unusual, inspection. 0530: Reveille, and then violent preparation by all concerned for the big event. Yes, it was to be a SQUAD DOG Inspection by a 4 striper, and this 'Feather Merchant' skipper was really anxious.

Well, we dressed in our little blue suits about 0800 so as to be ready by 0830. Naturally we stood around until about 0930-waiting. Once the inspection party got underway it went very rapidly and the Old Boy wasn't very hard on us. The inspecting officer was Captain McCorkle, Commanding Officer of DESRON 5, of which we are a part, and our Old Man really tagged him closely.

The Commodore was concerned about getting all the old, and high point, men off the ship, and he seemed to think there were not enough ratings aboard.

This ship was always 'Left Handed,' but lately the Reserve Officers seem to be doing what is convenient for them, and not what has been promulgated as policy. The other day we had to get the word on the latest point reduction from the can alongside. They were straight forward enough to announce it over the 1 MC General Announcing System so all hands got the word at the same time.

The inspection was over, and we wondered what the results would be. I was sure our E Division spaces were the showplaces on the ship. The Electrical Shop stood out with gleaming white paint work, no dust to speak of, good bright work and an air of workability about it. The men in the Division had done the work, and the praise would be theirs.

After Inspection Liberty was piped, and the Liberty Party shoved off in a light rain which gave mixed feelings about going ashore. At least the rain would settle the dust. The women and wine situation was still poor on a 4 hour liberty, but some sailors were getting up the hill into the residential area, and invited into homes; maybe getting a little saki and a chance to try to converse with the people. Some had gotten Japanese-English dictionaries, which helped a lot. Finally! Mail came in that had been hung up in Okinawa at the Fleet Post Office.

When I went on liberty, another guy and I went out into the country to see if there was anything to offer. He was well equipped for barter for the Yen is not much in demand and some things are not available to the Japanese so a black market flourishes. Anyway, we started thumbing and after several jumps we made a place by name, Haiki. It was no more than a small village, but the competition was not keen even though the yellow 'Out of Bounds' signs were plentiful. We were turned back by them on several occasions and each time after a considerable hike. It was a warm afternoon in the valley and the blues began to become uncomfortable so we started back to Sasebo.

As we passed a house we heard someone say, "Where you go?" and on a balcony was a kid that could speak, and understand, a few words of English. We cornered him and tried, in our most simple terms, to get a kimono or two. I even tried to get Pris her doily or table cloth. He didn't have any but we persuaded him to accompany us in our search for all the girls that owned such apparel. After much questioning we had him write the question in Japanese in case he shoved off. This he did while a small crowd gathered. The crowd formed immediately whenever we stopped, and we were surrounded by curious children.

After our short lesson we continued on up the street, followed by the small crowd of kids that we had attracted. At last we came to a small group of dwellings and after a few questions he found out that one woman had one to sell. As we were dickering and waiting another large crowd gathered and we were the center of interest again.

About that time a Jeep came up and a couple of Marines spotted the mob and stopped. I went over to tell them what we were doing, and after finding out the score they reached in the back of the Jeep and started producing cans of C Rations that we might use in trading. They came in handy and pretty soon people were running after gear to trade. I managed to get a small trinket, rather a doll in a small glass case about 3 inches square, for something or other, but there was not much else to buy, for money, or barter.

After exhausting the possibilities of Haiki we picked up a ride with two more Marines, and their Jeep. They were headed for Sasebo so we had a through trip and managed to look around town a little more. I picked up some stamps that had been canceled. The date on them was not quite like ours in that the year was 20 instead of 1945. They start time when a new Emperor ascends the throne.

27 OCTOBER 1945. SATURDAY. Navy Day was spent back in Nagasaki where the ship was 'full dressed' for the celebration of Teddy Roosevelt's Birthday. Cameras were permitted finally, and there were many pictures taken by Arispe, and others that helped identify the location of the ship, and included a shot of E Division among others.

A cruise book was being developed, and it was a shame that it was not started in Iwo Jima before the crew began to be disbanded, for there were many of my shipmates not in the book.

There was unrestricted liberty for about 10% of the crew. Liberty was better in Nagasaki than Sasebo because of the numbers of men on the beach in the latter place. In Nagasaki there were a few auxiliaries, and *Lamson*, and there was no crowd on the beach. The merchandise in the shops was less expensive than we had found in Sasebo. So much for the demand side of the equation. The men who had gone ashore had been able to pick up a few Kimonos, and other sundry items.

Rumors of our future plagued the ship. The last one that came down from the Quartermasters was that we would leave on 1 November; headed for Pearl, San Diego, Panama and the Atlantic Ocean. At 16 knots it would be December before we got around, but it would depend on the lay over. Personally, I would have liked to get back home by Christmas, but I thought it would be to my advantage to stay underway until January so I would have a better shot at Chief Electricians Mate while still attached to *Lamson*.

28 OCTOBER 1945. SUNDAY. Our fine liberty in Nagasaki did not last long, and we returned to Sasebo to moor at Buoy 24 with *U.S.S. Gherardi* (DMS30), *Helm* & *Flusser*. Another group was transferred, but there were several new men too, for there was an exchange of crew members between *U.S.S. Beale* (DD471) and *Lamson*.

29 OCTOBER 1945. MONDAY. Before we got underway, the Port Director, Navy 3912 sent four officers, and 53 enlisted men out to the ship in addition to the exchanges with the *Beale*; which was to stay out. The short timers were being put aboard the returning ships. We would be crowded on the way home, but nobody minded.

Two Electrician's Mates came aboard from *Beale*. Proehl, and Rothschild, and EM2C Winters was also added, and they would help stand watches until we got to the States where they would be discharged.

Ammunition was transferred to the mine sweeper, and we topped off the fuel tanks with 9,344 gallons at 60 degrees Fahrenheit in preparation for the long non-stop trip to Pearl. These older tin cans were long legged ships, and designed for such hauls.

At 1350 the crew was mustered at quarters, with no absentees, and at 1506, in accordance with a flag hoist from *Flusser*, *Lamson* departed for Pearl Harbor. 4086 miles were ahead of what remained of DESRON 5 as *Flusser* (DD368), *Helm* (DD388), *Lamson* (DD367) and *Ralph Talbot* (DD390) steamed out of Sasebo. The others of the Divisions represented had been lost during the war.

30 OCTOBER 1945. TUESDAY. On the Mid Watch the group was beginning to come around on an easterly course. The ships were 600 yards apart in a column, steaming at 13 knots. As the formation cleared Kusakaki Shima 7 miles to starboard our base course was changed and we were almost clear of the Japanese Islands.

1 NOVEMBER 1945. WEDNESDAY. Frank Kozlowski was advanced to EM1/C, still carrying his Planter's Peanut can. Amsler went to Electricians Mate Second Class, and Balland made EM3C. They would be discharged at their highest rate when we got back to San Diego, our ultimate State side destination.

10 NOVEMBER 1945. SATURDAY. What was left of Destroyer Squadron Five steamed into Pearl Harbor without any fanfare, just as it had so many other times. *Lamson* tied up alongside *Flusser* at berth D-1, Middle Lock. The Liberty Party was called away.

An article in the *Honolulu Advertiser* of 19 November 1945 was the only recognition that I can recall, of our efforts since December 1941. Some of the articles information is in the following paragraph.

There were eleven ships assigned to the current DESRON 5. *U.S.S. Drayton* (DD366), *U.S.S. Lamson* (DD367), *U.S.S. Flusser* (DD368), and *U.S.S. Smith* (DD378) were all that were left of the original Squadron. All had been heavily damaged, repaired, and returned to service at some time during the conflict. *U.S.S. Conyngham* (DD371), *U.S.S. Shaw* (DD373), *U.S.S. Bagley* (DD386), *U.S.S. Helm* (DD388), *U.S.S. Mugford* (DD389), *U.S.S. Ralph Talbot* (DD390), and *U.S.S. Patterson* (DD392) were replacements from other decimated squadrons during the war.

Shaw had been rebuilt after being heavily damaged while in dry dock with the battleship *U.S.S. Pennsylvania*, during the attack on Pearl Harbor. This Naval Unit was the only Destroyer Squadron of the Pacific Fleet to have served continuously from December 1941 until the Japanese surrender. Captain Francis F. McCorkle was the Squadron Commander, with his flag in *U.S.S. Flusser*, the original flagship of the Squadron, and one of the few that had gone through the war unscathed, although she had taken a round through the galley off Woetje, and been badly damaged in a collision with the *Drayton* off Pearl Harbor.

11 NOVEMBER 1945. SUNDAY. Barney Guidrey and I went ashore to see if we could find a good steak, and to celebrate V-J Day. We went out to Waikiki to Lai Ye Chai's for the noon day meal, and ended up in a fight with some testy LT (j.g.) because we were talking too loudly, upsetting the two women with him. We never got to the steaks, for Barney punched the officer in the nose, I manned the phone booth, keeping the JG off the horn, while the staff called us a cab, and on the way out I fanned a $20 to the waiter as we sailed out the front door. So much for our "Post War" celebration.

There had been a major change in the plans for *Lamson*, for the ship would not go to the East coast. A short stay in San Diego was scheduled, and then the ship would return to Pearl, and later become one of the target ships at the Bikini Atoll tests.

The Bureau of Naval Personnel had sent an All Navy message, requesting volunteers for a year of Electronics School. With all the Reserve technicians going home there were not enough in the fleet to take care of the new electronics gear. Radiomen, sonarmen, radarmen, electricians were eligible for training and conversion to Electronics Technicians. RdM2/C Brantley, RdM3/C Clifford, and I put in for the school at Great Lakes. We were all Regular Navy, and met the criteria.

12 NOVEMBER 1945. MONDAY. LCDR R.M. Ayer had orders detaching him as Commanding Officer, and his relief, LCDR George Ball came on board before we got underway. LCDR Ayer did not leave until San Diego. Mustered the crew at quarters, and at 0830 we began to fuel from a YO, taking on another 11,207 gallons of black oil.

1522. *Lamson* was underway for San Diego with the Captain at the conn, and the Navigator on the bridge. Lt. E.M. Adams was the Navigator, and Officer of the Deck as we passed buoy #6 to port, and entered the channel outbound at the rear of the Division. A bad recommendation by the Assistant Navigator, which the Captain caught, caused course changes that swung the starboard screw into the bank at 1554 1/2, about 400 yards, bearing 3330 from buoy #3. The Skipper called the crew to General Quarters to be on the safe side.

We stood out to sea to determine the damage while the rest of the outfit steamed on to San Diego. There was no hull damage, but the starboard screw was bent, and we limped back into Pearl on the port engine.

1753. Moored starboard side to *U.S.S. Twining* (DD540) at X-23 in Middle Loch. The whole crew was really pissed off to say the least.

13 NOVEMBER 1945. TUESDAY. Doc Carris, who had planned to ride to San Diego with us, left the ship for home. A diver came over from the *U.S.S. Altair* (AD-11), and reported that the starboard screw had one blade broken off about 2 feet from the tip. The other two blades were bent aft about 18 inches. There was no indication of hull, strut, or shaft damage.

16 NOVEMBER 1945. FRIDAY. Finally, a dry dock was empty, and *Lamson* was moved into Dry Dock #2 where the starboard screw was pulled again. This was the third emergency removal since 1942. We would not be home for Thanksgiving, and did not know how long we would be hung up in Pearl in another dry dock.

That night some of the boys broke into the beer locker, and drank up 10 cases of beer, leaving the empty cans in the 40 mm gun tubes, and on the Main Deck. This caused the Commanding Officer a great deal of unhappiness, and the crew was restricted because nobody would tell who took the suds. The restriction included the dry dock, and we were all frustrated as hell, managing to get Lt. (j.g.) Hixenbaugh who had relieved Lovejoy as XO, to restrict the Officers too. Later we were allowed to go into the dock to stretch our legs. When we left the dock we were still restricted to the ship yard, for the crew clammed up on the culprits; even though it was common knowledge who was involved. Good thing the skipper did not call in the Navy Security Agents for fingerprints.

A Board of Investigation was convened on the accident, but there was little to be done except to determine the facts and responsibility, for the Commanding Officer will take the blame. LCDR Ayer was being relieved anyway, and we all hoped it would be in Pearl. The new C.O. was a youngster, of about 26 years, and he seemed to be a nice guy.

On the 17th I sent a telegram to the folks letting them know that I would not be home for Thanksgiving. I missed my sister's wedding as well as a good dinner.

21 NOVEMBER 1945. WEDNESDAY. Our miserable dry dock restriction was about ended although we were permitted yard liberties. Most of us had tried strenuous athletics, and we were stiff and sore. Football, roadwork, walking, and swimming made the time go by more quickly, and relieved some of the discontent that had welled up in the crew. What a way to end a cruise.

23 NOVEMBER 1945. FRIDAY. The props were back on, and *Lamson* was back at sea, steaming singly, and headed for San Diego after a 10 day delay.

28 NOVEMBER 1945. WEDNESDAY. Lt. j.g. Neal Johnson was the OOD on the Mid Watch, and he logged that we were steaming singly on course at 15 kts. At 2155 we passed San Nicholas Island 33 miles to port. We would be in port early Thursday.

29 NOVEMBER 1945. THURSDAY. *Lamson* was directed to Pier 18, and at 0752 was tied up at the foot of Broadway to discharge passengers, and separatees. A light rain was falling, and I don't remember many people meeting the ship. It was a let down after all that we had been through, and except for the few married people that were met, I don't recall any jubilation at all. It was another day as far as most of us were concerned, but there was a mass exodus of 52 members of the crew, and assorted passengers.

I lost Amsler, Borrell, Kozlowski, and Kuhn as well as Proehl & Rothschild; who had come from the *Beale*. Lt. Apple, USN was detached at this time, having spent over two years on board, but he would go to another ship for he was Regular Navy.

By 0933 we were underway again, and at 1017 moored port side to *U.S.S. Smith* (DD378) at berth G in the stream along with *Flusser* and *Conyngham*. In the afternoon LCDR R. M. Ayer, USNR was detached, and left the ship at 1534. Not many people were sorry to see him leave, either.

The next day I got off on leave, saying "goodbye" to those headed home, and later was able to drive to San Francisco about the 7th to spend some time with the Roosman's where Connie decided to break off the engagement just because I told her I'd dated other women in Seattle. I was glad that I didn't have to marry her, for I did not need a family on the beach. I had two more years of obligated service, and did not know where I would be sent next.

4 DECEMBER 1945. TUESDAY. At 1124 *Lamson* was underway again. This time the destination was Pier 2 at the Navy Repair Base, San Diego for the removal of the quad 40mm mounts, and #1 20mm. This was done on the next day, and the ship was then moved to Pier 'G' to nest with *Flusser*, *Smith* and *Conyngham*, at the Destroyer Base.

27 DECEMBER 1945. THURSDAY. I had reported back from leave a couple of days before we were scheduled to get underway, and had gone home again on the 26th. My Dad took me back to the ship, and in the early light I managed to dent his radiator, causing it to leak. He dropped me off at the gangway and had to limp back to Wilmington. I hated to leave him with that problem, but I had no choice in the matter.

All during the day people logged out, and went over the side. Another group of dischargees left, including my striker Roger Trial. There were four of us left including Balland, Hargarther, and Hoffman to take the ship back to Pearl Harbor. 62 more of the crew had been transferred since our arrival, and now the officers were leaving. LTjg Phelan, Lt. j.g. Neal Johnson, Lt. j.g. W.A. Johnson, as well as Ensigns Bacon, Craig, and Shonkweiler were detached for demobilization.

People that I had steamed with for almost four years also went over the side, including CMM Jerry Giannatasio, CRM Chaisson, CFC Bracci, CSF Cherwa, and CTM Boyd.

1547- LCDR George Ball took us outbound for Oahu with LT Dan Hixenbaugh as the XO. We were underway for Pearl with 92 men, and 8 officers on board. *Flusser*, *Lamson*, *Smith*, and *Conyngham* headed for decommissioning, and later target ships.

1730- The Watertender in the Fireroom gave the engines a shot of water, and they were stopped. Again, the rest of the Division steamed over the horizon as they had done on 12 November. A decision was made to return to San Diego for repairs, but the crew was able to get it all back together, and by noon on the 28th *Lamson* was back on course for Pearl Harbor, and another liberty in San Diego was avoided.

31 DECEMBER 1945. MONDAY. The weather stayed nice, and the food was good. *Lamson* bobbed along gently on the calm sea, for there was little ammunition on board. Except for a few minor repairs there was little for the Division to do, and we stood watch on the Main Board, and took readings in the other spaces, and generally laid around.

The Muster Roll of the Crew dated 31 December 1945 showed the following men still on board from the original 21 of Company 41-184 that had met the ship in Suva, Fiji on 12 February 1942: Harold Hylton FC1/C, Leland Knight QM1/C, and Stanford Lichlyter EM1/C. I would be promoted to Chief Electricians Mate (CEM) the next day, and it would be a great way to start 1946.

LTjg Ralph Saul was the OOD on the Mid Watch, and his poetic log noted that we were steaming at 17 knots with Number 4 boiler on the line. Our next stop was Pearl Harbor, then at a later date the trip to Bikini, and poof!

A NEW CAREER CHANGE
JANUARY - FEBRUARY 1946

1 JANUARY 1946. TUESDAY. 00 - 04. *U.S.S. Lamson* was still on Course 248 degrees, speed 17 knots with #4 Boiler on the line.

04 -08. About reveille somebody threw a GI can down the ladder of the Engineer's Compartment to celebrate New Year's Day.

After breakfast I was called up to the Ship's Office and told that I had been promoted to Chief Electricians Mate (Acting Appointment) Temporary. I had a division of four, including myself with EM3 Robert Balland, EM3 Theodore Hoffman, and S1C Harold Hargarther. I moved into the Chief's Quarters with CMM Sessions, and CBM Smith. There were three of the 16 Chief Petty Officers left. Since I had no uniforms, I had to make do by putting a CPO hat pin on a baseball cap that I found. It was a beat up version, but it would suit the purpose until we got to Pearl where I could get the proper uniform.

The last few days at sea were spent well forward in the Chief's Mess, bouncing up and down and back and forth. I was still being called out for watches, and took the 4 - 8 for myself.

3 JANUARY 1946. THURSDAY. *Lamson* entered Pearl Harbor again, and was directed to moor at berth D-7 Middle Loch. At 1424 the next afternoon the ship was moved to B-24, starboard side to *Conyngham* (DD371), by the Receiving Station, almost directly across from the Fleet Landing, and a short distance from the Exchange and the Chief's Club. It was very convenient for all hands, and especially a new Chief Petty Officer.

Just as soon as the ship was secured the engineering plant was shut down, and power and water were taken from the dock. The crew was assigned living space in one of the air conditioned barracks at the Receiving Station just a short walk from the ship, and we ate at the Receiving Station Mess Hall. *U.S.S. Topeka* (CL-67), a new light cruiser, was tied up astern.

The Uniform Shop at the Exchange was very convenient, and when I shut the plant down I went over and bought my new insignia, a suit of grays, two more pants and shirts, hat and caps, spending almost $50.00 in the process. It sure felt funny going in and ordering a new uniform. I had originally planned to buy items a size larger than I normally wear until I realized that I was going to continue working as before, and would not be able to lounge around in the Chief's Quarters as I had seen my predecessors do. I gave my old familiar uniform away, mainly the whites, but sent those items home that I wanted to keep such as my tailor made blues, a suit of melton cloth blues that had been issued to me in boot camp, and my pea coat.

Balland left, and now there were just the three of us to do the work required to button up the Electrical System. The only time that I got out of my dungarees was when I went ashore. I gave Hoffman, who would be the leading electrician, some instructions on the Main Distribution Switchboard, and then took the *U.S.S. Lamson* name plate off the board as a souvenir, and remembrance of the miserable hours that I spent looking at it while on watch

Ship's Company began to decommission the ship, accounting for Title B material, coating machinery with preservatives, and stowing spares, tools and small equipment in secure store rooms. The crew of the *Topeka* (CL-67) let us know what they needed, and we would lay it out where it could be taken easily.

7 JANUARY 1946. MONDAY. My eyes were bothering me so I went up to Tripler Hospital again for another eye refraction and new glasses.

Since there were very few officers on board; the Chief's were assigned to the Quarterdeck and Jr. Officer of the Day duties. I was down in the Engine Room working on something when somebody yelled down the hatch that I had the watch, and dropped a web belt and .45 down on my head. I really took a razzing, but my shipmates concluded that the grays looked pretty good. The darn tie was killing me even though I bought shirts that had decent collars.

That .45 got heavy on the hip though. When my watch was over I could shove off if I wished, but since I was flat broke after buying the clothes, not drawing my Uniform Allowance yet, I was in no position to go ashore.

20 JANUARY 1946. SUNDAY. The ship was like a ghost now with everything secured except the laundry. Our mail had been stopped, for the Postal System had the word that the ship had been decommissioned on the 18th. Little did they know. Other than that, all was going well, and I felt like I was drawing a pension. About all we did was lounge around, stand a four hour watch every other day, and go to the CPO Club on the Base for a beer before dinner. Then I'd read, and go to bed. It was strange to be so free and able to go ashore any time, yet go to bed by 2100.

21 JANUARY 1946. MONDAY. *Lamson* was ready for the decommissioning ceremony. I had the Quarterdeck when the Captain came back from Destroyer Pacific Command with a message telling him to put the ship back together and get underway within five days. I bought a Val Pack at the exchange, for I expected to leave for Great Lakes, and without a sea bag.

26 JANUARY 1946. SATURDAY. Because the engineers had done the

decommissioning job properly; Number 2 boiler was lit off easily, and at 1045 the main plant was turned over once again for dock trials.

28 JANUARY 1946. MONDAY. *Lamson* was the only ship in the Division that moved on her own power, steaming to Middle Loch, on the other side of Ford Island, where the ship was secured to a buoy, this time D-5, with *Mayrant* (DD402), *Wilson* (DD408), *Smith* (DD378) and *Ralph Talbot* (DD390). *Lamson* was the center of the five cans so we were at the mercy of the Fleet Liberty Boats, and the landing at Pearl City was the closest stop. Everybody was so damn mad and disgusted that it was pitiful. Weeks of hustle and bustle, changing orders and indecision climaxed by a complete reversal of plan. If we had stayed in San Diego liberty would have been a lot better, and a lot of fuel oil would have been saved.

Another piece of bad news indicated that BuPers was not taking anyone from the Pacific Fleet for Electronics School. I resigned myself to my fate and started taking college courses at the base Education Office through US Armed Forces Institute. (USAFI)

31 JANUARY 1946. THURSDAY. Good News. Another message came in with the word that those who had applications in for ET conversion school prior to a certain date were not effected by the new policy on electronics school. Brantley RDM2, and Clifford RDM3 and I would go after all. Brantley had been aboard the same length as I, but was in a different boot company, having enlisted on the 11th while I entered on the 17th of December 1941. Orders were cut, and we would leave our old home on Friday morning after Pay Day.

My new address would be:

NTSCOL RADIO MATERIEL (EE & RM)

NAVTRACEN, GREAT LAKES, ILL.

1 FEBRUARY 1946. FRIDAY. Pay day. In my eagerness to get paid and get off I lost a good fountain pen to the guy behind me in the pay line. He borrowed it to sign his papers, and I moved away from him and didn't get it back.

After lunch, at 1230, six of us left the ship. Three were transferred to General Detail, Aiea, FFT nearest continental receiving station for reenlistment leave under authority of ALNAV 209-45: GM2/C Bob Beardsley, WT3/C, Bill Kees, and S1C Alton Northcutt. The three of us headed for school were transferred in compliance with Commander Western Sea Frontier Speedletter of 15 January 1946 to the nearest continental receiving station for further transfer to Naval Training School, Radio Material, NTC, Great Lakes, Ill.

I had been aboard *Lamson* since 12 February 1942, a little short of four years, and had advanced from Apprentice Seaman to Chief Electrician's Mate by hard work, good luck, and being in the right place at the right time. I was also the only one left eligible for Chief.

The three of us, who were headed for school, were not ordered to General Detail, Aiea. I was to report to Great Lakes Naval Schools Command by 14 February, but the orders left it up to me to get there as best I could. We were told that Aiea assigned transportation though, and when we got to Aiea the Yeoman at the receiving desk said, "Let me see your orders, Chief." That was the last I saw of them for five days. He told me where the Chief's Quarters were, and I was stuck.

I learned to wash and iron my new khaki clothes, how to play Acey Deucey, and cribbage too. It was not a complete loss, and I saved money too, for we were restricted awaiting transportation.

As ships came through Pearl, or Honolulu, headed for the States they were filled with passengers from Aiea. One afternoon our names were called and we were bussed to the Matson passenger docks in Honolulu where we marched aboard *SS Lurline* with a couple of thousand other servicemen headed home. I ended up in a large stateroom that had been fitted out with 12 bunks. It was still luxurious compared to *Lamson*, and even had a bathroom fitted out with a large porcelain bathtub that must have been great on the peacetime Honolulu runs.

We lined up for meals, but the crew had taken care of troops for years, and were well organized. Good food too. *Lurline* had been a troop transport since January 1942, and the civilian crew had seen a lot of servicemen come and go so they were used to the crowd, and treated us very well. The three days to San Francisco went by very quickly. From my point of view *U.S.S. Lamson* was just a memory that I preferred to put behind me for good.

9 FEBRUARY 1946. SATURDAY. It was early in the morning when *Lurline* pulled into the Army Port of Embarkation piers at Fort Mason, and the various service organizations directed the troops to demobilization activities. Brantley, Clifford, and myself found ourselves on a bus headed for Navy Receiving Station, Treasure Island for onward processing to Great Lakes.

I went out to Roosman's for the evening, glad that marriage to Corrine was not for me. I called home to let the folks know what was happening, and the next morning Connie and I rode bicycles a bit, and then went down town San Francisco. The only clothes that I had was my grey cotton twill CPO uniform. It was the first time she had seen me in other than civvies or the V necked gown. We went to a good clothing store, I think it was Hastings', and I bought a heavy black coat because I was about to freeze. It turned out to be a Bridge Coat, but I did not know enough about the

Uniform Regulations at the time to know the difference. The salesman in the store did, and I was forever grateful for that fact. We went back to Roosman's where I said my farewells. Connie said she would sell the ring, and send me the money, and we parted on a platonic note.

Treasure Island issued me a Transportation Request that modified my orders, and after we had lunch I had to catch the Chicago bound train in Oakland about sundown so I said, "Goodbye" to Corrine for the last time, and caught the Oakland ferry that made connections the train. I was completely on my own again, and not part of a draft. This was the first time that I had enjoyed this freedom, and it was a fine contrast to that period when I moved with sea bag and hammock enroute to *Lamson* in January and February 1942.

One stop along the way is still remembered. The diner had been taken off the train after we hit the Union Pacific tracks, and we were having a bad time with the lousy sandwiches that were costing a fortune. We pulled into Omaha, Nebraska about 2000 the evening before getting to Chicago. Everyone made for the Station and food. The Station Restaurant was crowded and a returnee spotted a City Canteen in the Station and away we went. It was a bit crowded, but we made out well for you could pick up a dozen sandwiches, and a pot of joe.

We were lucky enough to switch cars there too, and the last leg was spent in a comfortable chair car. The last morning it was only 6 degrees below zero.

13 FEBRUARY 1946. WEDNESDAY. When the troop train pulled into Union Station we asked how to get to Great Lakes, and were told how to catch the local North Shore Line for the Naval Training Station. I had asked the conductor where to get off, and he told me that we should disembark at the Main Gate of the Station. I was short about a mile, and the 2 feet of snow did not feel good. We walked across the Boot Camp to the Electronics School, on the north side of the station, lugging my Val Pack, and cursing my ignorance. There was another stop at the North Chicago gate that would have been much better.

After checking in, Clifford was told that he did not have enough time to complete the work unless he extended his enlistment. He would not extend, so he did not start classes, and was transferred back to sea. Brantley and I took a small examination, and my studies paid off, for I was put into the main class stream instead of the Refresher Course. Classes would start on Monday.

18 FEBRUARY 1946. MONDAY. The primary class started with lectures, arithmetic, and basic physics. Books were issued as well as a big slide rule. The time went by quickly, and I spent the weekend trying to recuperate from my fast trip from Pearl, and ended up by needing to recuperate some more because I caught something akin to the flu. That walk in over a foot

of snow didn't help when we got off the train about 1/2 mile before we should have.

I had to go to Milwaukee for a suit of blues, so three of us from Barracks 501, including Sayer B. MacMenamen who owned a car, drove up after classes ended. We were walking down the main street when we were accosted by three very lovely girls who needed dates for a dance that evening at Marymount Catholic Girl's School; but that was a different story. School was going to be more arduous than I had anticipated.

DIARY OF LT. EDGAR M. ADAMS

U.S.S. Lamson

DD367

October 28, 1944

The Philippines

We entered Leyte Gulf on October 29, a column of six cans, having left the tanker near Palau, two days previous. The weather was dismal, but there was no rain as yet, and everyone was topside taking a first look at the Philippines, that had been "The Country Beyond" for so long. In spite of the reports of the suicide raids on the CVB's of a few days previous no one seemed particularly apprehensive. We went to General Quarters (GQ) a couple of times, but nothing developed. It seemed much like any other tropical coastal region, except that the natives who paddled out in their outrigger canoes sometimes wore straw hats. They were peddling Jap currency. When we reached San Pedro Bay we saw a couple of things which showed there was a war on. The first was a corpse which we passed close aboard. I didn't see it, for I was below at the time preparing a message requesting a badly needed spare part, but all of the director crew and everyone topside saw it and said it was an American. I wasn't particularly sorry to have missed it. Two of the ships in the harbor were damaged. One, a 2100 tonner had only a foot of free board aft and another, a Liberty ship, was also badly down in the stern.

We luckily were able to get our spare part, and proceeded to anchor for the night. A storm was expected, and the weather was pretty foreboding. I had the midwatch and turned in early. When I climbed up on the director there was very little rain, it stung like needles so you had to turn away from it. It was a pretty dismal watch. The foul weather gear kept me just dry enough to make what water did leak in the more bothersome. The wind blew up to 65 knots, according to later reports; and I don't doubt them for it was strong enough to keep the ship heeled over five or ten degrees. She didn't ride into it as she does in moderate winds probably because of the large surface of the bridge structure forward, which gave the wind something to work on.

Looey was up on the fo'c'sle all night, veering chain, and hauling it in to veer again, trying to get the anchor fast; but it was no use. After dragging a couple of hours we got underway. This was critical too, for it had begun to rain harder and visibility was very bad; and the anchorage was packed with ships. The captain was on the bridge and you could tell he was working under strain. Somehow, however, he got us clear of the merchant ships and found a more sheltered anchorage, where we dropped the hook again. Up on the director I was trying to speed the passing of time and not having much success. I found that some of the phones and optical gear had not been covered and was wet. This peeved me, and I gave Westphall hell. Some can a few thousand yards off was firing starshells out over the land where the (battle) lines were. Every now and then the flares would flicker on in the rain and slowly settle as they burned out. They fired one about every three minutes throughout the night. I couldn't help thinking what a miserable job that must have been on a night like that.

Then suddenly the wind died down and it was so quiet that all you could hear was the gentle patter of the rain. It was so sudden it surprised you, and made you wonder if you'd dozed off. It was the storm center. The ship rocked there for a while of her own momentum. Then the wind sprang up from the opposite direction and blew like hell again. I saw Looey back on the fo'c'sle with Pevey and his crew. The *Flusser* streamed past and told us to join her, so we hoisted anchor again and cruised around till daybreak. It was great below at the end of the watch.

In the morning we picked up an LCM that had been badly mauled by the storm. She was nearly swamped and the engines had konked out. The two seamen who manned her were half dead from fright and exposure. They were afraid of drifting ashore behind the Jap lines. The Doc gave them a shot of whiskey and put them to bed, and in a few hours they were able to return to their station. Meanwhile the scavengers among our crew were sacking their boat. Judah got their rifles and personal gear and stowed it in the Wardroom, but a lot of other stuff was stolen. It makes you wonder to see your own boys acting like a bunch of asses.

During the day there were a couple more alerts that sent us to GQ, and we began to get the idea there was definitely a war going on. We spent most of the evening at our battle stations and on a couple of occasions the beach and some of the ships opened up with tracer and AA. There was bright moonlight, but we saw no planes.

The next morning (the 31st) Jack Smith took the boat crew and a salvaged part and went to help pull some PBYs off the beach. Then we went to fuel. There were uncertain reports of enemy planes in the area, and we were a little apprehensive while we were alongside the tanker. But nothing happened. We got underway and went to pick up Jack and his party. It was then that I saw the corpse. I don't know if it was the same one or not. He was all swollen up and floating there like a cork. He was floating on his stomach with his bottom sticking out of the water. Evidently the swelling of his torso burst the fly of his pants for they were in a bunch at his ankles and his long underwear was stretched tight and white across his grotesque buttock. I couldn't help thinking, "What an ungrateful way to die."

Sometime that afternoon we had swimming call. It seemed foolish, but I went in and the water felt fine. There wasn't much of a turn out. We hoisted our boat aboard and headed back for our anchorage. It was about 1700 and chow was just going down. Suddenly the bell for GQ started to clang. There was a mad scurry of feet, the clatter of tipped over chairs, and the feeling of, "Oh my God! This is it!" On the ladder to the bridge I glanced around and saw a great stream of tracers pouring into the sky from around the airfield about five miles away. The director was tracking the planes by the time I got up there. I was busy getting the battery trained out and didn't see the planes, but Westphall was giving a good description from the pointer's seat. "See him, Charlie, see him? It's a VAL! Lookit that son-of-a-bitch go! Here come the P38s, Jesus. Look at 'em go after him! They're firing! I can see their gun flashes. They're pouring it—he's smoking! See him smoking, Charlie? There he goes! There he goes!" The sun was just going down. It was the curving trail of smoke two P38s circling. By the airfield black smoke was billowing up into the sky. Evidently a fuel dump had been hit for it burned all through the night sending up rolling red flames and heavy smoke.

We were at general quarters all night. The moon was bright and full and all the ships in the harbor seemed helplessly visible in its brilliant light. And there were many planes in the air, and time after time brilliant clusters of tracers streamed up from the beach positions and from the portion of the horizon where the task force was patrolling. And there were white flashes of the 5" bursts high in the sky, and gray blankets of smoke laid by the small craft that silently steamed aback and forth through the silent hulks that were the merchant ships and transports. Planes were evidently all about the place, but not once did we see one. It was a long night, but no one ever became sleepy. Our positions were cramped, and our fannys got sore from our hard seats; but every time we were tempted to doze off the bright moon would remind us that we were goddamn naked down there, and that sooner of later something would be after us, and we'd better be ready to shoot.

1 November 1944

CDD-10

At daybreak we got underway, one division of us, and headed out to meet a convoy and bring it in. It was a dismal prospect at best; for convoys are a delicious morsel, and there were all kinds of indications that the attacks would continue through the day. We ate breakfast in shifts and stayed at our battle stations. The planes were still lurking about. We formed up in a star for best maneuverability and headed out. As we proceeded, the task force over the horizon gradually came into view. Evidently it was having a pretty rough time, for several times we saw their AA bursts slashing in the sky. Our course out of the Gulf would take us past them at about 5 miles, and at 8 miles they were well in view on the horizon. The third attack of the morning was coming in on them. Their broadsides were flashing orange and their wakes were boiling white. Some of the boys saw a couple of planes go down. All I saw was one Betty flying low on the water right through the task force formation. All kinds of millimeter were shooting at her, but she didn't seem to be taking hits, I don't know whether she got out or not.

Suddenly the *Mahan* opened up. She was about 4000 yards to starboard and was firing on her starboard beam. I slewed around to see what she was shooting at. The director located three planes way out there, but couldn't make them out. They never got close enough to shoot at, and finally disappeared. The task force had ceased firing. One can was smoking badly. We wondered where the Hell the air cover was. Everybody felt pretty rotten. The signs were clear. It was to be a rough day, and we were tired from no sleep the night before.

The log says the *Mahan* opened fire twice. I only remember once. That shows you how confused you can get when you try to recount an action. The log is right. After the war is over I can see the veterans smashing their fists on the bar and swearing they saw such and so. I'll laugh at them.

As we came abreast at about 5 miles, we received a message from the task force to drop what we were doing and join them. I guess the Admiral was a little worried, and I can't blame him. With no air cover, he needed cans for his outer screen and he was short. We came right and joined him. In forming up we passed the damaged destroyer close aboard. The starboard side of her fantail and gun four were mangled and black, but the fires were out. It was the *Claxton*. I had roomed with her Doc at the BOQ at Mare Island. I'll bet he had a mess on his hands.

Things looked quiet now so we secured from GQ for chow and a little sleep, we hoped. We got chow, but no sleep. I no sooner wiped my mouth than the bell started its clamorous dinging. The panicky scramble was on. In a matter of seconds I was on the director relieving Corson. He had the director trained out and tracking, but the guns were still in their sectors. Davis, on the rangefinder, was screaming at me to let them have it. But Guedry was just getting his phones on. I told him to tell the guns to match up and commence firing. It seemed like an age. Range was 12,000 yards. I saw gun two match up and screamed, "Commence firing!" By this time some of the other ships were opening fire. Then with a crash our guns started firing. The boys really put out. I heard Davis pull that target angle around to 300 and checked the fire. I asked Westphall to get another target.

158

"On target," and we opened up again. But he turned out to be going away too and the Captain had come right, bringing the gun two hard on the bridge. I gave, "Check fire." There were no other targets. I don't think we hit anything, but I'd won my bet with Westphall, he'd claimed the *Lamson* was through as a combatant ship, and I'd bet him we'd fire in the Philippines. We joked about it, but nobody laughed. We were all tired and scared. Another can had been hit.

There were still plenty of planes around, and it wasn't long before they came in again. We didn't know it until the van destroyer opened up, but we were on them in no time. For some reason the Captain told me to hold fire. There were Vals making an approach at about 12,000 feet. Finally the Captain gave me the go sign, but the planes soon were in their dives. We only fired a few salvos. The planes dove on one of the injured cans that had two standing by to help her. They were firing like mad, and they got one plane for sure. It burst like a Molotov cocktail at the end of its dive. One plane, but what a terrible price. One of the cans standing by caught a 500 pounder aft. Black smoke poured up from her deck house. You could see the flicker of small fires. Soon she was one great mass of red flames from the torpedo tubes aft, and the column of smoke was a great funnel shaped pillar five or six hundred volcanic gushes of red and black fire. Then she settled in the stern, pointed her fo'c'sle up into the sky and went down. The great black cloud hovered overhead, gloating.

They were sending out two P38s for air cover. Christ! Do they call that cover? There were enemy planes in all directions. The men and officers were beginning to snap at each other. I was as bad as any. There was no thought of sleep. I wasn't sleepy anyway. Like everyone else I was burning adrenaline. Combat came out with the straight dope, that there were four BBs, two CAs and 13 Jap cans on the way up from Mindanao, due to arrive the next afternoon at 1300. Wasn't that just ducky! Where and the hell is the Air Corps?

Somehow the rest of the afternoon went by. I don't know how many times we trained out and waited for the attack to come in, but there was always tension. After an hour or so, another tremendous column of black smoke made its appearance on the horizon. It seemed even larger than the other, and the general thought was that another can had succumbed to her injuries. Not until the next day did we learn that it was oil from the lost destroyer which had come to the surface and ignited again.

After sunset we were graced with an hour of darkness and were able to make a pretty good meal. Everyone was in hopeless spirits. Burkhart was bitterly fatalists and Apple was excitedly garrulous, Looey's slow drawling remark was a classic, "There's only two things we can count on now, good luck and the good Lord." It got a laugh, so maybe we weren't in such a bad shape after all.

I climbed back up on the director, and it wasn't long before the smiling moon climbed like Peter Lorre up into the sky. It was as bright as a searchlight. The men were being served chow on their stations. Corson was below having his when combat started screaming. Planes were coming in again and were close aboard. I got out on the bearing but was told to hold fire. They were coming in across the moon and there was no use showing our position. I think that most of the ships opened fire. One plane crossed our stern and flew right over the formation. His path could easily be followed by the movement of the tracer streams which all converged on one spot. He passed between us and one of the firing ships and their tracers came straight at us in a torrent. GAD! I thought sure they would be all over our decks. Why they weren't I'll never know. Shortly afterwards the destroyers formed up in a column. To gain our position we drew abreast of and passed the *Smith* close aboard. The banter that passed at that moment was something to hear. It was like Ebbets Field at a Dodgers-Giants ball game. Bronx cheers and pointless obscenities. O'Connell later remarked with a laugh, "There's an American for you. If it had been the British it would been 'Thumbs up,' or 'Some night, aye maitie.'" If it had been the French, it would have been, "Vive!" But being American it was the sign of the goose and, "Fuck you and hooray for me!" It was wonderful for morale.

As the moon climbed higher and higher the situation eased off a bit, until finally at about 2000 we could relax. Half the battery was allowed to sleep on their stations. Corson had to finish his chow, so I took the director 'till midnight. Nothing happened, and when I was relieved I stretched out on the platform to get some sleep. I got about five minutes, then, "Alert on the battery!" Some more bogies were located nearby. When they left we tried again to sleep, but they soon came back, and up we were again. The moon was high and the silhouette effect was gone, but it was awfully bright. I think the heavy ship opened up once or twice at long range, but the planes didn't come in very close again. Towards morning we got a little rest on our stations. I wasn't sleepy, but when I lay down I was asleep in ten seconds.

2 November 1944

The next day we cruised with the task force, went to GQ again, secured, and in general worried a lot and did very little. The rough day we had expected turned out to be a vacation. Nothing more was heard of the Jap task force of 4 BBs, 2 CAs and 13 cans. Overhead most of the day were a couple sections of P-38s. How we loved them. Just like at Finschaven we had loved them. During the night there were a couple of alerts and some firing, and everyone slept on their stations; but the strain was definitely off.

3 November 1944

The next day, the third, we left the task force alone and went out on anti-submarine patrol off the entrance. There was some tension, for we were all alone out there. The lookouts were doubled and everyone was kept on their station, half being allowed to sleep. There was some firing in the bay and where the task force was patrolling, but nothing developed in our sector. We saw a waterspout, the first I'd ever seen, at about 4000 yards, so we got a good view. The area around the spot on the ocean from which it rose was as if it were effervescent. After a few minutes it broke up and disappeared.

There were a couple hours of darkness before moonrise that night, and I asked Joe if I could secure all but two of the lookouts, he said OK, so I secured them. At about 0200 the Captain came up to the director and really raised hell. He blamed Judah and Hixenbaugh and I. The next day I spoke casually with Joe about it. "The Captain raised a quite a stink about the lookouts, didn't he?" Joe, innocently, "Yes. I'm sure glad I didn't give you permission."

"I thought you did."

"Did I?" Joe replied. I turned on my heel and left. The depths a small man will drop to because of fear for his superior.

4 November 1944

We were on patrol all day as before. Everything pretty quiet throughout the day and night, but everyone hanging close by their battle stations. The lookout situation changed every five minutes and everyone is rather sore on the subject. I thought it was being overdone. I finished reading "Moby Dick."

5 November 1944

Relieved of our patrol and went in to fuel. Everything was pretty quiet until evening, when, back on patrol with the task force there was a red alert. It didn't amount to anything. I'm still sleeping on the director, but many of the crew are sleeping below.

6 November 1944

Ammunitioned ship. The working party wasn't big enough, and they really worked in the hot sun. Some of the ammunition was for the *Mahan*, which was on patrol. When we finished we patrolled with the task force. There were a few alerts but nothing developed.

7 November 1944

Went out to relieve the *Mahan*. She laid to and we came alongside to give her ammunition. The Captain made a bad landing the first time and overshot, scraping the sides and bending in the 40 MM tub against the *Mahan's* forward bulwarks. We got the ammunition over in a hurry and went on out to our patrol stations. Another storm blew up in the afternoon. It rained and blew, and finally got so rough we secured the director and took the watch down to No. 2 gun shelter. It kept up through the night and everything was soaked.

8 November 1944

Still storming all day. It finally got so bad we headed in for the lee of Dinegat Island, hunting shelter. The wind was of typhoon proportions, blowing the water out into the low hissing combers. It must have run up to 50 or 60 knots. The air was driving with salt spray and the foam was blown out into white strings across the waves. We were rolling heavily, especially when we came about. Everything at such times slides across the decks with clash and clatter. I had the 8-12 at night. I never saw it so dark. It was like a misty cave topside, except for the chaotic wind. The waves hissing and tumbling were spectacularly phosphorescent. They were cloudlike formless emulsions, sparkling in places like a spangled carpet. It gives the impression of depth and endless flux and flow and galaxies at the beginning of time. The rain had ceased. It was a wonderful watch!

9 November 1944

The storm broke up today. The ship continued to take a pretty heavy roll, but the sky was pretty clear. It gave us a chance to get things dried out. Surprisingly, very little damage was done by the dampness that drenched everything. There was some rusting of exterior surfaces on the guns, but the men turned to in good force, and soon everything was in fine shape again. We stayed on patrol, no relief being in sight.

10 November 1944

Relieved on patrol this morning. We rejoined the task force and continued underway. We are on in four on the director now, and things are fairly easy. I sweated out my weekly hull report, the curse of Friday. Found water in the gun trunks, leakage from the pits during the storm, but no bad damage. A quiet day patrolling with the task force.

11 November 1944

Armistice day. Still patrolling with the task force in Leyte Gulf. Fueled ship about noon. Gave Spiser his exam for controlman third class and passed him. He didn't know too much, but I hadn't the heart to flunk him. He's such a good worker, and what with his wife due to have a baby…Aw hell. A few enemy planes came around at sundown and kept us at GQ for a couple of hours, but never came in. We secured when it was dark, and had a bridge game well started in the wardroom when considerable night activity developed and we went to GQ again for a couple of hours. It was so dark, however, that no one was particularly apprehensive. They came in close a couple of times, and there was quite a little AA from some of the other ships. Also lots from the beach. Really quite a sight. Now that we are secured I must get some sleep. There is liable to be more before the night is over.

12 November 1944-07:00

Not much sleep last night. We had to go to GQ again at 0330. The moon was up, and although only a crescent it made a fair path across the water for a ship to be seen in. We tried to secure once but had to come back again, and I've just come off again. The planes flew very close, but fire was not opened. We heard his motors once, but it was dark enough so that we weren't too worried. 2345 we had GQ off and on all day, though nothing developed very close until evening. Then we caught a glimpse of a dog fight about 10 miles astern. It was too far to see what was happening, but it must have been a pretty big affair because way beyond was the greatest cloud of air bursts I've ever seen. A portion of the sky which must have been several miles in extent in all three planes were oily looking from diffused bursts. We secured shortly after dark and it has been quiet since. I had the 20-24 watch. Guedry thought I was asleep and left his station for half an hour. What a sneaking trick! I should put him on report, but instead I had him wear the phones for the rest of the watch. From the way he pouted about his bad treatment, I know his conscience realized the justice of it. There was some unusual lightning tonight. One huge thunderhead some distance off seemed to be working overtime and discharged periodically. And when it discharged its exact form would light up like a light bulb. It was like the flash of a huge gun firing straight up.

13 November 1944

We were called to GQ at 0600. It was already half daylight, and we were a little concerned, as our fighters were not yet in the air. Nothing came in, however. The planes turned out to be just leaving rather than just arriving, and we secured in time for breakfast. During the morning we left the task force and went out on patrol, where we spent a quiet day. I got a few letters written. In the evening we had another alert, but again nothing developed and we secured. I turned in early to get some sleep before the mid-watch. At about 2230 my sound sleep was broken by a sudden call to GQ. I knew in an instant it meant business and scampered up to the director in my bare feet. Two float planes had passed overhead in the dark night at an uncomfortably low level. There had been no waning. It developed that there were thirty or more float planes around. An incoming convoy and the task force both were attacked, and a couple of times they started our way. Flares of amazing brightness were dropped. It was pretty tense. After over an hour, surprisingly, it cleared up, and we secured. Just in time for my mid-watch. It went by quickly, for Westphall, O'Connell and I had a fine argument on what a fire controlman should know.

14 November 1944

Started out the morning, as usual, with GQ. Again nothing developed, and we secured when the friendly air patrols appeared in the sky. The *Warramunga* relieved us on the channel patrol and we moved to outer patrol. The day was quiet with warm sunshine and an occasional rain squall. I slept all morning, and had the first dog (watch) in the afternoon. Just before darkness, after dinner we had an alert, and quite a scare. A bogey was playing around out about 20 miles. Suddenly he headed right for us, exactly as if he had seen us and was coming in. Range closed steadily: 17 ½ miles, 16 miles. We trained out on the bearing and were ready, but we couldn't pick him up. And we were all alone, his only target. 12 ½ miles, 10 miles, 9 ½ , 8 ½ , Jesus Christ! We passed into a rain squall. It was half darkness, but it didn't seem as if we could possibly be hidden. The sunset was right behind us. We were making high speed. 7 miles, 6, 5 ½ . "All guns standby." Where in the hell is he! There was a quiet, tense moment. It was getting darker, "Bearing changing right."

"Range opening." 7 miles, 8 miles. Darkness! We were OK. Whew! Back to the bridge game. "What was it?"

"Three clubs."

15 November 1944

What an unproductive day. With all the time in the world to myself, all I did was sleep and play bridge. At about 2030, Dunne had taken Smith's place at the table, and we were all a bit punchy. Dunne made the remark that he was tired of going to GQ at four in the morning and having his day completely ruined by five. It nearly broke up the game, for the resigned way he said it set all four of us off into laughter that brought tears streaming down our faces. We convulsed for five minutes steady, and ended up so weak that all life was lost to the bridge game.

16 November 1944

An alert this morning as usual, but no development, continued patrol all morning without incident and were relieved in the afternoon, to report from the task force to the harbor commander for duty. On the way in an air raid developed and there was considerable activity, tracers and AA all about. Planes were picked up as close as three miles but we were well covered by darkness and didn't fire. We anchored in darkness and secured at 2100. The anchor was frozen in the hawse pipe from being secured for so long, and it took a while to break it loose. The commissary is very low. We are hoping for a chance to provision ship soon. Otherwise we'll be on rice and malt tablets. Maybe there's mail for us, too. We're all in hopes over that, and it's one advantage to the harbor duty. I'm afraid it will be rough with air raids from over land, though.

17 November 1944

Cloudy and rainy weather all day kept the air activity down to a low level. We sent the motor whaleboat out bumming for chow. They managed to get some cream and sugar, but it rained so hard we had to call the trips off. The weather cleared some in the evening. After supper our usual bridge game was interrupted by GQ. The airfield, only a few thousands yards from our anchorage was under attack. The night was very dark. Shore based AA was firing a lot of tracers. They caught a plane in full searchlight beam and opened up on him with all kinds of 20 mm and 40 mm guns. It was a very spectacular sight in the dark night. The plane burst into flames and went down in less than 5 seconds. It was the first plane I had seen shot down at night.

18 November 1944

1100-So much has happened this morning that I'd better write it down while I think of it. Dawn GQ was uneventful and we secured. The weather was clear with about 3% cumulus clouds. Before I had time to eat breakfast they called us back to GQ. Being landlocked, we had no definite dope on the situation, and as usual we kept our lookouts alert but expected nothing to happen. There were P-38s in the air and everything looked O.K. On our starboard hand, over the airfield a P-38 suddenly started to dive, and shortly there was the rrrrrip of his gunfire. We didn't see his target until it started to smoke. Westphall said it looked like a P-47. It crashed. Then things started happening on all sides at once. A row of bombs splashed dead ahead along the shore, then an AP and some LCIs about 7000 yards on our starboard bow started firing like mad. We got on their target but he was already in his dive, a Hap (from reports) bent on a suicide crash on the AP. He was hurt and burst into flames about 200 feet up, but managed to crash the AK and start a pretty fair fire. At the same time the ships on the horizon on our port hand were firing. I had other reports to investigate and didn't train out there until all at once the director was a bedlam of yells about the plane to port. When we trained out I couldn't see him, and the director didn't report "On target." There was some delay on the account. By the time we fired he was within 4000 yards and heading straight for us. Then the 40s and 20s opened up. The *Flusser* was about 500 yards away in the next anchorage. The plane did a wing over and dove on them. He was big as life when it hit the water about 800 yards off. To me it seemed undamaged when it hit. It was an Oscar, I think, though it is hard to say anything with certainty after such excitement. Everyone was pretty scared and jumpy as hell. Other enemy planes were in the area. We trained out on a bearing where some were reported. The ships out there started firing like mad and we found the plane among the bursts and started tracking. I got the guns around and opened fire. Since he was coming straight at us it was impossible to tell what he was. He swung around to target angle 90 and Davis started screaming, "Check fire!" There was so much noise on the director that I couldn't understand him for a few seconds. It was a P-47, and what a storm of his own ship's fire he was going through. I pounced on the cease firing buzzer and stopped. The 20s opened up when he was way out of range, but the lads are young and we didn't give them too much hell. The P-47 miraculously didn't seem to be damaged.

Everyone is terribly jumpy. We don't like being anchored with air attacks coming in, but it looks as if that is how it will be for some time. There must have been 15 or so planes in that attack. There were many that I didn't see. Two ships were damaged by suicide dives; that's a rough kind of war.

1430. We've had two more alerts, that took us, breathless and shaking to our stations. Nothing got in, however. There are plenty of P-38s and P-47s in the air. God bless 'em!

2000. We were at GQ from four o'clock to sundown, and at anchor. Some planes came in and strafed the airfield, but we weren't able to see them. The tension was pretty great. Bogies were being continually reported 15 and 20 miles off, and many heavy low clouds made it so that in many sectors we could never have seen them until they were on top of us. Our only respite was a drenching shower that covered us for about an hour. It soaked us to the skin, but we breathed easier for it. Nothing serious developed, but when we secured at darkness, I felt as if I had been run through a wringer, and so did everyone else. If we could just have been underway it would not have been half such a strain. We played bridge tonight, but the game lacked usual chatter that made it such a good recreation before. Tomorrow we fuel. It's a dark thought.

19 November 1944

1100. When I arose this morning it was still partially overcast with occasional showers, visibility very limited on some sectors. At GQ around 0800, everything seemed fairly easy, with fighters in the air. Suddenly we saw two planes low over land making a run on some freighters about four miles off. No one fired until the last minute, when two 20 mms from one of the freighters started spitting feebly. Being low already, the planes simply nosed over and crashed. Actually there were three, though I only saw. One managed to crash his ship and start a fire. I am amazed at the cold deliberateness of these suicide attacks. They simple prove we have no real conception of the psychology of the Japanese mind. The Captain later said, "They are like the early Christians, to whom death in the arena meant nothing." Resent the analogy if you will. It's true.

That was the only event. We got underway and went over to fuel ship. For some reason there was little tension while we were fueling. In fact the whole morning had been easy. Maybe we're getting conditioned to it.

There were several canoes nearby while we fueled. One contained a total of 12 people I could see and who knows how many babies in the bilges. That must be the family size. Now we're back in our old anchorage.

2145. We were at GQ off and on all afternoon. At times things looked pretty grim, and the easiness of the morning was soon lost. Heavy clouds continued to keep our visibility maddeningly erratic. At about four o'clock we started hearing reports of various large groups of enemy planes approaching the anchorage. One group of 19 Vals kept coming in until we were nearly frantic. They were engaged by our fighters and, I guess, broken up, because they never arrived. Then the most wonderful thing happened. Out of the clear sky we were ordered to take a convoy to Hollandia (New Guinea). I never felt so relieved in my life, and you should have seen the faces brighten up as the anchor chain started clanking up. We got underway, but the area was still abounding with bogies and we had several more moments of tension. Once we tracked a Dinah directly overhead, but it was too high to shoot at and I wasn't sure of it's identification until later. It was the first I'd seen. Nightfall found us in the southern anchorage waiting for the LSTs to come out. Shortly after darkness, a couple of planes flew all around us and through the anchorage and caused a little tension, but it was very dark and not too dangerous. Several times some of the ships and the shore AA fired

20 November 1944

Morning found us still uncomfortably close to the storm center. Dinegat Island, which we had patrolled off of was in sight and stayed in sight all day. Evidently getting the convoy underway on that pitch black night had been excusably mixed up and delayed. But even if everything had gone off on schedule, we wouldn't have been much farther along. LSTs are slow cookies. So we were brought to our battle stations by the morning air raid on Pedro Bay. They didn't bother us, and we felt plenty cheerful about being on our way. Later we secured for a quiet day. A nice fresh breeze and heavy roll of the open sea kept cheerfully reminding us we were on our way. I had the 20-24 watch and it was wonderful. Half the sky was clear and starry, and the other half had broken "sheep flock" cumulus where the fingernail moon moved about furtively. We expected a typhoon, and secured everything, but it never came.

21 November 1944

1100. A conference in the wardroom this morning. Unless we get our study courses caught up, we don't go ashore at Hollandia. What a despicable example of advantage exploiting. It ruined my morning. Suddenly there was GQ. A Francis had flown directly overhead. We're still not out of it; one can see that. A group of CVEs were close by and the air was filled with Hellcats and TBFs. When the situation clarified there was little strain. A Betty was reported down over the convoy.

2100. We had another GQ this afternoon, but nothing developed, and it didn't dampen our good spirits much. With 20 knots under us as we left the convoy with our course set for Hollandia. I worked on my course all evening. Now I'm ready to turn in with writer's cramp, a stiff back and a bad humor.

22 November 1944

I spent the whole day trying to get caught up in the main course, copying the first six lessons over in ink. After writing all day, I still have a lesson and a half to go. Stood the 20-24 watch and it was a beautiful moonlight and starlight night. The bright half moon set just before I came off watch. Everyone at ease on the director, talking of constellations, signs of the Zodiac, and such matters inspired by the spangled sky. We enter Hollandia tomorrow early.

23 November 1944

We entered Humboldt Bay in the morning, and it looked good to us in spite of the haze of smoke from the hundreds of ships. The rugged jungle covered bluffs scarred with the brown furrows of graded roads and unsettling dust powdering everything over, might not be home but it is refuge. Today is Thanksgiving. We're still low on chow so it wasn't much of a Thanksgiving dinner. It was turkey, though. A bit stringy and a little strong from hanging in the ice box, but still turkey. I took a few work requests over to the tender, and worked on my course.

24 November 1944

Finished up my lessons and am now up to date. Tomorrow I make liberty. Today I had charge of the liberty party and it was a mess, because of the boats shortage. I didn't get back until 8, but we only lost two men.

26 November 1944

A group of us went ashore yesterday. It took us a while to get there, for the boat had to act as a taxi for some gold braid and run all the way across the bay and back before it could make the short trip to the FPO lading. Anxious to have a few cold beers we scrambled up into a gravel put by a dusty road and broke open a case. It was warm. We drank it anyway. After about half an hour of chit chat and alcoholization Smith and I decided to take off. A gravel pit by a dusty road is a hell of a place for a party. So he and I and a fellow named Piper from the Smith and I each shouldered a case of beer and headed for WAAC camp. It was a good size camp, well barricaded with woven wire fences and MPs. We chatted with the MPs and hung around for an hour or so without turning a wheel. Then Jackson collared a cute little gal on her way to the chow line and after about a twenty minute period of laughing cajolery talked her into finding a couple of friends and joning us. When they showed up they were a bit on the portly side, but our taste was affected by the long weeks sans women and we didn't mind a bit. After a short argument with a couple of MPs we took off down the road with our beer on our shoulder and the gals on the arm. Under a couple of palm trees overlooking the surf on the sea side of the peninsula we spread our blankets and proceeded to open our beer with our forty fives. There was a lot of small talk and laughs, a few songs, and the warm beer. The moon was up and bright enough to cast shadows of the palm heads on the ground. After a while we were all feeling pretty good. I got the urge to swim in the surf, so I stripped to my skivvies and went in. The water was only knee deep for a long way out and bottom was coral, but it felt good and was fun. In about 20 minutes when I came out the gals had decided they wanted to go in, so we all stripped to our skivvies and proceed to cut our feet on the coral. It was fun. Afterwards there was more beer, some chatter, a few songs and a little shameless smooching in the bright moonlight. The boat was waiting for us at the landing after we dropped off the girls. We were tired, and drunk, and red with the gumbo dust that coats everything on the teeming beach. It had been a good evening.

Today I had a little hangover, but not bad. My watch didn't come until the 16-20. But it was a hectic day. Twenty of thirty passengers came aboard with all their luggage, and sacks of mail for Leyte. We leave to go back up tomorrow morning. It's going to be rougher than ever, for we are to act as fighter director in the landing areas during two operations. There are the wildest kinds of scuttlebutt as to the places we are going to land. Everyone is terrifyingly pessimistic. The other night Jim Davis came into my room and started chatting. He said he figured we'd be sunk for sure, that the *Lamson's* luck has run too long. I told him he was exaggerating the dangers. It was a bold front. I feel the same way as he and everyone else feels. This is it. That's always the way it is before an operation, especially if you have a few fresh memories to unsettle your confidence. It was the same way at Arawe, and Gloucester and Saidor.

We are really loaded up with provisions. The forward mess hall is completely filled and all the storerooms and every nook and crannie. We have enough dry stuff for a couple of months, and we'll probably use it all before we get more. This past three days has been a maze of working parties. We've had recreation, but not rest.

27 November 1944

En route to Leyte. It was pleasant day, everyone more influenced by the good cruising than by the prospects of the coming operations. There has been lots of chattering with officer passengers, and reading of magazines that came in one shipment of mail. The word is gradually getting out on the nature of the operation, and the more the word is gradually getting out on the nature of the operation, and the more that comes out the more dismal it looks. The plan seems mad, there are so many places from which its units can be attacked. However, Manus seemed stretching things pretty far, and it worked out with no strain. One is too liable to appraise the wisdom of a military operation according to his own margin of safety, and that margin always looks so slim at the outset.

28 November 1944

Another easy smooth day of cruising, the water oily, glassy, with a glare on the horizon that melts it into the sky. We are six cans in a scouting line, a nice way to make a trip, easy station keeping. Tomorrow we will be close enough to expect alerts from enemy planes. Somehow the dread of things ahead had vanished. Maybe we are used to the idea. Entering Leyte Gulf holds no particular scare any more, probably because the coming operation sounds so much worse. A week ago it was the kettle.

29 November 1944

We enter Leyte Gulf tomorrow. Had one alert but the planes turned out to be friendly. A bridge game in the wardroom after chow this evening. It was hot and thick with smoke. We knocked off early. Apple was there with this sensational observation-Des Div 23 was under air attack at 6 o'clock tonight at the exact place we will be at dawn tomorrow. I went up on deck to cool off, and sat down on a ready box by gun one. What a beautiful night. The full moon, being an amorphous mass of cumulus clouds, was about half way to the zenith. The waves surging aft glittered softly in its light. Looking up towards the bridge, there was the still barrel of gun two pointed upward silhouetted against the bright clouds, and a lookout standing at the life lines, and the bulk of the bridge and foremast swaying back and forth against the sky as the ship moved with the sea. Enjoy the moonlight while you can. You'll hate it tomorrow night.

30 November 1944

I must say our arrival in Leyte Gulf was a bit disappointing. I racked out after noon chow expecting to be awakened by the ringing bell, but slept right through to supper time. And at night so far it has been cloudy and rainy so that the big grim moon can't bother us. The morning, however, was not uneventful. As we approached the channel one lone Kate came in low and we fired a few rounds at it before it turned off at about 6,000 yards. It was a deflection shot for us and I had to check fire when it passed behind the *Flusser*. I was a bit slow in doing this and the *Flusser* took a little of our shrapnel. Lots of our long missing mail came aboard tonight, and we've had a wonderful evening of it. Word has it that a can out on patrol caught a suicide Val right down through the director bridge and CIC with 24 lost. Guess it's not so quiet as it seems.

1 December 1944

At anchor in Leyte Gulf, the day cloudy and rainy. If there were any excitement it would have to right on top of us for us to see it. We fueled ship about noon. Transfers came in for a FC2/C and GM 2/C. When I submitted S---- and S---- [names omitted by editors] the Captain said, "No, we would not use transfers to get rid of bums." (Both ..... have service records like something from a sociology book-drunkeness and disorderly conduct, breaking arrest, AWOL, etc. not one shipboard offense.) I argued stoutly that they were not bums, but the men who according to their shipboard records were most deserving of a transfer. I didn't care a damn what they did on the beach if they were good men on board ship, and both of them were. We went 'round and 'round all afternoon. Other officers were consulted, and finally, against his better judgement, he gave in.

In the evening we were about settled down for a quiet, rain enveloped night, when word came through that a sub or possibly several were in the gulf and had fired fish at the task force. So it was special sea detail and under way on a hunter killer. We thought we had one twice during the night and went to GQ, but both were false alarms. The first one came during our bridge game, and when we ran out on deck it was like wrapping your head with black felt, it was so dark it seemed to contract about you. And was it raining! We were all soaked. When we secured, the bridge game started again and lasted until the mid. This ol' Doc and the fat man clipped our wings good. The mid watch, luckily, was dry. The full moon was hidden deep in the heavy clouds, but the light shone through in a diffused sort of way and lit the scene with a weird and misty light. I was pretty sleepy by the time the watch was over. A man should sleep while I can.

2 December 1944

Still patrolling on the hunter-killer for the subs. No results yet that I know of. Air activity has been moderate. There were a couple of alerts, but nothing developed. At sundown a plane fired a fish at the task force. They weren't far off, and we saw plenty of their AA but it was never very tense for us. Still cloudy and rainy all day, but showing signs of clearing up a bit tonight. A plane is reported shot down in Surigao Straight shortly after dark tonight, so the weather doesn't preclude air action. We'll be at GQ before the night is over. Better get sleep while I can.

3 December 1944

My prediction was wrong. The weather closed down and it rained all night, so it was quiet. There were a couple of alerts during the day, but nothing developed. This afternoon we gave up the hunter-killer, came into the bay and anchored. A can was lost in Ormoc Bay last night. It's group really had it rough-continues air attack all night, but they got in some good licks at shipping there and shot down some planes. But as far as we know no survivors from the sunk can were picked up by friendly forces. Tomorrow night our division goes up, with some LSMs to supply some of our troops that are hard pressed. We're hoping it won't be so rough as we're only going about half as far up. Tom Weeks is being transferred in the morning a Form "G" for anxiety neurosis. It's tough to see him go, for he's a fine officer; but the Doc says that if he were to stay on another month the results could be permanently harmful, and that's enough for me.

December 4

Underway this morning at 0800 and picked up the LSMs and LCIs at the southern anchorage, and started down the east coast of Leyte. The day was cloudy and overcast, visibility about 8-10,000 yards. If we were to be attacked it would be sudden. We got on the radio and asked about air cover, and they didn't seem to know what we were talking about. Besides, the rain had so muddled up the airfield that the planes couldn't take off. Things didn't look so good. We went to GQ right after noon chow as a precaution. As we rounded the south end of Leyte we could see Mindanao off about nine miles. All kinds of native sailboats were hanging around the horizon. It didn't take much imagination to give them slant eyes and radio sets. There were supposed to be subs around. However, hour after hour went by and nothing happened. Some one got a bright idea and hooked up the movie PA system and turned it on loud. The ship was suddenly throbbing with a hot Cuban rumba: Cui, Cui, Cui, ca. About the same time we received word that they were sending us P-38s for cover. The weather had opened up. The good news and the loud music combined to make the afternoon almost festive. Smiles broke out, and moral popped up to the sky. We passed some canoes close aboard. They were Filipino, alright, and waved and stood at attention in a simple moving way. There were many villages along the southern tip of the island. Some of the houses are European. Civilization here is a far cry from New Guinea, Now it is dark and we are heading up the west coast of the island. We should start unloading at about 0930. Things at present well under control.

5 December 1944

What a night that turned into. Gad! I feel as if I have just run from Marathon to Athens. The weather cleared at about the time the landing craft hit the beach, and the moon came out. It was half full., and only occasionally would the clouds veil it to any great extent. Very fortunately it was pretty high when the clouds broke. So there was little silhouette effect. But still it seemed terribly light; the other ships were clearly visible to us at 4,000 yards. Shortly the float planes started appearing. They were all around in numbers from one to eight or nine. We had a night fighter, but not much success with him. However, he was good for morale; and no one was particularly scared until the first bomb was dropped. We had a black cat too, and when a plane appeared crossing our bow with a dim red light we thought it was he, though we tried to get him in our sights to track. But he was terribly hard to see in the gray sky. He circled around us in a most harmless sort of way; then suddenly "Crack!" a bomb exploded astern. It was a shot in the dark and a bad one, for it missed by a couple of thousand yards; but it caused the old man to start raising hell, and it wasn't long before he had convinced everyone that if we ever got out it would be a miracle. To make matters worse the LSMs were terribly slow on the beach, and when we finally got underway we were hopelessly behind schedule, and had visions of a bad morning in unfriendly territory. My idea was that the men should get some sleep so as to be ready for it. I argued with him until he finally gave up to end the argument. However, they didn't get much sleep.

The planes started coming in two or three at a time strafing. When they did this I felt more sure that they couldn't see us, however, scuttlebutt has it that the *Drayton* was hit and two dead from one of these runs. But there was no sleeping while it was going on. Two more bombs were dropped and both again were guess shots missing by a long distance. I was even more sure they couldn't see us. Up to this point the Captain had been steaming along quietly at 10 or 12 knots, as he should. Then, over the phones "Speed twenty!" Good God! It boiled up the water astern until it was a glowing swirl a thousand yards long. I don't know why we slowed, but he did after a short time, and I breathed again. Then came the good news that Hellcat coverage for us would start at the first gray streaks of dawn. And they were right on time, and everyone felt better. Yesterday we were glad for the darkness; today we were glad for the daylight. The morning thus far has failed to bring any concerted threats, although the Hellcats shot down one of the shoppers in the early grays of the morning twilight. We're still a long way from home, though; and there may be more before it is over. The weather seems closing down, though.

2035. I had no sooner written the above words when the clang of the bell sent me madly up to the director. It never fails that when, after waiting hours for nothing, you finally secure, along comes an air raid that is the daddy of them all. By the time the battery was rearmed, the melee was on. I caught a glimpse of three planes diving to starboard and screamed into the loud speaker "Action starboard!" expecting the guns to fire locally until the director got on, but not succeeding. We didn't get off a shot with the 5 inch. Fortunately the planes didn't choose us as a target, but dove on the

174

LSMs and LCIs which were in a tight formation. (We were maneuvering violently.) We got squared away just in time to get on some planes diving to port, and fired several rounds at them. While we were shifting from one to another as we saw them choose other targets, I saw three coming down from starboard again to go right over us. It was too late to do anything, and there was an awful moment. Why they didn't choose us to dive into, I'll never know, but they too dove on the formation of barges. The 40s and 20s were shooting like mad, but I don't think it hit anything. It all happed so quickly, and I was so preoccupied with finding for a target the guy who had us in mind, and being terrified all the while, I have no idea of my own as to the identity of the planes, where they came from, how many there were, or where they were. However, one thing is certain. It was another suicide attack and plenty heavy. Prato counted eight crashes and I don't doubt that he missed a few that the P-38s shot down. At least three of the barges were hit and one was cut neatly in half and went down. One destroyer was grazed, but not badly damaged. It was a futile attack on the part of the Japs, but it left us all shaking like so many leaves of aspen. We milled around for some time before we decided it was over, circling the milling smoking barges at about 30 knots. When all the survivors were picked up we started on again. Miraculously the two others had been hit could still run on their own power. Later we took one of them alongside to get his casualties. The motor whale boat took some off the other. There were some nasty burn cases, and one, I later learned from the Doc is critical. As I write this the ward room is a litter of stretchers and bandages and sweaty faces. There was another attack when we were all started again, just before sunset. Again we were surprised, though we hadn't secured from GQ, by their coming in over land. This battle was a rather general one. In addition to our group (three cans and the crippled barges) there were a couple of odd cans on the horizon, and the task force hull down on the starboard hand. These planes came in low and I had plenty to think about: the chance of hitting the ships scatted around; the chance of hitting the P-38s who were attacking the formation; getting the most dangerous target; etc. Thus the action was a confusion of check fires, resume fire, unmask the battery, shift to port, etc. Again I let two planes go right over us, but again they chose another target. The gods were with us today. I only saw a couple of planes, but there must have been more than those. The task force and the odd cans were firing like mad too. These suicide planes weren't so determined. One of them turned and hauled ass over the mountain. Another, however, wandered around aimlessly through the forests of ack ack and finally decided to dive on the *Mugford*, Clodius's old ship. Wham, red flames! And he hit. Right aft of the stack.1 Clouds billowed up, and we started talking post mortem for the *Mugford*. She'd been our companion in the air attack at Cape Glouchester, and several of the night snooker raids in the early New Guineas campaign. Gradually, however, the smoke subsided and finally the good word came that everything was under control. Then we started waiting for sunset. Gad! It took its time coming. When it did the F--- and we rang up 25 knots and left the crips to care of the darkness. We secured from GQ and everyone laughed and told wild tales of what they had seen, figuring the day was over. But it wasn't. A big bogy searched the bay as we sneaked in the dark. He passed us within 1000 yards and circled around for some time. Now we are anchored, and I am wondering how the rest of this night will turn out. The moon will be out about 2300. Gad, I can't keep awake I write this. Better close for today. It's been the roughest two days of the war to this kid. And one wonders how long the luck of the lucky *Lamson* will last.

6 December 1944

2100. We're well on our way again, and tomorrow looms as a day of judgement. If we get through it, the worst will be over, for the moon will be waning and our most critical operations will be at night. Right now we are at GQ, but resting easy. It is dark out with no moon until 11 or 12. I left Coreson in charge on the director and came below for a smoke and a cup of coffee. Tomorrow at dawn we make a landing at Ormoc Bay. We will stay around and bombard until at least 10 am. During that time it would be a swell set up. We have a road to command, and will blast anything that comes down it.

Today has been anything but easy, but I did get a good night of sleep last night-eight hours like a dead man. There were alerts in the bay, but we didn't go to GQ. The sleep was too important. In the night, we transferred our patients, all of which were doing OK. Carris is a fine Doc. In the morning we transferred Strueving and Spring. They were happy boys, and I felt glad for them. They had both been through the whole war on the ship, and deserved a break. The others watched them leave with eyes like lost souls. They knew what was ahead for them. In the same boat were our codes and operations plans and secret gear, being removed for security purposes. It was as if they intended expending these cans. That's the first time I ever saw it done (removing secrets before an operation, that is). Then we got underway and formed up with the LSTs we were escort to the beachhead. Heading south again, we had lots of good air cover; but the recollection of yesterday and the promise of tomorrow made everyone terribly jumpy. You could see the hopeless feelings in the faces of the men all around you, and feel it in your own. The clouds and squalls made visibility uncertain, and bogies were being reported all afternoon. Some guerillas reported 25 bombers and 36 fighters heading south in the late afternoon. Just at dusk we picked up eight unidentified planes visually, but soon lost them in the clouds. We counted the minutes while the sun moved painfully downward and the sky slowly darkened. When it was dark we breathed again. We were rounding the southern tip of the Leyte. Some enemy planes are hanging around, but can't see us in the dark. The range keeper developed trouble, and we started envisioning ourselves going through tomorrow in local control. But the boys worked in the darkness and fixed it up so that we expect it to last the day our, and possibly more. When the moon comes up there should be some excitement, for we were undoubtedly seen; but I'm sure that if we keep our heads and steam slowly they won't be able to see us when the moon comes up either. But tomorrow---who knows? Wade, the torpedoman, is on the sick list with shot nerves. He's only one jump ahead of the rest of us.

I got no sleep that night, though I lay down on the director platform once or twice. Each time, however, a plane came over and brought the whole ship to the ready. Towards morning what was left of the moon had come out, but it wasn't enough to create any real hazard. But one plane (maybe it was two planes) worried us a lot, he flew over us again and again as if he actually had us spotted. Each time we thought he was making a run. Morning was getting close and the planes were all around. It looked as if we were in for a dawn fracas.

7 December 1944

We were miserably tense. But dawn came and the planes left. We had it all our way at the landing. But we'd wondered how long it would be before the first suicide attack would come in. We took our station 2000 yards off Albuerra and searched the shore for activity. The bombardment ships were pounding at the beach head and the APDs were coming into position. We saw some troops crossing a field and gave them a few salvos of air bursts. The action brought everyone's spirits up considerably. We saw some troops in the streets of the town but we waited. Some amphibious tanks were coming up from the south, travelling close in shore. As they neared the town shots started splashing around them. The fire was coming from the south corner of the town. We trained out and gave them ten or fifteen salvos. The fire stopped and a cloud of dust covered the area. But after a bit the firing started again and the ducks turned out into the gulf. We gave the house another pasting. This time the forties raked them too. The look outs reported a plane coming in low from the north. Some of the ships were firing at it. We got on it with the director. It was a P-40. Before I could stop them the forties were firing. The plane was hit and had to return to base. Our spotting plane arrived on the scene and called for a salvo southeast of the villages. We gave it to him and he gave us a spot and called for rapid fire, I gave him six salvos. It must have been a fuel dump or ammunition, for it went up in a blaze of glory, burning and exploding as long as we watched it. Our spirits soared.

The beachhead by this time was crowded with ships, and you could tell from the activity that the assault waves had moved inland rapidly. At our battle line five miles to the south our artillery began to open up, dotting the blue hillside above Albuene with gray puffs of smoke. We were shooting at a shack where we had seen some activity. The can down the shore from us was shooting at a clump of trees at the water's edge. He hit something, for he started a fire. There was no sign yet of an air attack. Our own planes were all around. Everyone felt pretty good. There were no more targets, so we pulled out a few thousand yards and took a breather.

Everyone had a sandwich for breakfast. The last of the ships were now on the beaches; it was 0930 or 1000. Suddenly one of the ships down the bay started firing. At length we found his target. It was a twin engine plane flying fairly high. We opened up on him as he passed us and shot at him as he went away. Our pattern and control was good; the bursts were all around him. When we last saw him he was smoking badly. He was later reported to have crashed. I remember announcing over the speaker system, "The last we saw of the plane it was smoking like hell. Good going." I was conscious for a moment of a feeling of foolishness for showing my excitement. The lull that followed was tense. The first plane had arrived, and it wouldn't be long before the rest would be out. Everyone searched the sky anxiously. There were only a few clouds. Although there had been little sleep for anyone the night before there was no drowsiness. We were all living on adrenalin. Our anxiety was well founded.

Soon the radio was cackling with reports, and the fighters were heading out to the west. We ran our speed up to 25 knots. The gunfire of the destroyer pickets on the horizon west announced the fight was on. The P-38s were wreaking havoc in a large formation of planes. They were falling like flies. Some of them, no doubt, were suiciding under control but it looked as if many were shot down. I wasn't watching it too closely, for I was worried about the other sectors where other attacks might come. When quiet had settled in again we looked around to see the results. Two columns of smoke were rising persistently on the western horizon. There were several ships close together out there and we couldn't tell what had been hit. The radio told us "Valentine" has been hit and is beyond salvage. "Jesus! That's the *Mahan*." We felt the shock doubly. First because we all had friends on board her, and second because we were relief picket and would take her place in that hot corner. At 25 knots we headed for the columns of smoke. We passed fairly close to the first one. It was an APD burning from stem to stern. Two ships were alongside playing fire hoses on her. It was easy to see they'd never save her. Ten minutes later we were near the *Mahan*. She was abandoned and burning. You could hear the popping of her ammunition. Her bridge and foremast and stacks were tangled steaming wreckage. Smoke was pouring from her wardroom. Casualties, it seemed, must have been terrific. The other picket was dead in the water with her life nets down taking on survivors. Her decks were crowded but there were still many in the water. We lowered our boat and sent it to help. Word got around that Captain Campbell got off OK. We were glad to hear it; he was a fine skipper.

We steamed around straining our eyes for planes until the water was clear of survivors. We were between an island and the peninsula of Ormoc. To the west was the hazy outline of Cebu. As the whale boat came along side we spotted a plane over the island. At the same time reports of bogies all around started coming in. No time to be picking up a boat! We ran up flank speed and started maneuvering. The other can did the same. For what seemed like an age we circled and twisted, scared to death, training out on one bearing after another, investigating reports by lookouts, investigating reports by the planes and radar. Some were friendly; some were not; some were never seen at all. A large plane appeared and reappeared low on the western horizon. We sent out the fighters, but the passed by him without seeing him. Nothing came within range of our guns, but a small attack got in to the bay and hit another APD. Evidently they came in from the southwest. The last LSTs finally left the beach and the convoy began to form up. We found a lull and got our boat aboard. Then after another spell of anxious twisting and turning we started in to take our place with the convoy. The other picket stayed out there. Half way to the convoy we saw she was shooting at the *Mahan*. After a while she put a fish into her and steamed to join up.

It was about one o'clock, the day better than half over. We felt a little better now that we had plenty of company. But we were creeping along so damned slow. And God! There were long hours of daylight left. Also it was clouding up a lot. If it would only rain it would be fine; but with just clouds—you can't be sure of what might come out of them. There was a lull as the convoy crept southward. Maybe the BBs in the van opened up once. I don't remember. At about three o'clock we were passing between the small island south of Bay and the mainland. Bogey reports had been coming in for ten minutes of when we were alerted. Captain rang up flank and cleared the channel quickly.

We were well clear of the channel when we spotted the twin engine plane high overhead. We got on him but couldn't get a good shot. Our fighters were up there, but he had lots of altitude on them. Also, I don't think they saw him. He ran off north, then turned and came in at us or maybe it was another, don't clearly remember. Captain handled the ship beautifully. The plane tried to get astern but he was held broadside by a tight turn to the right. When he came in he had to keep coming right to keep his bead on us. Meanwhile, the five inch and forties got in some solid licks. I think some damage made it hard for him to come right, for he wasn't turning fast enough to catch us. We saw him let go his bomb, which soared through the air like a projectile and hit with a shattering crash about fifty yards astern. The plane sped on to port, and I paused to collect my wits with the guns trained to starboard. Then someone screamed that he was coming around to come in again. Madly we swung the guns around to port, but in the middle of his turn he winged over and crashed. There was a cheer from the guns. Here was a low and fast one between the island and Leyte. By the time I could get the director around to starboard two had been shot down by some beautiful firing of a can in the channel. The other was coming at us, dipping his wings and weaving. Somehow he got on our stern and stayed there. It was hopeless with only guns three and four to bear and the rangefinder blanked off, but we set minimum range and fired. I was screaming at the bridge to unmask the battery. The last I hear from them was "Coming left." There was no doubt he had us, for the plane was in perfect control.

I saw him come right a hair and pull his nose down a little, just as if he were setting his sights. When his guns started flashing everyone in the director ducked. On my pigeon's roost I leaned over as best I could and waited. There was the crash and momentary hot blast which stung my face. Then there was steaming and hissing and the mad physical struggle for men to get out of the director. Bracci was clawing past Corson who was trying to free himself from his phones and leave at the same time. I held Corson back and let Bracci get out. Then, when Corson tried to leave he was held back by his life jacket strap being caught on the range keeper knob. I hauled him back and freed him. On the director platform I frantically looked around for a way off. The bridge on the starboard side was wrecked and burning. Stupidly I started for the ladder to the bridge, but the smoke which enveloped the port side sent me back. The foreward spray shield was the only way. Judah helped me and I got down to gun two with no strain. I started heaving projectiles over the side, but someone stopped me. There were men in the water. I climbed over the spray shield and down to gun one. There was a crowd on the fo'c'sle among them some badly wounded. There was Banas dumbly dabbing at his right eye with a bloody handkerchief. Another burned and black with oil lay on the deck. For a while I tried to help, but it was soon apparent that I was in the way. So I sat on the capstan and looked at my hands. On the back of the left one was a wrinkled fold of dead skin; on the right a great water blister was rising. I knew my face must be the same way.

The Doc was there doing a wonderful calm job with the wounded, stopping bleeding and giving morphine. When my hands started to hurt I asked him for a sirrette and he fixed me up. I looked at my watch. It was 3:05. Somehow I was surprised to find it was still running- as if any catastrophe was bound to stop a watch. Some ships in the convoy were still firing. There was a tug standing in and the *Flusser* was maneuvering to port. Danny and Judah were doing a good job directing the activities on the focs'l, while the Doc worked the wounded. They were getting ammunition off gun one and saving empty powder cans for floats. I remember seeing Dunne standing like an orator on the ready box calling on everyone to keep their heads. Somehow it struck me funny. Someone said there were orders from aft to abandon ship, and the uninjured started climbing down life lines. There was a salvage tug standing in and the Doc told me to wait and see if I couldn't get over to the tug direct. The tug came in and started playing hoses on the fire. It didn't look as if they intended to bother with the men on the fo'c'sle. The water hissed as it fell on the gear around gun two. The fire was licking at the ready boxes in the gun shelter. They still had their ammunition. Danny and the Doc pleaded in hollers with the Captain of the tug to get the wounded off the forecastle. We were worried about the magazines. Finally the tug started edging in and brought her bow to our bull nose. The wounded in stretchers were passed over and then the rest of us jumped across. The decks were already filling with men, who had been pulled out of the water. Doc took the badly wounded into the mess hall and set up his sick bay with the help of the chief pharmacist's mate of the tug.

I stood out one door and kept those who weren't badly wounded from going in and getting the way. I looked at *Lamson*, and she was a mess. Her stacks and bridge were a twisted mass of smoking wreckage. I felt like crying, but that was just shock, I think. After a while the men from the fantail started coming aboard, some direct from the ship and some from aft life rafts and out of the water. There were some bad stretcher cases who had to be set on the deck outside, for the mess hall was full. The doctor would get to them in time. Speiser was in pain with a leg pretty badly riddled. Charlie Hogue lay white faced in the stretcher. He didn't look too bad until you saw some dots of red on his forehead and a puncture in his chest. I bent and said a few words to him. He asked about Jim Davis and the others on the bridge. I told him I was afraid they were all lost. "I'll be with 'em in a little while," he said.

After a while the Doc told me to come in and get fixed up. He lay me on the table, pulled the dead skin off my face and hand, dusted me up with a sulfa powder and bandaged me up. Afterwards I wandered around aimlessly talking to the men. My face was beginning to swell and the loops of bandage over my nose and chin kept slipping. I went to the scuttlebutt and tried to drink, but I couldn't find my mouth with the stream of water. There was a cup there, and it worked all right. Talking with various men in the crew brought the answers to a few of the questions that were in my mind.

Ginnatassio saw the Captain leap from the bridge almost the instant the plane hit. Jack Smith was dead on the quarterdeck. Joe was dead, and Cris, and Thompson, Kirslic. No one got out of the forward fireroom. "Had anyone seen Humphrey or Herrera?"-No. (I could have transferred both of them and their wives both pregnant.) Looey Woods standing in his shorts with the Doc said he'd have to go aboard with the salvage party. "The hell you are! You're not going anywhere." Looey had a chunk out of his bottom the size of a dollar bill and a couple of holes in his thigh. Topside they had decided to attempt salvage. The fires were pretty well out, and the *Flusser* would stand by. The convoy was on the horizon. There were two and a half more hours of broad daylight. We'd have a few fighters, but it seemed like a terrible risk; and both the *Flusser* and the tug were loaded with survivors. In fact, at the time it didn't seem like a risk at all, but rather a certainty. The poor *Flusser* would catch hell first, then us.

I took another drink from the glass at the scuttlebutt; my lips were like wieners. The water went down uneasily. I went to the rail and tossed it. Looey was lying on the deck in the Captain's cabin. We talked quietly for a while. Then there was scurry topside and we knew something was up. I went out into the passageway so as to be able to get to the weather deck in a hurry if need be. The passageway was jammed with terrified men from the weather deck seeking shelter. (The plane who had crashed into us had strafed us from the fantail to the bridge, and the picture of those blazing guns was plenty fresh.) We heard the *Flusser*, off to the starboard firing; and the crowd in the passageway surged to port. I stepped back into the room and lay on the deck, terribly naked without my life jacket. The tug's 3"/50 was shooting; then the starboard fifties opened up. They must be close now. Looey later said that when he heard the fifties open up, he reached out and felt the bulkhead. "The son of a bitch was plywood!" The firing stopped and silence for a few seconds. Nothing had happened. I lay there and waited. Maybe it was ten seconds or a miute. Then the firing started again. This time it was to port. The crowd in the passageway surged to starboard. It was a nightmare of time-time as the prime elemnt of the universe, like the current of a stream, carrying us relentlessly on and on and on. Why were we alive? The momentum of life itself. It seemed as if the guns were firing a long time. Some ponderous force was carrying me along. Then there was a long silence, followed by the sounds of normal movement and normal life. It was over. I got up and went into the next room with Looey. He said, "Brother, I'm telling you._____." The sun was about set. There'd be another half hour or so of light. I decided I'd better get my life jacket. It was in the sick bay. When I asked the Doc about Charlie, he said, "Charlie is going to be all right." Confidently. Was he being confident to ease the strain for me? My left eye was almost swollen shut now, me and the Doc added some to my bandages, which were all slipping and falling apart because I had moved around so much. He gave me a bunch of sulfa pills. After that I wandered a lot more.

Darkness was awfully slow at creeping in. We were making four knots. The *Lamson* was riding her cable off to port, for her rudder was down left. A salvage party was getting ready to go aboard as soon as it was dark.

And dark it finally became. I sat on deck and watched the last gray fading in the west, and felt safe. Westphall was in a cot nearby. His back was sprained-or something. I asked him how he felt and he said it wasn't so bad if he didn't move. Then he wanted to relive himself. I welcomed the excuse for activity and groped below and got a urinal. When he had finished I took it below again. There were a bunch of men gathered in the galley, smoking and drinking coffee. I tried a cup and a piece of cheese. The coffee was in a large bottle. Near it was a note: "If the coffee should run low, call me at any time on gun one." Signed by the name of one of the ship's cooks of the tug.

Then there was a can of pineapple juice. It tasted delicious and I gulped at it. Then I went into sick bay again. Holt, one of the 20 mm gunners, was lying there with shrapnel in his belly and burns. A couple of pals were telling him he'd done more good firing and asked me wasn't that right? "Ya, you got in some good licks, Holt." Who knows? Maybe he had. I went out on deck and tossed the pineapple juice, cheese, and coffee. Westphall was pretty uncomfortable and couldn't sleep. I went below and got him a sirette. Chaisson was up there and he administered it to him. My hands were too stiff. It was very dark. That was fine. The salvage party got *Lamson's* rudder amidship and we made six knots instead of four. I started telling people we'd be in Pedro Bay by day light. That was wrong. Hutton had a half sheltered place on the boat deck, I sat down and chatted with him for quite a while. Then it started raining and I went below to where Looey was. I couldn't see very well when I lay down to sleep. In the morning both eyes were shut.

Thus the fateful day ended. It is not completely described by any means, and no doubt there are many inaccuracies in the way I remember it. And many events, and thoughts and impressions I have lost or left out because they didn't seem important. But every thought and act was important and meaningful and dramatic. It was a day such as Hemingway would write a hundred pages on.

The next day I spent in darkness, and I don't remember much that happened. I must have slept a lot of the time. The *Flusser* had left us during the night taking Charlie and Speiser and a couple of other badly wounded whom quick hospital care could help. Other ships were with us in the morning. We were transferred to the hospital ship in the late afternoon. They had me on a stretcher, though I could have walked easily. At length they set the stretcher down uncertainly. I told them I could walk if someone would show me where to go. There was a woman's voice among them- a nurse. When I got up to walk, the arm that came around me to guide me was hers. It was soft. I liked that.

Later on they fed me with stew that had meat and potatoes and carrots in it. I don't think I'll ever taste anything so delicious. The Doc and Captain came around and said a few words, of temporary goodbye.

The hospital ship got underway to leave San Pedro Bay on the morning of the 9th. My eyes had opened, I looked out the port; but I didn't see the *Lamson*. She must have been off to starboard. It was a cloudy day. The nurse made the "routine" talk about what to do in case of attack and we had to abandon ship. She said the Japs seemed to leave the hospital ships along.

During the day the *Lamson* men who could, wandered around the wards and talked with everyone, and with some wandering of my own I found out pretty much what happened on the various stations on the ship, and how those I was especially interested in made out. Herrera and Humphrey were both all right; so I could rest easy on that score. Charlie Hogue had died, good natured, dogmatic Charlie who he had ribbed so much about the merchant marine. Floccari, with his leg amputated, was fast going in an oxygen tent. Stanberrry and Jim Davis were badly burned, but seemed to be all right.

There were a lot of Army men in the ward with arms and legs in casts or amputated. Across from me was a young parachutist, who had accidently been shot by another man who was cleaning his gun. He was a very nice young fellow, simple and quiet spoken, and natural. The fellow above him whined a lot, and said a lot of things that got on my nerves, like, "I don't care if it hurts. If it's good for me, that's all I want to know." (As if taking a shot of penicillin was being brave.) And so on.

The Army nurses were fine. They worked right along with the medics, and did a lot of cheering up as well as dressing wounds. There was an especially pretty one that came on all night. Once I asked her, "How about one of those wonderful eye washes, Queeny?" She said, "My name is Miss _____ and I'd love to give you an eyewash."

Floccari died the first day out.

I visited a lot with Stanbury. When I first saw him bandaged as he was nearly from head to foot, I hardly dared speak to him but when I left him it seemed as if he were fine. His mind was clear and he enjoyed talking. He told me how he had been on the port wing of the bridge and had flattened up against the bulkhead where the challenges are written when the plane came in, and how it seemed as if the hand of providence had saved him.

Not until the second day did I find the ward where Jim Davis was and he was asleep with one leg in a cast and burn bandages covering his face, shoulders, and arms. I came back after a couple of hours and talked with him for a while. He, too, seemed to be fine; though his jaw was broken and wired to set, causing him to have trouble talking. His mind was clear, and he told how easy it had been to drift off with the ether when he had been in the operating room to have his fractures set. And how he would have to have his uniforms cleaned up when he got back to the states.

The next afternoon when I walked in to talk to him, my heart sank. Two doctors were working with him like mad, listening with stethoscopes and passing their hands before his eyes. I tried to talk to the nurse, but she was busy. Out on deck, I gazed out at the vacant sea. The weather had cleared; it was blue and calm. After 15 minutes I went back. There was a curtain around Jim's bunk. I felt miserable. He had seemed so well; and he wasn't the kind of guy that should die in a way, cheerful, home loving Jim. He should have had such a happy life with so many friends.

On the way back to the ward I met the nurse of our ward, who knew of my interest in Jim. "Your friend died."

"Yes, I know."

"That's the way it is with burns. The third or fourth day there is a crisis. I've seen it so many times, and there's nothing you can do."

"Oh."

"Stanbury is going to die too. We've known it from the start."

"It's a dirty god damn way!" I was sorry I said it.

That night Stanbury's case was on everyone's mind. Somehow we felt that if he lived through the night, he'd be O.K. We resented the seeming callousness of the nurse's prediction-like a weather man forecasting rain-though it really wasn't. Stan was on a stretcher in a room by himself with a yello bottle of plasma hanging from the ceiling, a long rubber tube leading to the needle in his foot. Outside on the weather deck, his window, were Clancy and Sherman, quietly watching though there was no indication of activity inside. I joined them in the light of the floodlights which played on the green stripe and red cross on the side of the ship. Inside was Stan and we watched seriously. This was not morbid curiosity at all. Stan was liked by everyone and he liked everyone. We were pulling for him in the yellow light of the window. Clancy and Sherman were no closer to him than any one of the thirty men aboard ship, but they were watching. They were good kids, those two. At nine thirty the decks outside were cleared and we went inside.

The next morning Stan was still alive, but his temperature was 105. We were to arrive in Hollandia that afternoon. The nurses were marvelous. They tended to him; and when he insisted on talking they joked with him. They brought nurses from all over the ship to visit with him. They'd stand in front of him so he could see them. Stan loved that. "Gee! Everyone this one is prettier than the one before!" And he made elaborate plans to have all of us get together in Hollandia at the end of the ship's next trip. In the afternoon when the ship docked and they were ready to evacuate the patients, he was still holding out, but his temperature was still 105. The ward doctor and nurse didn't want to move him in an ambulance and drove him the mile and a half over the bumpy dusty road to the base hospital. There he was put in a ward practically unnoticed and he died that evening.

The day came in, when we were still quite a way out Looey and I went up on the boat deck to the burial as sea of Charlie Hogue, Jim Davis, and Floccari. There were the white cloth covered forms with flags at the rail, and the chaplains (Catholic and Protestant,) and the ship's company in whites at attention. A few words by the Captain of the ship, some scripture by the Protestant chaplain, a little ritual by the priest, and the boards were raised. Astern the white bubbling wake reached back into the eternal blue and gray of the ocean.

My bandages, except for my right hand came off on the third day, and they paintd me up with gentian violet, with formed a purple crust. My face, puffed, crusted, bearded, discolored and ghoulish. When I looked in the mirror I scared myself half to death. But I was so much better off than most of the rest. Looey to lay on his stomach and couldn't get up and around much. Gusberti, the signalman, was so bandaged up that you had to help him smoke a cigarette. And on and on down the list. And the Army boys with their amputations and the prospect of the states and home loomed big.

At the base hospital we were in Quonset hut wards. Evidently they were very crowded. We were exasperated when after 36 hours the doctor had not so much as looked at our wounds. Looey was in the same ward. After 48 hours he called the Corpsman to him and asked him to get the chit that he had filled out when he came in. He wanted to check to see if he had put down Christian Scientist as his religion. Chow was bad too, and the seamen who came around to visit with us said it was the same way all over.

After a while, though, the chow got much better; and the doc got around to us and took care of us. And it wasn't so bad. It was a thrill to see how well the burns were healing up day by day. Eventually I could shave and then the blue crust was soaked off and replaced with an ointment that Omigod itched, and then the new skin and the last scabs coming off. Only the right had seemed to come along slowly.

One day I got up and went down to the docks with Hogan, my 40 mm gunner's mate. The *Flusser* was out there at anchor and we thought we could get some definite dope about the ship, and maybe some beer. We caught a boat and went out there. I talked with some of the *Flusser* officers. They thought they had seen the Luzon operation ahead of them, and after Ormoc Bay, they weren't at all happy about it. I certainly didn't envy them. I found that the ship was in Manus and read the Captain's report on the damage. There was plenty of it. Also there was a list of seamen that I had counted lost. They told be of the heroisms of Solomon, our Chief Pharmacist's mate, who tended the wounded on the fantail, though horribly burned himself, and refusing to leave the ship until he had all his patients safely across, later to die of his burns. They were really swell on the *Flusser*. Hogan and I left with 3 cases of beer. We took two to the hospital to pass out to the men; and took the other for ourselves, hoping to line up some WAACs, as Jack Smith and I had done before. We were a dismal failure and ended up drinking the beer ourselves.

25 December 1944

Christmas- after a good X-mas dinner of turkey, cranberry sauce, fruit cake, and ice cream I am sitting along in the hospital chapel-rec hall. It is an open building with a canvas roof stretched over a frame. Cloth woven into woven wire form the walls and the breeze blows through making it cool at midday. I am enjoying my X-mas cigar. The set up lends itself to reflection and thoughts naturally drift to past X-masses. My first thought is that X-mas in my life has not been the joyous occasion that day should have been. Last X-mas we were on our way to Cape Gloucester with the invasion armada, nervously apprehensive as one always is at the outset of the operation. Before that there was San Diego and the dismal crowds in the rain. And before that there were the school worries that always accumulated at that time, just before the final exams and the first of the big debate tournaments. But then I thought of some happy occasions and they recalled others. The X-mas that was all John's glow-when he returned from the lumber camp laden with lavish presents especially for Mother and Sue and Amy, brought the first good size accumulation of money he had earned. And it's ritual of Dad ceremoniously taking "Trails Ploughed Under" from the shelf, opening it up to the "Savage Santa Claus." And Jiggi tooting his X-mas present of a chocolate flavored rubber bone from under the X-mas tree, and mindful of the pretty wrapping carrying it to his big blue pillow before trying to unwrap it. Yes, X-masses have been good.

12 January 1945

Riding homeward on the crest of the wave. It's a great feeling. Great swells from the SW gather us up and hurl us forward until, having passed, it sets us down in the trough for the wave which follows to pick up again. If we were clipper seamen of sixty years ago we would be gratefully conscious of the favorable winds and sea. Not being clipper seamen we are simple grateful for the fact that we are heading homeward; and the cold, which daily (almost hourly) grows more and more bitter causes much shivering and discomfort. It has been hazy for the past three days. Tonight it is clear. That means we can expect much colder weather, so the Captain says. There is no one to question his prediction. We have been in the tropics too much of the time to have developed much weather consciousness. There it is either clear, cloudy, rainy, windy; never cold, seldom stormy.

The ship, with its gutted, twisted shell of a bridge, is a miserable looking sight, but she handles easily, and it is as comfortable as every below decks. Watches are not as rigid as they have been and close station keeping is not required. The *Haradon*, with whom we are travelling, is damaged also. The bridge is the 20 mm platform with a pelorus and a canvas shelter jury rigged. The signalman perches precariously on the mangled director platform. The OOD wears phones which connect him with the JOOD on secondary con where the helmsman and quartermaster perform their duties.

I stand the OOD watches during the day, and since so little is required in the way of station keeping ("Keep astern of him and keep him in sight") it isn't much of a test of ability. However easy our watches, we are doing a great deal in preparation for the yard. It is clear that there will be no carelessness or easiness on the part of the officers this time. Our last lesson is too clear in our minds, and the Captain would never permit it anyway.

Corson had most of the preliminary work completed when I got back on board at Pearl. He's efficient and smart; it saved me a lot of work.

Bill Judah's feud with the Captain came to a head when the question of who would take over gunnery in my absence came up. The Captain bypassed Judah and put in Corson. I was afraid he would do that. Judah resented it, as he naturally should, and quit. As a result, he is no longer in gunnery at all, and will probably be transferred in the yard. I feel a distinct loss. Bill's common sense and likability were an asset to the department in many ways; and his old joviality will be missed in the wardroom.

The new exec, everyone says, is fine; -and the more I see of him the more I agree. He is capable and confident; and has the courage and tact to prevent the Captain from making his position only nominal, as was the case with Joe. In so doing he removes a lot of the friction between the Captain and the department heads and division officers. And personally he is liked, with out sacrificing any respect. That is a good combination and makes the future look much brighter.

Painting by Grant Powers, U.S. Marine Corps, depicting USS Lamson (DD-367) blowing up before sinking following her use as a test ship in the "Able Day" atomic bomb test at Bikini Atoll, 1 July 1946, part of Operation Crossroad. (Image donated to the Naval Historical Center by Miss Barbara Gilmore)

THE WRECK OF THE LAMSON, CIRCA 2007

The editors of this volume are grateful to Andrew Pitkin for graciously providing images, seen here and on the cover, of the remains of the Lamson. Pitkin wrote:

I am a British anesthesiologist living and working in Gainesville, Florida. I started diving in 1992 and spent many years diving wrecks in the English Channel as well as the caves in Florida and Mexico. I had always wanted to dive the wrecks in Bikini Atoll and when I got married my wife (who also dives) and I planned to visit Bikini as a belated honeymoon. We always thought of it as probably being a once in a lifetime trip, but as it turned out that may be the case as diving operations in Bikini have been suspended indefinitely because of problems with air transportation in the Marshall Islands. However, we made a number of friends on the trip who we have remained in touch with. We dived Bikini in September and October of 2007. The obvious highlight there is the USS Saratoga, with all the remaining wrecks being bonuses. The USS Lamson is a good dive because it is upright with lots of features still intact and she is relatively shallow compared with many of the other wrecks there, giving you more time to explore.

Object at the center of the image is a coffee cup.

An aft gunmount with a fish in the foreground.

Sinks

LAMSON'S LINEAGE

U.S.S. Lamson (DD 367) was laid down on March 20, 1934 at Bath Iron
Works in Maine alongside her sister ship *Drayton*. She was launched two
years later, on June 17, 1934, and commissioned October 21, 1936.
However, DD-367 was the third *U.S.S. Lamson* to serve in the United States
Navy. Launched on September 1, 1920, DD-328 was a four-stack *Clemson*-
destroyer. She had been laid down on August 13, 1919, at the Bethlehem
Shipbuilding Corporation's San Francisco yard. On April 19, 1921, she was
commissioned, and joined the US Atlantic Fleet, at Charleston, South
Carolina December 28, 1921. Throughout her career, DD-328 served along
the eastern seaboard, and in the Carribean.

DD-328 crossed the Atlantic, starting in Boston in 1925, and sojourned in
the Mediterranean for one year. Upon her return to American waters, she
joined the Scouting Fleet. 328's career was relatively uneventful. American
had a proud peace time navy in the inter-war period, but the country was
still isolationist in its view, and pledged harmony and disarmament
frequently. Thus, there was little for destroyers such as DD-328 to do, other
than to conduct exercises, fleet maneuvers, and show the flag overseas.
After only nine years in service, she was struck from the Naval Register on
October 22, 1930. Four years later, in Baltimore, she was scrapped.

Before both DD-367 and 328, had seen service, DD-18 had become the
first *U.S.S. Lamson*. Laid down in 1908, in Philadelphia, she was launched
June 16, 1909, and commissioned February 10, 1910. A *Smith*-class
destroyer, DD-18 was a four-stack vessel like DD-328, and also served in
the Atlantic Fleet. Unlike DD-328, however, DD-18 was more torpedo boat
than destroyer, and participated in three naval operations. She weighed
anchor from Key West, on May 7, 1916, and sailed for two days to the
Dominican Republic. US Marines landed in the Dominican Republic, in
response to unrest in the country, imposing an eight year military
occupation under Rear Admiral Harry Shepard Knapp.

After her return to Key West, DD-18 left once more, this time bound for
Vera Cruz, Mexico. Only two years earlier, US forces had occupied Vera
Cruz. Mexico as the nation was fighting a civil war, and John Pershing, and
his expeditionary force were roaming the countryside in search of Pancho
Villa.

With America's entrance into World War I, DD-18 assumed patrol duties in
the Azores, and escorted convoys from the Portuguese islands to Brest,
France. Fulfilling her role as escort, she rescued the crew of merchant ship
Finland after it was torpedoed by a German U-boat. A month after the war's
end, she left Europe, and returned to Charleston. On July 15, 1919 she was
decommissioned and sold later in the same year.

Why were three American destroyers named *Lamson*? Roswell H. Lamson (1838- 1903) was a naval hero of the American Civil War. Born in Burlington, Iowa, he entered the Naval Academy in 1858. He graduated during the turbulent year 1862, and took command of the wooden screw steamer *U.S.S. Mount Vernon*.

According to "Lamson of the Gettysburg: The Civil War Letters of Lieutenant Roswell H. Lamson, U.S. Navy," Edited by James M. McPherson and Patricia R. McPherson "Lamson always seemed to be where the action was in the naval war...he was captain of the big deck guns on *U.S.S. Wabash* that did the most damage to enemy forts at Hatteras Inlet and Port Royal." The description of Lamson as a man 'where the action was,' seems apt. In addition to *Mount Vernon*, he commanded gunboats on Nansemond River, took control of *C.S.S. Planter* (which was sailed out to meet the Union fleet, by escaping slaves) pioneered new techniques for clearing naval mines, and commanded *U.S.S. Gettysburg*, receiving wounds at Fort Fisher in 1865.

Although Roswell Lamson's achievements are not widely known, it is no surprise that three different destroyers were named after him. The unsung heroes, whose actions had a profound effect but were overlooked by history, have always characterized the christening of 'Tin Cans' and the men who sailed them.

The *USS. Gettysburg*, a ship commanded by Roswell Lamson during the Civil War. (Naval Historical Center)

USS Lamson (DD-18) running trials in 1909-1910.
Photo by J.W. Dawson, Philadelphia.
NH 55479

Lamson (Destroyer #18) under way; circa 1912. (US Navy- Library of Selected Images)

Lamson at her mooring in 1910. Note the large awning running the length of the deck, as well as the short smokestacks (the smokestacks were raised by 1912). –(US Navy- Library of Selected Images)

"Full steam ahead" seems to be the order of the day as DD-328 charges through rough sees in the mid-1920s. --(US Navy- Library of Selected Images)

BIBLIOGRAPHY

- Griggs, William L. Preludes to Victory: The Battle of Ormoc Bay in WWII. Hillsborough, New Jersey: Atlantic Press, 2002. (Also see: http://www.ormocbattle.com)

- Kappes, Irwin J. *The Battle for Leyte Gulf Revisited.* Military History Online. 11 June 2010. 2003.

- Mcpherson, James M.; Mcpherson, Patricia R. Lamson of the Gettysburg: The Civil War Letters of Lieutenant Roswell H. Lamson, U.S. Navy. New York, Oxford: Oxford University Press, 1997.

- Morison, Samuel Eliot. History of the United States Naval Operations in World War II: Leyte: June 1944-January 1945. Edison, New Jersey: Castle Books, 1958.

- Phelan, Richard A. Tin Can 367: The Beginning, Life and End of United States Torpedo Boat Destroyer and Its Crew: 1936-1945. Bloomington, Indiana: AuthorHouse, 2008.

- Toppan, Andrew C. Bath Iron Works. Charleston, South Carolina: Arcadia Publishing, 2002.

www.ingramcontent.com/pod-product-compliance
Lightning Source LLC
Chambersburg PA
CBHW072002090426
42740CB00011B/2057